FAST AND FURIOUS

RICHARD GARRETT

Fast and Furious

THE STORY OF THE WORLD
CHAMPIONSHIP OF DRIVERS

with a foreword by
GRAHAM HILL

ARCO PUBLISHING COMPANY, INC.
New York

Published 1969 by
ARCO PUBLISHING COMPANY, INC.
219 Park Avenue South, New York, N.Y. 10003

Library of Congress Catalog Number 69-12570
ARCO Book Number 668-01840-2
All Rights Reserved

© Richard Garrett 1968

Printed in Great Britain

For
Anthony and Simon

Contents

	Foreword by Graham Hill	xi
	Introduction	xiii
	PART ONE: OVERTURE	
1	The Rules	3
2	In the Beginning...	5
3	A Grid of Drivers	19
4	Motor Racing is a Business	27
5	Curtain-raiser	34
	PART TWO: TRIAL OF STRENGTH	
6	The B.R.M.: A Grand Prix Car for Britain	43
7	Round and Round the Houses	51
8	Jack Brabham: Man of Two Worlds	58
9	Lightness and Simplicity Amid the Sand-dunes	65
10	Lotus: Almost a Legend	75
11	The Fastest, Most Dangerous, Circuit	82
12	Honda: The Sun Will Eventually Rise	91
13	And So To Le Mans	100
14	A.A.R.: or the Dream of Daniel Sexton Gurney	108
15	The Anatomy of a Grand Prix	116
16	Cooper-Maserati: Keeping a Name Out in Front	124
17	The Biggest Switchback in the World	131

18	Enzo Ferrari: Ride a Prancing Black Horse	140
19	A Funny Thing Happened on the Way to the Chequered Flag	147
20	The Last of the Lone Wolves	159

PART THREE: END OF A YEAR

21	What Happened in the West	175
22	Conclusions Are Not Necessarily Comfortable	180
23	What Happened in the End	194

Epilogue   199

Index   201

Illustrations

Between pages 24 and 25

Husband-and-wife act
Drivers at home
Machinery at factory
Before the storm
Flying Scotsmen
Putting the lid on
Ready to go

Between pages 88 and 89

Dutch landscape
German trackscape
Urban speedway
Sand-dune spectacular
Car passes car
Car passes man
Into the pits
Out of the pits
Ferrariscape
Towards a conclusion
Bendsmanship
Denny Hulme in his Repco-Brabham (old style)
Jack Brabham in his Repco-Brabham (new style)

ILLUSTRATIONS

Between pages 152 *and* 153

Arrival
Departure
Those responsible
Stop-watch wives
Conversation pieces
Tribute to Bandini

All photographs by the Author

Foreword

by GRAHAM HILL

Surrounding every racing car there are people. A lot gets written about the cars, but not enough about the people. Maybe that's our own fault. Perhaps we don't go out of our way enough to court publicity. If that's so, we ought to mend our ways. After all, motor racing today is a mass spectator sport. People are interested in people. They ought to be told more about the human side of the business.

Richard Garrett's book is a refreshing change in this respect. There's enough about the cars in it and there's certainly plenty of action. But most of all it's about people. The people who make up motor racing. It's about the drivers—and about the men they drive for, the engineers, the mechanics and pretty well everyone else who takes part in Formula 1 motor racing.

As a professional driver, my whole life is obviously aimed at winning races and the World Championship of Drivers. In 1962 I was lucky in this respect. Since then I haven't quite made it. But that doesn't mean to say that I haven't enjoyed my motor racing. I have. Every minute of it.

And that's another reason why I think this book is important. The whole picture's there. It even told me a few things that I didn't know.

I can recommend it to everyone who follows motor racing—and, come to that, to anyone who doesn't. Motor racing is exciting, and so is *Fast and Furious*. That's why I'm glad to have had this opportunity to write a foreword to it. It's about the lives of people like myself and my friends, rivals and colleagues. I hope you enjoy it as much as I did.

Introduction

If there are any mistakes in this book it's nobody's fault but mine. No writer could possibly have been given more assistance—both in the finding of facts, and in the checking of them. Motor racing, especially at the height of the season, is apt to be a somewhat tense occupation. There is not only the question of trying to win races, but also the problem of getting to them. Racing drivers, team managers, engineers, mechanics, and what-have-you tend to be birds of passage. They are seldom in the same place for very long at a time, which adds considerably to their difficulties. None of them can have relished the intrusions which the production of this book demanded. Nevertheless, all of them were a good deal more than polite. I learned to marvel at the way in which most of them unhitched themselves from their many immediate problems and gave their attentions to answering what must have been a lot of tedious questions.

Grand Prix motor racing is a realm in which something always seems to be happening. For example, when I was writing the first chapters it looked as if Mercedes, after their brief return in 1954–5, had retired from the sport for good. Then, when I was about halfway through, a newspaper came out with a report that they had decided to come back. The object, if one was to believe the story, was to brush up the Mercedes image with the younger generation. The report was hotly denied, which—as everybody in the newspaper industry knows—does not necessarily mean that it was untrue.

For another example, at the start of 1967 it looked as if Bruce McLaren had finally made it as a constructor of Formula 1 cars. He was making do with a somewhat underpowered V8 engine, but that was only for the time being. A V12 was just round the corner. Unfortunately, however, the engine was late in arriving, and Bruce, for the sake of a competitive ride, had to switch horses and join Dan Gurney for three events.

Truth, then, is something of fairly short duration. Within a matter of weeks, or even days, it can be rendered false. That is something which anyone who writes books about motor racing has to face, and anybody who buys them has to put up with.

Similarly, any given Grand Prix is only a living affair of human toil and mechanical marvels until the next one has taken place. After that it just becomes a collection of statistics, chewed over lovingly by intense enthusiasts and forgotten by everyone else.

You cannot, however, write a book about motor racing if you don't show it happening. You might just as well give a lecture on Beethoven without playing his music, or publish an article on some painter or other without showing any of his pictures.

For this reason I have included accounts of Grand Prix races in 1967, and used the 1967 World Championship as a structure on which to build quite a lot of the narrative.

'And that', I seem to hear somebody say, 'is a pretty foolish thing to do. The book will be out of date almost as soon as it's written.'

Actually, it won't. There are a number of things which are common to all seasons, and which don't and cannot date. There is the struggle of mechanics to get the car ready in time. There is the tumult of sweat and ingenuity, which sometimes collapsed in a pitiful pile of disappointment, as the race progresses. There is the attitude of engineers to their profession, and the attitude of drivers to theirs. And there is the complexity of human and mechanical problems which become solved and then disintegrate to form new ones.

These are the eternals of motor racing. Actual races only serve to illustrate them.

During the research for the early chapters I read through a great many books and magazines. One which proved to be particularly valuable on the historical side was *World Championship* by Gregor Grant. It is now, alas, out of print.

I also received considerable help from members of Shell International Petroleum Company Ltd., from Shell-Mex and

B.P. Ltd., and from Shell operating companies in France, Belgium, Holland and Italy. Shell, indeed, deserves my special gratitude, for it was this organisation which first encouraged me to write about motor racing, and set me off on a long trail which eventually led to this book.

The present-day Grand Prix driver is a true professional, and a very busy one at that. I must confess, however, that I had no misgivings about asking Graham Hill to write the foreword. I knew that, in spite of his enormous number of commitments, he is the most generous of people. I am extremely grateful to him for undertaking the task.

Finally, thanks to my publishers, who originally talked in terms of 40,000 words, and who treated me with tolerance and understanding when I turned in rather more than that.

R.G.

Hadlow, Kent
1968

PART I

Overture

I

The Rules

After the last war the responsibility for international motor racing was taken over by an organisation named the International Association of Recognised Automobile Clubs. Such a cumbersome title couldn't expect to survive, even when it belonged to the very Establishment of motoring. And so, presently, it became shortened to Fédération Internationale Automobile, which inevitably became abbreviated to F.I.A. In this respect it resembled its companion body, the Fédération Internationale Motorcycliste, which looks after motor cycling. That is nearly always known as the F.I.M..

But if the F.I.A.'s earlier name was impossibly long it was none the less descriptive. The membership is composed of delegates from national automobile clubs (the Automobile Club d'Italia in Italy and the R.A.C. in Britain, for instance). Together they pool ideas and exercise a good deal of influence.

The F.I.A. carries out its motor-racing responsibilities through a committee commonly known as the C.S.I. (Commission Sportif Internationale). It hammers out the rules, approves (and sometimes disapproves) of innovations, and sits in ultimate judgement over all disputes.

Currently, the C.S.I.'s rules for World Championship events are that each shall be a Grand Prix classic (i.e. an approved race with a certain amount of history behind it); that it shall be run over a distance of not less than 182·5 miles and not more than 250 miles; that it shall last for at least two hours; and that the cars shall conform to the current Formula 1 regulations.

The system of scoring is 9 points for first place, 6 for second, 4 for third, 3 for fourth, 2 for fifth and 1 for sixth. The Championship used to be decided on the results of the drivers' best six races in the World Championship series. In an attempt to make it more competitive the C.S.I. revamped the rules in this respect at the end of 1966. Now the World Championship is fought out on the basis of a driver's best nine races. Five of these must be from the first six races of the season, four from the remaining five races.

Grand Prix races counting for the 1967 World Championship (with which quite a lot of this book deals) were the South African, Monaco, Dutch, Belgian, French, British, German, Canadian (for the first time), Italian (in 1967 wearing the title of European Grand Prix—it changes every year), United States and Mexican Grands Prix.

And that's it. Other information about rules and regulations are introduced at appropriate places in the narrative. Any attempt to wedge these ones in would merely hold things up. So there they are. Down on paper. Out of the way.

2

In the Beginning . . .

Count Antonio Brivio was a man of impeccable manners. Enzo Ferrari, for whom he used to drive, once paid tribute to the 'gentlemanly chivalry', which he habitually displayed at the wheel of a racing car. Mostly, he drove Alfa Romeos, and he usually finished fairly well up. His greatest success was when he won the Mille Miglia of 1936. In that year, too, he came second in the Coppa Ciano. But, otherwise, Count Brivio accomplished nothing very remarkable. His name appears in numerous books, but usually in lists of drivers. Writers never treated him to the kind of rhapsodies they reserved for the Nuvolaris, the Rosemeyers and the Chirons of the sport.

Presently Brivio married and retired from motor racing altogether. It might have finished there, but he was a man of influence; a responsible and, above all, tactful character. His days as a driver were over, but somebody had the excellent idea of electing him the Automobile Club d'Italia's delegate to the Commission Sportif Internationale.

In the middle of 1949 the C.S.I. was in session to consider plans for the following season. Among those present was Count Brivio, and Brivio put up a proposition. There is no available record of what he actually said. What it amounted to, however, was 'Why not have a World Championship of Drivers?'

The idea found favour. A system of scoring, heavily influenced by the methods of the Fédération Internationale Motorcycliste, was devised. They also drew up a list of races which would count towards the Championship.

Initially, a driver would be awarded 8 points for a victory, 6 for second place, 4 for third place, and so on—down to 2 for fifth place. A bonus of one point was awarded for a fastest lap. If two drivers tied for position the points were to be divided. It was all reasonably straightforward, and not unlike the system used today. They dropped the fastest lap point in 1960, when a single point was awarded for sixth place. In the following year they stepped up the winner's reward to 9 points.

In those early days, however, it was not unusual for a car to be used by more than one driver during the course of a race —or, indeed, for a driver to use more than one car. When, for example, the outcome of the first year's World Championship was being fought out at Monza in 1950 Ascari overtook Farina on the fourteenth lap. Shortly afterwards the former's gearbox packed up, and he trudged back to the pits to pick up Taruffi's car, which he drove until that, too, broke down.

What, then, did one do on such occasions? The F.I.A. devised a rather complicated points-sharing system, which survived until 1958. After that the driver had to make the full distance in one car.

The World Championship was for Formula 1 drivers. Not every race, however, counted. To earn points, an event had to be a *grande épreuve*, and the committee finally settled on the British, Monaco, Swiss, Belgian, French, and Italian Grands Prix. The 500-mile classic at Indianapolis was also included, but never used. It was not until the United States Grand Prix was introduced in 1959 that an American event featured in the Championship.

As a slight complication, there was the added provision that not every result should count, but only the best. The reasoning was a trifle vague on this score. As originally drafted, the rules seemed to be somewhat uncertain as to whether the best four or five performances would count at the end of the season.

When Brivio suggested the idea of a World Championship he struck a resounding blow for Italy. Whatever else may have been uncertain at the time, one thing could be counted upon. The resulting champion would certainly drive an Italian car. Almost equally certainly—though the arrival of Fangio from South America posed complications—he would be an Italian driver.

During the 1930s the dictators (influenced, perhaps, by the chariot races of ancient Rome) saw in motor racing a powerful prestige-builder. Mussolini started it, and for several years the red Alfa Romeos of Italy were virtually unconquerable. But then Hitler decided to get in on the act. He even gave the sport a Körpsführer named Huhnlein to supervise the efforts of the Reich.

The efforts in question were personified in the giant supercharged Mercedes and the no less gigantic Auto-Union. The latter, designed by Ferdinand Porsche (who, ironically enough, also designed the first Volkswagen), was a pig of a car to drive. Its massive engine, situated at the rear, gave the back wheels a marked tendency to unstick. But the car was so long, and the driver perched so far forward, that it took some time before news of any happenings at the rear reached him. By then, unless his reactions were superlatively quick, it was too late to do very much about it.

But, provided it didn't kill its driver, the Auto-Union was remarkably competitive. In nobody's hands did it perform better than those of Rosemeyer, a young driver who had come into car racing from motor cycling. Eventually it did for poor Rosemeyer, but that was on some eccentric record bid along a stretch of autobahn. The car was slammed by a blast of wind as it came out from beneath a bridge. Rosemeyer was buried with full military honours.

The last year or so of motor racing before the outbreak of World War II saw the Germans soundly whipping all other comers, including the Italians. And then everything closed down for the duration.

The fighting was hardly over when France, the cradle of motor racing, staged the first post-war event. Known as the 'Cup of the Prisoners', it was held in the Bois de Boulogne, and won by Wimille in a Bugatti. That was on September 9th, 1945. The crowd was huge, the enthusiam enormous, but the circumstances were somewhat straitened. However, it was a beginning. The St. Cloud G.P. of the following year was more significant. It showed that, along with whatever art treasures the Italians may have hidden from prying hands during wartime, there was a laudable stock of 158 Alfa Romeos. And, what's more, they had stood up to storage remarkably well.

During the war years two men had spent a good deal of their time dreaming up racing cars. One was Raymond Mays. The other was Enzo Ferrari, one-time racing maestro of Alfa Romeo, and now planning to build his own cars. By 1950, when the World Championship was established, Ferrari's project was far ahead of Raymond Mays'. The Germans were busy rebuilding Germany. Neither Britain nor France had any really serious competitive machinery. Italy had the cars and, as it happened, most of the top drivers. The only question waiting to be answered was: who would win? Would it be an Alfa Romeo or a Ferrari?

There were, of course, dramas behind the scenes. At the end of 1948 the Alfa Romeo team dropped out of motor sport—never, it appeared, to race again. The problem was the old one of money. Alfas said they couldn't afford to go on. Fortunately, however, the Italian Government obliged with a grant of £50,000. The great marque lived to race again, though not for very many years.

The first race in the World Championship series was the British G.P. (wearing, that year, the mantle of the European G.P.) at Silverstone. The King and Queen were in attendance, and so were Mr. Mays and his B.R.M. The latter, with the former driving it, performed a couple of demonstration laps, and everybody thought that it looked jolly good—which is more than they thought later in the year at the *Daily Express* International Trophy, when it never got away from the starting grid.

Enzo Ferrari was not there. As happens from time to time in motor racing, there had been a dispute over starting money (twice during the past sixteen years Ferrari has threatened to retire from racing. But on each occasion the situation has been saved by funds contributed by the Italian motor industry. The Italian Government, after its hand-out to Alfa, seems to have been less ready to come forward.).

Thus the first event in the series was dominated by Alfa Romeos, which processed round the circuit, took the first three places, and put up tolerably high speeds in a race which was not particularly exciting. The winner was Farina, who began the season as he clearly intended to end it. For, on September 3rd, 1950, at Monza, Dr. Nino Farina won the Italian Grand Prix and thereby became the first World Champion. His age at the time was forty-two.

The second event in that first year of the World Championship was at Monaco. Two things cause accidents in motor racing: mechanical failure and human error. In this case, however, it isn't stretching things too far to blame it on a wave.

It was a blustery day, with heavy seas breaking over the sea wall. One of them deposited a nasty little pool of water on the track, just as the pack was coming round for the first time. Farina was busy overtaking Gonzalez when his wheels touched it. He slid, crashed into a stone wall, and then bounced back into the riot of oncoming cars. Gonzalez and two other drivers were involved immediately, and then six more. Fangio who, with some very deft manœuvring, managed to avoid the mêlée of swerving, soon-to-be-crumpled machinery, won the race at an average speed of 61·33 m.p.h.

The only injuries from the multiple shunt were one cut chin and one sprained wrist.

Fatal casualties in Grand Prix racing are happily rare. This is no doubt due to the fact that, to compete, a driver has to be very good indeed. Nevertheless, it is a sombre thought that of the first four World Championship title-holders only Fangio survives. Farina eventually retired from motor racing after more crashes than most people even think about—let alone experience. In spite of the immense mauling his body had received over the years, he seemed prepared to drift contentedly into old age. And then on his way to the French Grand Prix of 1966 he was killed on a patch of road in the French Alps. He was fifty-eight years old.

Alberto Ascari, who was World Champion in 1952 and 1953, had known more about the dangers of motor racing than most people. In 1925 his father (Antonio Ascari)—then on his way to what everybody predicted would be the top—was killed in the French G.P. at Monthlery. Young Alberto was seven at the time. His mother, understandably, lived in the fear that he might follow Antonio's example. There now seems to be a kind of inevitability that Alberto would take up the sport, for he often used to accompany his father to practice sessions at Monza. Sometimes he was allowed to sit beside him in the car.

But this awareness of the perils of the sport was always with him. Ferrari recalls how on one occasion he asked Ascari why he was so severe with his children. The driver replied: 'I don't want them to get too fond of me. One of these days I may not come back and they will suffer less if I have kept them a bit at arm's length.'

It was, perhaps, just as well. One day Alberto Ascari didn't come back.

During the 1955 Monaco Grand Prix he was lapping like a scalded cat, with Stirling Moss's Mercedes hot on his heels.

As Moss came out of the tunnel, the Mercedes engine packed up, but Alberto knew nothing of this. He pushed on, down past the station, through the tunnel and lined up for the chicane. But here something went badly wrong. The car hit the straw bales, bounced off a bollard, shot into the air, flew over the top of a cabin cruiser moored at the quayside, and tumbled into the harbour. When the spray and the steam had subsided it was possible to see Ascari tearing off his helmet and then swimming strongly for the land. Frogmen helped him ashore, and he was packed off to hospital with a broken nose.

Some days later he turned up at Monza, where a 3 litre Ferrari sports car was being tested. Ascari seemed to share the view of horse riders that after a fall one should get into the saddle again as quickly as possible.

During the midday break he asked whether he could do a couple of laps in the sports car. Without even bothering to put on a helmet he climbed into the driving seat and shot off. The first lap went splendidly. On the second time round, however, he spun off on one of the bends. It is an easy bend: one that Ascari had taken innumerable times before in much faster cars and in much more desperate circumstances. Possibly he had a black-out as the result of his injury at Monaco. There's also a possibility in the story of a labourer who, knowing it was the lunch break, walked across the track. Ascari is supposed to have seen him, and swerved to avoid him. Later the workman is said to have confessed the whole matter to a priest. But this tale has never been substantiated.

Alberto Ascari died on the way to hospital. The precise cause of his death will always be a mystery. In much the same way nobody can convincingly explain why, in 1958, Peter Collins came to grief at Nurburgring when he failed to take one of the right-handers and plunged into the bank. It was not a particularly difficult manœuvre. He had done it innumerable times before, and the circumstances were no more pressing than on any other occasion. Nevertheless, something went wrong, and whatever it was cost Collins his life.

Fangio survives and is at present running a very prosperous business in Argentina. Among his interests is a large motel about 250 miles from Buenos Aires.

Hawthorn should have survived. Nineteen fifty-seven had been an unlucky season for him. At the start of 1958 I visited him at his Tourist Trophy Garage in Farnham. 'What's your immediate ambition?' is probably a pretty trite question, but one is apt to ask it. Hawthorn replied with a wry smile: 'Just to win a Formula 1 motor race.' During the course of the year he won it at Rheims. But he did much more than that. Thanks to good placings in other events, he ended the season as World Champion.

Then came news of his retirement. He went on record as saying that motor racing had become 'too dangerous'. He told reporters that he meant to take up flying. One day, driving from Farnham to London in his Jaguar, he lost control of the car on the Guildford bypass. It was a nasty spot, where there have since been several other crashes. But this one ended Mike Hawthorn's life. The young man (he was only twenty-nine) who had survived all the hazards of the circuits died beside the main road.

More leading drivers have been killed in practice, in minor events, and in circumstances which have had nothing to do with racing at all, than have perished in the *grandes épreuves*. Indeed, when one considers that nearly 160 qualifying events have been held since the World Championship was introduced in 1950, the figure is almost dramatically small. Nevertheless, it is an unhappy coincidence that many great drivers have died violently.

For instance, Camille Jenatzy, who was the second holder of the World Land Speed Record, was shot during a wild-boar hunt in the Ardennes. Raymond Sommer was killed not in a *grande épreuve* but at the wheel of a 1,100 c.c. Cooper in a minor event. Robert Benoist was executed in Buchenwald. Fagioli, at the age of fifty-four and after over twenty-six years in motor sport, was killed in a small race devised as a curtain raiser to the Monaco G.P. of 1952.

Fangio was the acknowledged master. Not since Nuvolari had there been a driver of such immense skill. There were few situations from which he couldn't extract himself. But even his genius wasn't proof against fatigue.

In early June, 1952, he had been driving a B.R.M. in the Ulster Trophy race at Dundrod. He left immediately afterwards for Monza, where he was scheduled to drive a Maserati 'Six' in the Grand Prix. From one of the Channel ports he drove right through the night, arriving at the circuit too late for practice. Consequently, very weary, he set off in the race from the back row of the grid. Before very long he overshot a bend, and ended up in hospital with multiple injuries.

That long night's drive was one of Juan Manuel Fangio's very few serious mistakes.

The hazards of motor racing are not confined to machines which either break down or go out of control. One British Grand Prix (at Silverstone in 1951) was brought to a peremptory halt by a cloudburst. The rain flooded the circuit and the final was stopped after only six laps.

Nineteen fifty-five was a fearful year for the Argentine Grand Prix. The temperature in the shade was 140 degrees F.—on the circuit it was estimated at about 180 degrees. The redoubtable Fangio and his fellow countryman Mieres both completed the race and drove the whole time. Admittedly, they had to stop at the pits occasionally to be drenched with water, but they made it.

Other drivers were flaking out from sunstroke and exhaustion. Of the two Ferraris competing, the first was variously driven by Gonzalez, Trintignent, by Gonzalez again, and then by Farina. The other began with Farina at the wheel, who was relieved by Maglioli, who handed over to Trintignent, who finally returned the car to Maglioli. The story goes that it was all so confusing that afterwards they had to call in a firm of chartered accountants to work out the allocation of World Championship points.

In the end everyone seemed to assume that everyone else was suffering from sunstroke. On one occasion Stirling Moss was resting between spells at the wheel when he suddenly found himself being picked up and taken to an ambulance. It took a good deal of talk to explain that, really, he was quite O.K.

For Farina this must have been an intolerably difficult race. Before leaving for the circuit he had been injected with painkilling drugs. During the previous year, in the 1,000 Km Race at Monza, he had been driving a 3 litre Ferrari when the fuel tank split. The car burst into flames while it was travelling flat out. Farina managed to jump clear once it had slowed down sufficiently, but he was badly burnt. These burns were still causing him considerable discomfort.

The Argentine Grand Prix (it ceased to count towards the World Championship after 1960) was the scene of some quite extraordinary happenings. On one occasion somebody forged a set of passes—with the result that the starting grid was swamped with people and it became almost impossible to get the cars away. On another occasion a mechanic pushed a car over Stirling Moss's foot before the start.

But the worst event of all occurred in 1953 (the year when the cloth helmets for drivers were discarded and crash helmets became compulsory). Enormous crowds turned up to watch the race. They were in a somewhat excitable frame of mind, but the police said that everything was under control.

By the 32nd lap it became clear that this was wishful thinking. As Farina loomed up in his Ferrari, a spectator ambled across the track. Farina swerved violently, went into a slide and catapulted into the crowd. Fifteen people were killed and thirty others ended up in hospital. The Ferrari was badly damaged, but Farina escaped with a sprained ankle.

Thankfully, it is not often that a racing car goes berserk and takes a toll of spectators. The greatest tragedy of this kind was the Le Mans disaster of 1955, when eighty-one people were killed. When, in the last Mille Miglia (1957), the Marquis de Portago lost a wheel off his Ferrari, eleven spectators died; and fifteen perished with von Trips, when he crashed at Monza in 1961. Finally, there was the case of the bridge at Aix les Bains. This was a Formula Junior race organised with an eye to stepping up the town's appeal to tourism. Clearly, the administration wasn't all that it might have been—otherwise nobody would have dreamed of allowing the public to crowd on to this flimsy footbridge. Eventually the inevitable happened. The bridge collapsed. A number were killed, plus Christopher Threlfall, who was approaching the scene in his car and ploughed into the wreckage.

If wandering spectators and rickety footbridges cause accidents, so, sometimes, do animals. Back in 1928 the driver Bordino lost his life in the Alessandria G.P. when his Bugatti hit a stray dog. Mostly, however, the fur and feathered world seems to have a healthy respect for the sport. Accidents of this kind are rare. There was, however, the time at Monza in 1952 when Tony Gaze had to receive first aid after being struck in the face by a bird. And at Silverstone in 1958 Behra's B.R.M. developed a slow puncture after running over a hare.

But by far the worst episode in recent years occurred in the Belgian Grand Prix at Spa in 1960. Alan Stacey was travelling very quickly in his Lotus when a bird literally flew into his face. The shock sent him off the track and into a field. Stacey was killed instantly and his car caught fire.

Luck is continually cropping up in motor racing. Hawthorn had bad luck out in Argentina in 1954 when, after a spin, the crowd (that Latin American enthusiasm again!) gave him a helpful push—and thereby caused him to be disqualified.

Stirling Moss had better luck at Monza in 1956. A 'shunt' may be defined as 'an accident causing damage to the car'. It is, on the whole, something to be avoided. On this occasion the word takes on its other significance, which is to do with railways. Moss had run out of petrol. Just as he was coming to a halt, Piotti's Maserati gave it an obliging biff at the stern. Nothing could have been better calculated. Moss and car leapt forward and just managed to coast to the pits.

But it isn't always so simple. Sometimes you have to get out and push. The record in this respect probably belongs to Jack Brabham, who pushed his Cooper half a mile to finish third in the 1957 Monaco G.P.

Brabham's effort is no doubt impressive as a feat of physical strength. For sheer spectacle, however, there's surely nothing to beat Ascari's achievement in the German G.P. of 1953. After four laps one of the Italian ace's front wheels came off. Somehow he managed to keep the car under control and drive back to the pits on the brakedrum. He then took over Villoresi's car for the next ten laps until, to judge by the sound of the explosion, it blew up literally.

The two elements which seem to pose the greatest threat to man are fire and water. In the Dutch G.P. of 1953, however, the trouble was gravel. The track had recently been re-surfaced, and many drivers suffered cut faces from flying fragments of stone. One of the cars had all the paint stripped off it by this process.

In the French G.P. at Rheims in 1961 Jim Clark had his goggles shattered by stones. The paint was stripped from his helmet, and his face was cut. This was due to the heat of the day melting the tar and causing the gravel to break loose.

Back in 1933 that famous driver Sir Henry Birkin was driving a Maserati in the Tripoli G.P. His sleeves were rolled up above the elbow, and his bare arm touched the exhaust pipe. The burn turned septic. Eight weeks later he died of blood poisoning.

When, in 1961, B.R.M.s took part in the British G.P. for the first time, there must have been many who recalled Birkin's fate. The cockpits became so overheated that when the race was over the drivers' hands were blistered. Fortunately, on this occasion the injuries were not serious.

The standard comic scene of motor racing took place in 1958 when the G.P. circus foregathered in Rheims. Among them was Harry Schell, who had recently invested some hard-earned cash in a Vespa 'minicar'. One day when the car was parked outside the Lion d'Or Hotel a group of his colleagues manhandled it up to the first-floor landing. With a lipstick, somebody lettered the words '*A Vendre—Occasion*' (For Sale—Second-hand) on to the windscreen.

Verging on comedy was the time when Horace Gould's throttle connection broke at Nurburgring in 1956. An obliging lady in the crowd handed him a safety pin, and he managed to carry out an emergency repair. As he drove off to the pits, he was heard to call out: 'Thank God you weren't wearing elastic ones!'

As the governing body of motor sport, the F.I.A. has to exercise some sort of restraining influence. The task is not very easy. On the one hand, it must ensure that Formula 1 is the ultimate in speed and power. On the other, it must try to see that not too many people are hurt. The restraining influence is wielded by means of the regulations governing the cars.

When the World Championship was founded the current regulations for F1 cars were that their engines should not exceed $4\frac{1}{2}$ litres unsupercharged, or $1\frac{1}{2}$ litres supercharged. The formula had been introduced in 1947 and it remained until 1954.[1] Then it was modified to $2\frac{1}{2}$ litres unsupercharged. In 1961, it was modified again—this time to $1\frac{1}{2}$ litres unsupercharged. Finally, in 1966, the present regulations were introduced, putting a 3 litre limit on unsupercharged engines and $1\frac{1}{2}$ litres on any which happened to be supercharged. In 1961, self-starters became compulsory.

Throughout the years, the question of fuel was always cropping up. Before the war, some people condemned the sport for becoming 'a contest of fuels' and certainly some very potent brands of liquid dynamite were being used. Since then,

1. In 1952 and 1953 the World Championship was fought out with Formula 2 cars, which had a limit of 2 litres unsupercharged or 500 c.c. supercharged on their engines.

at various periods, 100-octane petrol, aviation fuel, and a free-for-all, have been in vogue. In 1958, the situation stabilised itself with the regulation (which still applies) that commercially available petrol, as supplied to motorists at any filling station, must be used.

The rule is a good one. It enables oil companies, which have spent a great deal of money supporting motor racing, to cash in on their successes by advertising. It also helps to improve the breed, for motor racing offers unique opportunities for research into combustion.

During the past seventeen years ten drivers have become World Champions. Fangio holds the record by having won it five times—the last four times in succession. When, in 1957, he won it for the last time he was forty-seven years old. And that is another record.

Jack Brabham comes next, having won it three times. But he enjoys the further distinction of having been the first man to win the World Championship of Drivers and the Formula 1 Constructors' Championship. The latter was introduced in 1958, and is nearly always won by the manufacturer of the car driven by the champion. The one exception was in 1958, when Mike Hawthorn (in a Ferrari) won the drivers' award and Vanwall won the constructors' prize.

But then 1958 was a somewhat odd year. Although Hawthorn won the Championship at the end of the season, he only came first in one race (the French G.P.). Both Stirling Moss and Tony Brooks won three races, but, in spite of this, they ended the season with fewer points.

At twenty-seven Jim Clark was the youngest driver ever to become champion. Hawthorn was twenty-nine when he won it; Phil Hill and Ascari were both thirty-four. Graham Hill and Jack Brabham (when he won it for the first time) were thirty-three. John Surtees was thirty (having already been World Champion motor-cyclist seven times).

The years of the cliff-hanger endings were 1962, when Graham Hill's triumph depended on the outcome of the South African Grand Prix held shortly after Christmas; and 1964, when everything hinged on what happened in Mexico City.

In the latter race Graham Hill, Jim Clark and John Surtees all stood a chance of winning the Championship. Fairly early on in the race, Hill was ruled out after a shunt with Bandini's

Ferrari. Clark, who had led for the entire event, came to a shuddering halt with one lap to go, when his engine blew up through lack of oil. And that left Surtees—who came second, and thereby secured the Championship. Dan Gurney won the event.

Motor racing has become highly commercialised. It is no use regretting the fact. It is an extremely expensive business, and if it weren't for the interest of the oil companies and the tyre firms and the accessory manufacturers it would probably perish from lack of funds.

Nevertheless, there is a danger of forgetting that it began as a sport—and a sport, in the minds of many people, it still is. Now and again you find an example of really great sportsmanship coming into it. There are many instances, but nothing can touch the Italian G.P. of 1956. If Fangio was to win the Championship he had to win this race. The South American star was engaged in a fierce battle when his steering went wrong. He came into the pits.

The Ferrari team signalled to Musso to come in and hand over his car to Fangio. The Italian ignored the signals. Later, however, he came in. He remained there long enough for the mechanics to do whatever they had to do, and then went back on to the circuit. Fangio was left there, staring despondently into space. Then Peter Collins, who was well on the way to winning, was called in for a tyre check. He summed up the situation immediately, jumped out of his car, and handed it over to Fangio. The South American smiled broadly. He gave Collins an affectionate pat on the shoulder, climbed into the cockpit, and went off to win the race and the World Championship for the fourth time.

The World Championship seems to go in phases. For the first eight years the Italian cars predominated, just as, perhaps, Brivio hoped they would. Alfa Romeo finally left the scene at the end of 1951,[1] and Mercedes made a brief comeback in 1954. In that year Fangio was champion—spreading his drives over Maseratis and Mercedes. In the following year he was World Champion again—this time using a Mercedes exclusively.

And so for a short while the Silver Arrows of Mercedes thrilled spectators, and that massive martinet Alfred Neubauer

[1]. Alfas resumed motor racing in 1964 under the banner of Autodelta—though only in Grand Touring and sports car events.

—with his three stop-watches strung round his neck and his little black and red flag—dominated the pits. And then they all departed. Three years later Neubauer retired from motorsport management, just like the huge supercharged cars he master-minded and which in some strange way he resembled.

And so back to the Italians. Until 1959 Ferraris had been the mount of champions on four occasions; Alfa Romeo—twice; and Masaretis one and a half times (the half was when they shared Fangio with Mercedes).

But in 1959 the British domination of Formula 1 racing began. In the previous year Mike Hawthorn had been the first British driver to win the Championship. In this year Jack Brabham became the first driver to win it in a British car. Since then, apart from 1961 and 1964—when Ferraris were the winners' cars—British machines have won every year (with the possible exceptions of 1966 and 1967, when Australia might reasonably claim the honour).

3

A Grid of Drivers

The Formula 1 racing car and the ordinary family saloon have a number of elementary features in common. They both have self-starters, steering wheels, and so on. But there it ends. Graham Hill once compared the two breeds to an expensive wrist watch and a grandfather clock. The heart of the former beats faster. It is a much more finely engineered and, in some ways, more delicate instrument.

It is tempting, though inappropriate, to use a similar analogy when comparing a racing driver with an ordinary motorist. The former has to be immensely tough. Nowadays there is no off-season in Formula 1 racing. When things slacken off in the Northern Hemisphere there are events in South Africa and the Tasman series to keep the drivers busy. And then there are saloon-car races, sports-car events, and even a rally or two. During 1966 Jim Clark competed in something like 100 events. Quite apart from the work involved, this meant a great deal of travelling. Indeed, top racing drivers must figure high on the lists of airlines' most constant customers.

Most of them will welcome the advent of supersonic passenger flight. The travelling is, on the whole, a bore. Bruce McLaren, who builds cars as well as races them, is one of the few who manage to put it to good use. He spends most of his time in the air writing long reports.

'After an event,' he once told me, 'I try to convey as much as possible to my engineers. They end up knowing about as much as I do.'

The others read. 'If you don't read, you go through hell,' Jackie Stewart (who finds it difficult to unwind) said. The literature of action is most popular with them. There are few top drivers who haven't read the whole James Bond *œuvre*. At one time Frank Harris's massive *My Life and Loves* enjoyed a vogue. Graham Hill took 55,000 miles of air travel (he bought it in New York, finished it in New Zealand) to get through it. According to my calculations, Jim Clark put up the fastest time on this book.

Richard Attwood is one of the few serious readers. He applies himself to technical articles in motoring magazines. 'I'm hoping to make myself technically minded,' he says.

Possibly drivers have more courage than the average man. Certainly they have immense powers of concentration, are competitive and very determined by nature, and often have a degree of mechanical ability. Brabham, of course, is a brilliant engineer, and so are John Surtees and Mike Parkes. Graham Hill, Jackie Stewart, and several others have had some sort of mechanical training. Bruce McLaren and Dan Gurney have both picked up a tolerably profound knowledge through the very business of motor racing.

The worst moments in top motor racing are those immediately before the race. Jackie Stewart, who nevertheless manages to be extremely affable on such occasions, tends to be withdrawn. 'I never like to be enthusiastic,' he once told me. 'I get this tense feeling. Rather than let it out, I try to keep it in. I sort of hold it inside me, if you see what I mean.'

There are others who don't hold it inside them. They became garrulous and are glad to talk. Graham Hill isn't a bit happy to talk. 'I become thoroughly unsociable,' he admits. 'I want to save everything for the race. Of course, there are a lot of people milling around, and they come up and wish you good luck. But it's not really the best time to approach me.'

Some while ago a heart specialist named Peter Taggart, who races in his spare time, made a disturbing discovery. As he lined up on the grid before the start of a race he noticed that he sometimes suffered from a pain across his chest. Other drivers would probably have dismissed it, but Dr. Taggart knew what it was. It was a symptom often associated with heart disease.

Not unnaturally, it worried him. One evening, after a day's racing, he was having a drink in the club house when he overheard a snatch of conversation from a neighbouring table. 'What I don't like about motor racing,' the speaker observed, 'is the pain you get in your chest before the start.'

This alerted him. He made enquiries among his friends, and found that several of them suffered from it.

His next step was to carry out some research into the matter. Enlisting volunteers, he attached a pair of electrodes to their chests, and connected them to a small transmitter (about the size of a miniature transistor set), which was housed in their overall pockets.

The transmitter sent out a signal, which was picked up by a tape-recorder on the edge of the track. Later the information from the tape was fed into a standard electrocardiograph recorder back in the Middlesex Hospital. The results provided a vivid picture of what the drivers' hearts had been doing before and during the race.

Normally, the average adult heart beats about seventy times a minute. Dr. Taggart's experiments showed that a racing driver's heart began to beat at the rate of over 150 to the minute fifteen minutes before the start of an event. During the race itself the rate went up to anything from 185 to 210 continuously.

He next carried out work on ordinary motorists. These tests revealed that, sitting in the car before starting, the rate went up to eighty-five beats a minute. In dense traffic it increased to between 100 and 140, and whenever a nasty incident (such as a near miss) occurred it went up to 150.

The significance of these experiments is not yet clear, though they certainly seem to show that racing drivers go through brief but considerable periods of tension. Most drivers are vague on the subject of nerves. They take the view that if you get into trouble it is probably your own fault. They also say that if you're not nervous you won't do well. Bruce McLaren compares this to the entertainment business.

Lorenzo Bandini, whose tragic death followed his crash in the 1967 Monaco Grand Prix, once told me: 'Perhaps "fear" isn't quite the right word for what one feels. "Apprehension" might be better. One has to consider the possibility of an accident—to accept the fact that it *could* happen. Apprehension helps one to see the danger. It makes one able to sum up a situation and so it assists one's control of events.'

Jonathan Williams, one of the newcomers to the top ranks of motor racing, looks at it another way. 'I fool myself,' he told me. 'The body of the car is like a suit of armour. Admittedly, it's only about one-sixteenth of an inch thick, but when I've got it on I feel that nothing can touch me. If you saw the road through the floorboards you'd be very alarmed. But you don't. You're only frightened when you've lost control—and I mean *really* lost it.'

All of which can, perhaps, be likened to that feeling of false security which most of us experience at the wheel of a car.

One day, perhaps, a psychiatrist will produce a fascinating book entitled 'Sex and the Single-seater'. Until it appears, the best one can do is to report that most top racing drivers, just like people in any other walk of life, are married. The exceptions are Jim Clark, Mike Parkes, Richard Attwood and Jonathan Williams.

Parkes once said to me: 'As long as one races, it's not fair to have dependants. Women may say that the danger of motor racing doesn't matter; but, deep down, it does. I've seen wives who, though they'd never admit it, are terribly worried'.

In his book *Jim Clark at the Wheel* Clark says: 'Naturally, I would like to get married and settle down like anyone else, but I have not felt free to do so during my years on the race track. Of course, this is purely a personal outlook, and I know many Grand Prix drivers who are happily married and whose wives willingly accept the additional risks involved in their husbands' profession. But personally I should not feel happy about asking any girl to share these risks with me.'

Attwood and Williams take a similar view—though both admit that if the right girl came along their resolution would probably crumble.

In spite of anything their husbands may suggest, most motor-racing wives are undoubtedly nervous. The standard occupational therapy is to accompany their husbands to meetings, to gaze at stop-watches and to keep lap records. As Bette (wife of Graham) Hill once told me: 'It gives me something to do. I couldn't watch Graham dicing with somebody. I'm not one of those wives who hang around. I'm one of the team.'

In spite of the fact that they have three young children, Mrs. Hill is able to get to most of the events. Her mother and father-in-law are usually available to move in to Graham's house at Mill Hill and take over. Mrs. Brabham (the Brabhams have three sons) is less fortunate, and has to miss out on a number of events. John and Pat Surtees have no children and, therefore, no problem. Jackie and Helen Stewart have a young son named Paul, and the McLarens have a daughter named Amanda. Somehow, Mrs. Stewart and Mrs. McLaren manage to get to most of the big events.

Husbands, defending their position, are apt to point out the advantages which motor racing offers in the way of foreign travel. 'In what other occupation,' they argue, 'would you see so much of the world?' It is a line which may, possibly, deceive themselves, but fails to take in most of the wives. They know that the interiors of airliners, 5-star hotels, and motor-racing circuits are much the same the world over. And these are about all they see on their excursions. There is no time at all for sightseeing. The race is usually on a Sunday and early on the Monday morning the Formula 1 circus sets off home—to get ready for the next event.

Jack Brabham, Jim Clark, Graham Hill, Chris Amon and Chris Irwin have their own aircraft and fly to events whenever possible. Indeed, with Clark, Hill and Colin Chapman all airborne, the Lotus team becomes rather like a branch of Transport Command.

In one year the R.A.C. alone issues something like 15,000 competition licences. If figures from other countries throughout the world were added to this the total would be enormous. And yet only a mere twenty or so become Graded Drivers—or, in other words, are right at the top of their profession. The most common way of becoming a Graded Driver is to win some World Championship points. Occasionally, however, drivers are admitted to this exclusive category after they've done outstandingly well in some other type of motor race (such as the 24-Hour at Le Mans, or the Targa Florio).

Graded Drivers may not take part in Formula 3 events, nor are they able to compete for the European Formula 2 Championship (though they can take part in F2 races).

For drivers in lesser categories motor racing is apt to be an expensive business. The *Weekend Telegraph* once reported the budget of an enthusiast who raced as a hobby and was apt to be pretty successful. In 1966 he had been prepared to spend £1,000 on the sport. When the year was over he found that, in fact, it had cost him £773.

At the top, by contrast, the rewards are very large indeed. Some drivers receive annual retainers, others earn monthly salaries. All are paid starting money in addition to this—plus bonuses for successes. In a Grand Prix event a driver who has done well in the previous year's World Championship series may well earn £1,500 just for turning up at the race. Ten per cent of the prize money is usually given to the mechanics. The rest is split between driver and entrant on a fifty-fifty basis.

A driver who's right at the top of the tree may gross about £50,000 a year, or even more. But he is one of a few. The average Formula 1 driver probably makes about as much as a middle-management executive in industry. On the other hand, he has none of the executive's security. He works in a job where retirement comes early and there's no pension scheme.

At forty-two Jack Brabham is still driving—and shows no sign of retiring. Graham Hill is thirty-nine. But there are many, younger, drivers who are no longer a permanent part of the Formula 1 scene. Innes Ireland and Tony Maggs are two of them. They are drivers of talent whose names are well known. But such is the intensely competitive nature of Grand Prix racing these days, they can no longer rely on getting any drives.

Very wisely, most of the senior drivers have plans for alternative occupations when the time comes. Jim Clark has his farm in Scotland; Graham Hill is a chairman of a firm called Speedwell Conversions Ltd.; Mike Parkes is a top engineer at the Ferrari plant; and Scarfiotti is heir to a cement factory. Brabham and McLaren will, presumably, continue to manufacture racing cars.

In comparison with horse racing, motor racing may seem to be somewhat underprivileged. The first prize for the 1966 Derby was £74,690, whilst the first prize in the British Grand Prix was only about £2,500. When the steeplechaser Arkle was injured, 500 well-wishers sent the horse 'get well' cards. Nobody has ever sent such a card to a bent B.R.M. (or whatever). When Jackie Stewart was badly injured in the Belgian G.P. of 1966 he only received a hundred cards and letters.

Over in North America the rewards are higher. The prize money for the Can-Am series alone amounts to about half a million dollars. By winning the Indianapolis '500' a driver can make more than he would by winning every race in the World Championship series.[1] It is hard to say what the total

1. A driver who qualifies to start and only completes two laps will have earned himself about £2,000.

Husband-and-wife act Jackie and Helen Stewart
Mike and Linda Spence

Drivers at home Graham Hill and his wife Bette
Chris Irwin

Machinery at factory Building Ferraris at Maranello
Assembling a Ferrari racing engine

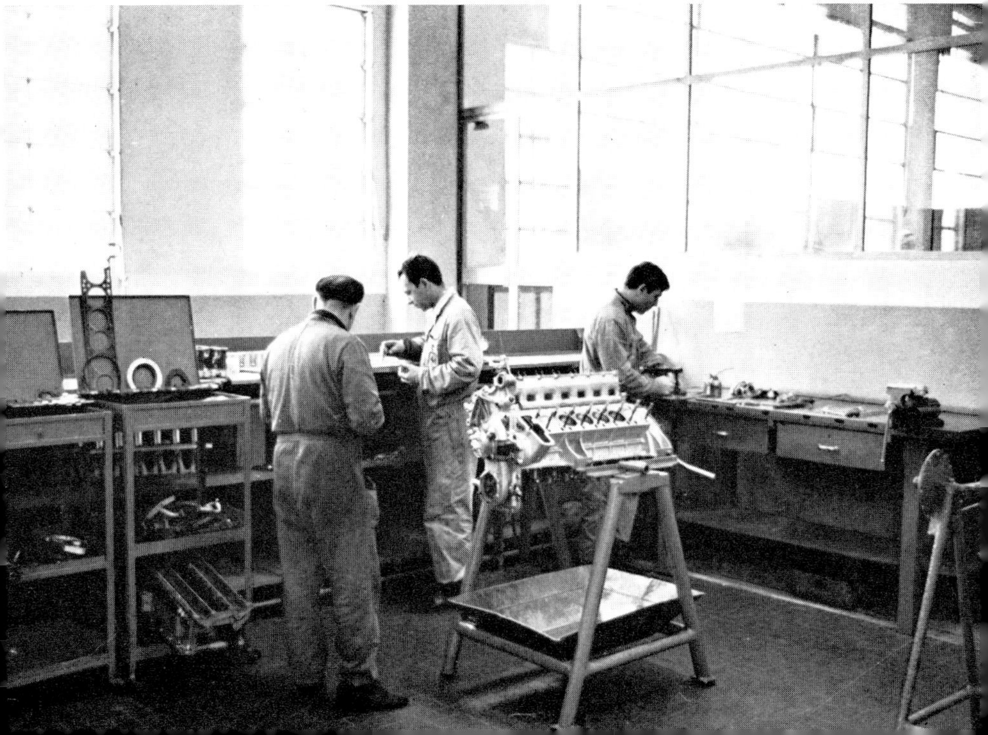

Before the storm

Pedro Rodriguez
Dan Gurney

Chris Amon
John Surtees

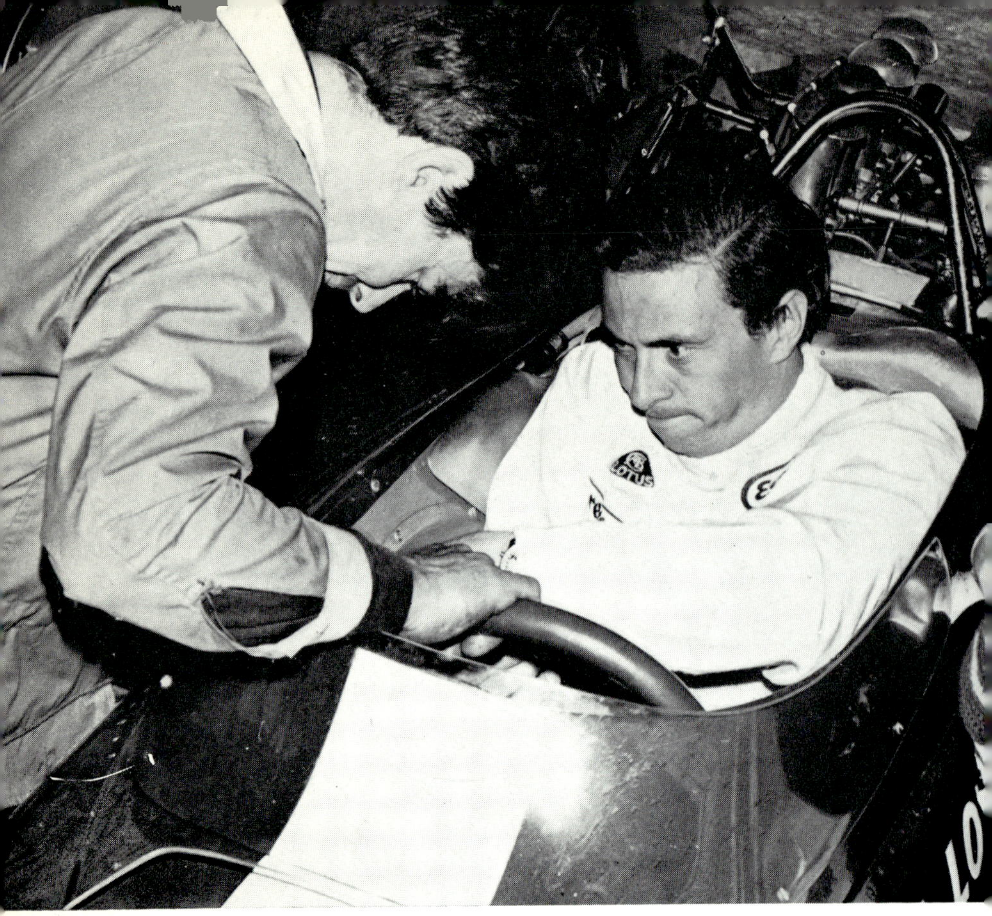

Flying Scotsmen Jim Clark tests the steering position
Jackie Stewart with Tony Rudd and mechanic
(loyally wearing cap in Stewart Tartan)

Putting the lid on
Jack Brabham

Graham Hill

Ready to go   Mike Parkes
              Dan Gurney

(including all the advertising benefits) amounts to, but it must be well over £50,000.

Certainly, what with drag racing, Indianapolis, and so on, an accomplished American driver can comfortably make between £30,000 and £40,000 a year—which is one of the reasons why so few of them come to Europe. It is hardly worth the plane fare.

Britain might reasonably be accused of a somewhat parsimonious attitude towards the honouring of her famous drivers. Back in 1958, Mike Hawthorn became the first British driver ever to win the World Championship. In the same year Tony Vandervell was the first manufacturer to win the newly created Formula 1 Constructors' Championship. When the New Year's Honours List was published it contained the usual array of deserving civil servants, meritorious politicians, and what not, but never a word of Hawthorn or Vandervell.

Currently, Jack Brabham, Jim Clark and Stirling Moss are the only members of the motor-racing fraternity to have received honours. Graham Hill and John Surtees, both former World Champions, have received no recognition from the state. In the 1967 edition of *Who's Who* only Brabham, Clark, Moss, Graham Hill and Colin Chapman are mentioned. John Surtees received an invitation, but he was away in America at the time. He sent his form in too late for publication. Raymond Mays, founder of the B.R.M., does not appear.

Regarded, simply, as failure to recognise success, this lack of enthusiasm by the Establishment would seem to be sufficiently reprehensible. It becomes even worse, however, when one considers the enormously healthy effect which British prestige in the sport has had on car sales in the export market.

One imagines that in a few select homes the cellars must be bulging with bottles of champagne. It has become the custom in some important motor races for the sponsors to present 100 (in some instances, 300) bottles of the brew to the driver who does best in practice. Without exception, however, racing drivers tend to be remarkably abstemious. Many of them don't drink alcohol at all; most confine it to the odd glass of beer or wine. Few of them smoke. Piers Courage gets through about ten cigarettes a day—mostly when he's talking. Chris Amon goes on a cigarette and coffee jag when he's doing a more than usually strenuous stint of travelling, though he tries to give the former up during the days before an important motor race.

On the whole, drivers tend to be sympathetic to the idea of taking exercise, though they usually lament the fact that they don't get enough of it. Graham Hill works off surplus pounds in a gymnasium, Mike Parkes used to keep himself fit by occasionally bicycling to work and by walking upstairs to his 8th-storey apartment. Most drivers cite water ski-ing as their recreation, though shooting is also becoming popular (Jackie Stewart used to be a champion clay pigeon shot before he took up motor racing). In his *Who's Who* entry Jim Clark lists 'Parking in London' as one of his pastimes.

But the thing which singles racing drivers out from ordinary mortals is their competitive spirit. Graham Hill has put it this way: 'I'm like a painter with his canvas and brush. For me, the canvas is the circuit and the brush is the car. I use the car in an attempt to prove that I'm the best driver.'

Jackie Stewart has a punishing urge to do well in pretty well everything he undertakes. The one exception is golf. His handicap is 12, and he seems reasonably content to leave it at that.

And from Richard Attwood: 'It's like chess. If somebody beats me I don't feel "Well done the other bloke". I feel what a clot I must be. Yes—I get annoyed. I hate to feel I've been outwitted.'

Thus, in the final analysis, success is what counts. But racing drivers are tough with themselves. A driver's verdict on his own performance is not necessarily reflected by the result of the race. If he feels that he has won by default, or driven less than well, he is unlikely to join in the cheering—even if he has won. In this respect Graham Hill's analogy of an artist and his brushes seems to be particularly apt. Like people in more creative occupations, top drivers are immensely self-critical. They are continually striving to improve their performances. And that, for many of them, is the purpose behind it all. Ask a top racing driver when he is likely to retire and he'll probably tell you: 'When I don't get any better.'

4

Motor Racing is a Business

Motor racing is a million-pound business, and yet the only people who make any money out of it are the leading drivers. The main reason for this is the enormous cost involved. Ten years ago you could buy a Formula 1 racing car for between £3,000 and £4,000. Nowadays, that might, with a bit of luck, pay for a gearbox—or about half the price of an engine. According to one reliable estimate, a 3 litre F1 car, as competing under the current regulations, will set its owner back anything up to £15,000.

Understandably, perhaps, teams are reluctant to discuss their finances. Rob Walker, one of the last of that dying breed, the private entrant, says that running one car (a Cooper-Maserati) costs him £35,000 a year. From this, of course, prize money, starting money, and contributions from firms which support motor racing have to be deducted. When all the sums have been worked out at the end of a reasonably good season Mr. Walker's net loss is probably about £12,000.

A story which continues to circulate is that the annual cost of motor racing to B.R.M. is around the £100,000 mark. A spokesman for the company, however, vigorously dismisses the figure as inaccurate—and too much of a simplification. It seems that B.R.M. (with the help of other firms which support them) try to break even on their actual racing activities—but this doesn't include the cost of the cars.

And according to Colin Chapman of Lotus: 'You can't make a profit out of motor racing. You try to break even. You have to watch expenses. But there's a conflict of objectives—you can't reconcile the idea of winning races with that of making a profit. It costs a lot of money—and is thoroughly uneconomic—just getting to the race on time.'

Why, then, in an age which is dominated by the profit motive, do people continue to go motor racing? In Mr. Walker's case the answer is beautifully simple. He enjoys the sport, has many friends in it, and he can afford to indulge his passion.

Ferrari, Lotus, Honda, Cooper, Brabham, and to a lesser extent McLaren, are all in business to sell cars. Success on the circuits is an admirable form of publicity. Furthermore, they argue, the very high standards of engineering required by Grand Prix racing is apt to rub off on to the rest of their output. Ford in America (not F1 constructors, but heavily involved in GT and sports car racing) go so far as to claim that it's good for factory morale—a conclusion with which none of the other constructors is likely to disagree.

And so we come to B.R.M., which doesn't build cars for sale—though its parent company, the Rubery Owen Group, makes a good many components.

The first thing which has to be remembered is that Sir Alfred Owen, head of the group, is a great patriot. This may sound to be a somewhat naive statement, but it happens to be true. When he was first approached by Raymond Mays about the problem of producing a successful Grand Prix car for Britain he saw the sense of the argument. And, what's more, he persuaded many other influential people to participate.

Then came the failure of the original enterprise. Sir Alfred bought it up. One reason was that he felt that he'd made a promise and he meant to keep it. The other was that he still believed in the idea. In spite of all the doubters who surrounded him, he thought that success would come—and when it arrived it would be good for Britain and Rubery Owen.

Sir Alfred may be an obstinate man, but, like most millionaires, he has a habit of being right. The interests of his group are vast, and there is no doubt that a victory by a B.R.M. helps to sell such diverse merchandise as castings and filing cabinets.

Motor racing is glamorous. A good many enterprises—they include newspapers and cigarette firms, oil companies and airlines—see in it an opportunity to keep their images shining. One interesting example concerns an old-established engineering works owned by George Lister and Sons Ltd. at Cambridge. The factory runs a service to industry, and is also concerned with restoring iron gates for churches. Any connection with motor racing may seem to be somewhat remote.

In the late forties Lister's felt that their image needed a shot in the arm. And so they embarked on a motor-racing programme. It was very successful. It helped to re-establish the factory, and they have since pulled out of the sport. Nevertheless, they still have a caravan at Silverstone to which the firm's customers are invited.

On a much grander scale is the case of Mercedes Benz in the mid-fifties. In the course of just over a year, they spent something like £1 million on racing. Then, their mission accomplished, they withdrew.

Nevertheless, without the support of the petrol companies, the tyre companies, and the components manufacturers, Formula 1 motor racing would be in very sorry straits. It is estimated that in the course of a year all the oil companies throughout the world put about £2 million into the sport. Nearly every major team has an oil company somewhere in the background. For example, in 1967, Shell supported B.R.M. and Ferrari, Esso were behind Brabham and Lotus, and BP contributed to Cooper and Honda. 'Support' in this sense means a retaining fee of about £30,000 a year, plus about £2,500 in bonuses, plus free fuels and oils (which, according to one oil company's figures, is worth approximately £4,000 a year). These figures only give a rough indication, for, like everything else in motor racing, it is a matter of negotiation and there are no hard and fast rules.[1]

And, of course, at any given moment an oil company may decide to withdraw its support. A typical case is that of Dan Gurney and Mobil. When Gurney set up as a Formula 1 constructor towards the end of 1965 he was heavily backed by Goodyear tyres and Mobil. Then came a change of policy within the latter. No reasons were published, but it doesn't require any great stretch of imagination to see an indication in the firm's advertising. The emphasis has always been on economy runs (as opposed to speed trials). Latterly, moreover, there has been a pronounced emphasis on road safety. The slogan of the current Mobil campaign in the United States is: 'We're in business to sell you petrol. We want you to live.'

To find out more about oil company participation I talked

1. Written before BP and Esso decided to withdraw. For the full and rather sorry story, see Chapter 22.

to a member of the Shell International Petroleum Company. He told me: 'We try to dispel the impression that oil barons hand out bags of gold at the beginning of the season, just for the privilege of advertising victories, and afterwards just sit in the grandstands and watch what happens. It may have been like that fifty years ago. It certainly isn't like it today. We don't support motor racing because it's a sport and we're good sports. We're not being charitable.'

If charity is not involved what *do* they get out of it? The publicity element is obviously important. After any Grand Prix event you have only to look at the papers and see the rash of advertisements from firms which, in one way or another, have contributed to the victory. But Shell claim that they receive an additional reward in the facilities which motor racing provides for research.

'This is very valuable,' I was told. 'The idea isn't just that we hope to win a race. We hope to gain knowledge. For this type of research, a very exotic engine would be needed, and the cost to us would be prohibitive. As it is, we are able to study engines which are the most advanced, the most critically demanding, of any automotive power unit in the world. And this, of course, gives us an opportunity to test new fuels and oils.

'You can't put a price tag on this kind of thing. The engines would cost the earth. Those in Formula 1 cars are used in all parts of the world, in all kinds of climate. They have to use commercially available petrol; and yet, for example, the compression ratio of the H16 B.R.M. is 14:1 and it's probably turning at the rate of 12,000 r.p.m. Moreover, if it breaks down it has to be repaired quickly, regardless of cost, for motor racing is governed by deadlines.'

So—motor racing helps to improve the breed of petrol and lubricants. Apparently, it also helps in other matters too. Three years ago the B.R.M. engine was suffering from cam wear. The tappets were breaking up under the steel cams when the engine was going at full blast. B.R.M. couldn't find an answer to the problem and so they took it to Shell.

Metallurgists examined it and came up with a special hardening process. The problem was solved: the results pigeon-holed. Nobody thought any more about it for the next eighteen months. And then, the same trouble occurred all over again—though, this time, it was affecting the development of an ordinary family car. The B.R.M. solution was applied. Once again it worked.

The method of oil company sponsorship varies. Some prefer to sign contracts with individual drivers. Others prefer to support teams. 'In the long run,' I was told by a member of the latter persuasion, 'there's more milage in teams. Bentleys, Alfas, Ferrari, everybody knows about them, but who remembers the drivers?'

Nevertheless, even these people reserve the right to sign up an outstanding driver—a World Champion, an ex-World Champion, or somebody who, fairly obviously, is going to make it one day.

By tradition, the oil companies supply overalls to the racing mechanics, the tyre companies supply them to the drivers. On recent evidence, however, there are signs that this state of affairs is breaking up. More and more teams now seem to have all their outfits supplied by the tyre firm.

This is symptomatic of the tyre war which has been blazing across the Grand Prix world during the past two years. For a very long period indeed Dunlop had a virtual monopoly in the world of Formula 1 motor racing. From 1946, however, the American companies began to take an interest in motor sport. To begin with, their activities were confined to the U.S.A. Firestone began manufacturing tyres with a flat tread surface ('slick' tyres, they call them) for midget racing. Then they developed the idea, and applied it to drag racing—until, by 1958, Firestone slicks seemed to be essential equipment for hot dragsters.

Meanwhile Goodyear, after a protracted period of motor-racing hibernation, were beginning to reawaken to the sport. Among other things, they took a considerable interest in World Land Speed Record bids. Craig Breedlove, current holder of the record, used Goodyear for all his runs.

Inevitably the activities of Firestone and Goodyear eventually spread to Europe and Formula 1 racing. Dunlop found itself fighting on two fronts. On one side it was a battle for technical perfection. On the other it was a matter of money. The ordinary motorist is already benefiting from the former— just as racing teams are enjoying the rewards of the latter. Possibly, the only people who are not gaining anything are Dunlop. They may now be committed to a situation from which, if circumstances were different, they'd gladly withdraw.

Retainers, on the whole, are less common from the tyremakers than they are from the oilmen. Bonuses and free tyres are more the kind of things to expect, which is probably just as well. Entrants and drivers are obviously deeply concerned with the development of tyres. But, since lives and victories depend on them, they are likely to use whichever make seems to be most appropriate for the race.

Back in the days of motor racing at Brooklands, about 12,000 people used to turn up for a big race. At Silverstone today the figure is more likely to be 100,000. This is highly desirable and the organisers could well do with more. For putting on a major event is a very expensive business. There are several opinions about the cost of mounting a Grand Prix meeting. The most plausible puts the figure at about £80,000. Of this, about £30,000 can be accounted for by starting fees and cash prizes.[1]

The responsibility for finding this money belongs to the organisers, who make little or no profit out of a Grand Prix event. Much better, from a business point of view, is a club meeting—where the prizes are very moderate, and the entrants actually pay to compete.

Clearly, the public contributes to the bulk of the expenditure. In addition to this, there is usually a sponsor, who guarantees to make good any loss. In Britain the *Daily Mail* traditionally sponsors the British Grand Prix when it takes place at Brands Hatch, whilst Silverstone is the *Daily Express*'s pitch. Both papers decline to give any idea of what these ventures cost them, although I understand that the expense is comparatively small.

In other countries local tourist boards often contribute to the cost of meetings. It is estimated that the annual 24-Hour Race gives a boost of something like £1½ million to the economy of the Le Mans area of France. When in the mid-twenties it was decided to build a motor racing circuit at Nurburgring one of the main objects was to create work for the unemployed in the Cologne-Coblenz region (among its most active protagonists was the late Dr. Konrad Adenauer, who was then mayor of Cologne). But a secondary, though scarcely less important, objective was to introduce tourism to the Eifel

---

1. The value of the machinery on the starting grid is far above £200,000, and none of it can reasonably be insured—the premiums would be far too high to be worth while.

district. And so on. Scratch a European Grand Prix and the likelihood is that somewhere you'll find tourism as part of its purpose.

Motor racing used to be the sport of the well-to-do. Now it is a mass-spectator industry, which somehow manages to negotiate a precarious tight-rope bridging the abyss between profit and loss. At the beginning of 1967, everything was going well. Nevertheless, it was a somewhat chilling thought to consider what might happen if the oil companies and the tyre companies and the rest of big business decided to pull out. Could Formula 1 racing survive? There are many people who, at the time, said it couldn't.

Happily, though, there's another way of looking at it. When carrying out the research for this book, I visited all the major entrants. My first question, invariably, was: 'Why do you do it?' The answer always came quickly and completely spontaneously. 'Because I enjoy it', they all said. And then, as if aware of their business responsibilities, they dug around for more practical reasons.

Grand Prix motor racing is primarily a matter of enthusiasm, and the enthusiasm for it is enormous. With such powerful emotional backing it seems unlikely that anything could kill it off.

5

Curtain-raiser

ON November 18th, 1965, the Formula 1 constructors met at the C.S.I. offices in Paris. The meeting which lay ahead of them was going to be a difficult one. With C.S.I. officials they had to hammer out regulations which would govern F1 racing for the next four years.

The $1\frac{1}{2}$ litre limit on engines had never been particularly popular. When it was introduced, supposedly in the interests of safety, in 1961 it produced an outcry. Many people inwardly blamed the French, who hadn't produced a Grand Prix car since the Gordini. The drivers, especially, were against it. They felt that it gave them too few opportunities to prove their skills. Furthermore, it was an anachronism. Apart from weirdies designed to break specific speed records, the Formula 1 racing car was supposed to be the absolute in power in speed. Now it was nothing of the kind. There were several sports-racing cars and prototypes capable of much quicker performances.

Among the leading members of the C.S.I. are organisers of motor-racing events. They believed that more powerful cars would increase the appeal of F1 events to spectators. But now that it came to the point, the constructors had doubts.

The situation is best summed up by the feelings of Jack Brabham. As a driver, he welcomed the kind of changes which were likely. As a constructor, however, he saw the difficulties. Coventry Climax, which were manufacturing the engines for most of the British cars at the time, has already refused to build a 2 litre version. B.R.M. were only too well aware of the enormous cost of building and developing a new engine—plus a car to contain it. Probably, if things had been left to the constructors, the regulations would have remained where they were.

But they knew that this was impossible. Before the C.S.I. meeting they had accordingly agreed to press for a 3 litre limit. Knowing how the collective mind of the C.S.I. worked, they suspected that it would be cut back to something smaller.

On this day, however, the C.S.I. didn't run true to form. To most people's amazement they agreed. The new regulations stipulated a 3 litre limit on engines—or, if anyone wanted it that way, $1\frac{1}{2}$ litres supercharged.

To describe the reactions to the decision as an outcry would be to over-dramatise the situation. There was, however, a strong body of opinion which believed that it could, conceivably, put at end to Formula 1 racing. Where, they asked, will the engines come from? There'll never be enough cars to make a race.

Other people reacted in different ways. Bruce McLaren had hoped that production-car engines of up to 5 litres might be allowed. Colin Chapman was prepared to go along with the idea of a 3 litre limit, though he considered that the maximum number of cylinders should be restricted to eight. And so it went on. In the end all the constructors did what they clearly had to do—accept the situation and plan accordingly.

The possibility of using a $1\frac{1}{2}$ litre supercharged engine was quickly dismissed as impractical. Unless some method of cooling the gas could be found it was likely to produce explosions just when nobody wanted them. When this type of engine ran on alcohol it was all very well. Alcohol vaporises very quickly in the inlet tracts. As it does so, it cools down. But commercially available petrol was quite another matter. The only possible solution would be to use a heat exchanger, and that would immediately introduce a host of other problems and expense.

And so 3 litres unsupercharged it had to be. The constructors came up with all sorts of ideas. Some modified existing sports-car engines, others built entirely new ones. At one end of the scale was Jack Brabham, who staked everything on lightness and simplicity. At the other was B.R.M.'s chief engineer, Tony Rudd. Rudd produced a fantastic H16 engine, the like of which had never been in a car before.

Brabham's solution was a short term one. Rudd's was a

long-term effort. When it was first shown to the Press at the B.R.M. works in Lincolnshire Sir Alfred Owen warned journalists not to expect too much too soon. By 1968, when the various bugs will have been beaten out of the systems of the new cars, the accent will be on sheer power. That is when the H16, with its enormous development potential, will come into its own.

The new regulations came into effect in 1966. As everybody now knows, Brabham got it right. He won the French, Dutch, British, and German Grands Prix—the World Championship by a handsome margin and the Formula 1 Constructors' Championship.

Winter in the Northern Hemisphere is a time when constructors contemplate the lessons of the previous season, put in development work on their cars, and consider who they wish to drive for them in the coming year.

At the beginning of 1966 John Surtees was once more listed as the number one Ferrari driver. He'd won his World Championship in a Ferrari back in 1964, was heavily tipped as the likely Champion of 1966, and was expected to do no less well for his team in sports-car races.

But then came the drama. The racing director of Ferrari was a gentleman who owned a women's underwear factory in Milan. His name was Dragoni, and his position in motor racing was a curious anomaly, for he never received (nor, one gathers, asked) any payment for it.

Surtees and Dragoni had never hit it off. A series of squalls turned into a tempest on the eve of the 24-Hour Race at Le Mans and ended with the driver walking out. Scarfiotti took over his place in the team. John Surtees, looking tired and worried, returned to England.

Motor racing is a mass of 'ifs'. The big *if* in this case is what might have happened had Dragoni and Surtees managed to co-exist until the end of the year. For, shortly before Christmas 1966, it was announced that the former had resigned from his position at Ferrari's, and the duties of racing manager were to be taken over by a well-known motor-racing journalist named Franco Lini.

However, it's no use speculating. For the latter half of 1966, Surtees drove for Cooper-Maserati and ended the season by winning the Mexican Grand Prix for them. He then transferred to Honda, became the sole Honda driver, and began to apply his by no means inconsiderable technical ability to the developments of the Japanese Formula 1 racing car.

His place in the Ferrari F1 team was taken by Mike Parkes.

The other drama of 1966 concerned Graham Hill. Hill had begun his career as a professional driver with Lotus. He joined B.R.M. in 1960, and won the World Championship in 1962. He soldiered on with them, apparently very happy, until the end of 1966. And then came the shattering news. He was to quit B.R.M. and rejoin Lotus.

There were all sorts of rumours. He had won the Indianapolis '500' that year in a Lola Ford. Some people said that Ford (who are closely connected with Lotus) were behind the switch. There was talk of astronomical sums of money. Hill himself said that he had been with B.R.M. quite long enough, and that it was time for a change. Lotus, whilst welcoming him back into the fold, had nothing to say.

And so, at the start of 1967, the following line-up of Grand Prix drivers appeared:

Lotus was in the remarkable position of having two ex-World Champions, Jim Clark and Graham Hill, in its team. Brabham had himself and New Zealander Denis Hulme. Honda had John Surtees, Cooper-Maserati had Jochen Rindt and Pedro Rodriguez. Gurney had Gurney and his fellow Californian Richie Ginther. Rob Walker had Jo Siffert. Bruce McLaren was driving for himself. Ferrari had Mike Parkes, Lorenzo Bandini, Ludivico Scarfiotti, Chris Amon, and Jonathan Williams to choose from. And B.R.M. had Jackie Stewart.

But B.R.M. is in the unusual position of having what might be described as a 2nd XI. Tim (son of Reg) Parnell is, technically at any rate, a private entrant. He hires his cars from B.R.M. and enjoys an unusually close relationship with the factory. There are even occasions when he actually works for B.R.M., such as the Tasman Series, when he acts as team manager.

Thus, for 1967 only Jackie Stewart was under contract to the B.R.M. works team. But Tim Parnell had a further pool of talent consisting of Mike Spence, Chris Irwin and Piers Courage. The last two had been promoted into Formula 1 racing after an unusually promising season in Formula 3. It was a situation which recalled Jackie Stewart's fantastic jump to the top.

With Stewart as number one driver, B.R.M. reserved the right to select a number two on an *ad hoc* basis from Tim Parnell.

On the eve of the Tasman Series, and when constructors were feverishly (for motor racing is, by its very nature, a feverish business) preparing their plans for the coming year, the South African Grand Prix took place on January 2nd, 1967, at Kyalami.

The first South African Grand Prix was won by Whitney Straight at the wheel of a Maserati in 1934. Since the World Championship was introduced it has featured in the series since 1959—with the exception of 1964, when it was dropped. For a number of years it took place round about Christmas time, and was the concluding event in the series. More recently, it was pushed forward into the New Year. In 1967, therefore, it was the first of the eleven events which would determine the outcome of the Championship.

In the past the race had been mostly held on the coast at East London. In 1967, however, it was moved to Kyalami near Johannesburg. After Mexico City (altitude: 7,000 feet above sea level) it (at 6,000 feet) is probably the highest Grand Prix circuit in the world. This, in itself, poses problems. There's less oxygen in the air, which tends to rob engines of power. As it turned out, the South African G.P.—like the Mexican event—was won by a Cooper-Maserati. It also turned out to be a monstrous car-killer. Out of the eighteen projectiles which set off from the grid, only eight finished.

Any motor race which seems to be won from the word 'go' is bound to be dull. At first the South African Grand Prix looked like becoming the kind of procession we'd all become used to in 1966. The two Brabhams were well out in front, and they gave every sign of staying there. Whilst nobody would dream of begrudging this brilliant marque any success which comes its way, this kind of ascendancy lacks spectator appeal.

However, anyone who jumped to conclusions was in for a surprise. They misjudged the necromancy of Kyalami. This race was to spring a heap of surprises. Jack Brabham's engine was the first of the two in his team to fail. At forty-one laps it overheated and brought him into the pits. After that the race was never quite the same for Brabham. Denis Hulme went on in first place, just where he'd been all the time. He remained there for fifty-nine out of the eighty laps, and then he, too, ran into trouble. The fuel pump (they had to pack dry ice around it) caused his first pit-stop, and then there was a spot of bother with the brakes. All this cost him a lot of valuable seconds, and the remaining fifteen laps were not nearly enough to regain them.

The other supremos of motor racing had come to grief comparatively early on. Jackie Stewart's B.R.M. faded out after only three laps. Mike Spence's motored for thirty-one laps but was never very competitive. Graham Hill, in his Lotus, experienced all sorts of trouble. During the first six laps he spun twice, ran over a kerb, broke a wishbone, and tore away an oil line.

His team mate, Jim Clark, was slightly more successful. His Lotus survived for twenty-one laps, after which it retired with overheating troubles. The wings of Dan Gurney's Eagle were clipped when a rear-suspension mount was pulled out later on in the race.

And so there it was: disaster, disaster, disaster—up to a point. But the race was going on, and some very extraordinary things were happening. John Love, driving a somewhat elderly 2·7 Cooper Climax, was leading. Pedro Rodriguez, who had lost second and third gears (due to a broken selector), was in second place—after his Cooper-Maserati colleague, Jochen Rindt, had been compelled to call it a day. Rindt had been driving a somewhat sick car with the kind of panache you expect from a driver who considers that an F1 machine should go at ten-tenths and that's it. Unfortunately, if a car is ill enough it will expire—no matter what the driver thinks. This one finally died when the oil pressure failed.

Ken Tyrrell recalls with amusement the day when Tony Maggs and John Love were driving for him in Formula Junior, and one of them was to go forward into the Cooper F1 team. 'Their records,' Tyrrell once told me, 'were almost identical. Maggs had a more classic approach—a beautiful style. Love had more of the "get out of the way, I'm coming through" attitude. They had both won more or less the same number of races, but Maggs was a good deal younger than Love. For this reason, John Cooper chose Maggs.'

Alas—one hears little of Maggs these days. Love, on the other hand, has been Champion of South Africa for 1964, 1965 and 1966. And there he was, in this very hard-fought and punishing South African Grand Prix, looking (to the crowd's huge delight, for he is a Rhodesian) as if he was going to win it.

A mess of pottage may be a cheap price for a birthright, and a tiny fault in an auxiliary fuel pump is the damnedest thing from which to lose a motor race. John Love's Cooper had two fuel tanks. When supplies in the main tank were running low the job of this pump was to bring up reinforcements from the auxiliary. And it failed. Love and his Cooper came into the pits.

The service was superb. Within a matter of seconds he was back in the race and driving very, very quickly indeed—in spite of the fact that his engine still seemed to be missing.

There were seven laps to go.

Rodriguez ignored all temptation to hunt for the missing second and third gears (which would probably have wrecked the gearbox), and motored away with masterly skill until he won the race. He thereby secured 9 points towards his World Championship total, and earned himself a contract with Cooper-Maserati. John Love came second, Surtees third, Hulme fourth, Bob Anderson fifth, and Jack Brabham sixth.

It seemed unlikely that the South African G.P. provided many clues to what might happen in the rest of the series. Several cars (notably the B.R.M.) were obviously in the need of further development. Ferrari and Bruce McLaren weren't there at all. John Love, in spite of his 6 points, is hardly a serious contender for the Championship, for he seldom races outside Africa. None of the cars which competed were the ones to be used for the brunt of 1967 Grand Prix racing. Anyway for whatever it may be worth, here is how the World Championship stood on the evening of January 2nd, 1967:

1. Pedro Rodriguez 9 points
2. John Love 6 points
3. John Surtees 4 points
4. Denis Hulme 3 points
5. Bob Anderson 2 points
6. Jack Brabham 1 point

And so to Europe . . .

PART II

Trial of Strength

6

The B.R.M.: A Grand Prix Car for Britain

SOME circuits seem to suit certain cars. In 1963 Graham Hill, at the wheel of a B.R.M., won the Monaco Grand Prix. He won it again in 1964, and then in 1965. In 1966 he was less successful, but B.R.M. kept up its record. In that year the race was won by Jackie Stewart.

Ferrari won the Argentine Grand Prix for four years in succession, and Lotus did the same thing at Spa. With these two exceptions, no other marque can come within range of B.R.M.'s record at Monte Carlo.[1]

This is an extremely difficult course. It is very twisty, hemmed in by hotels, with a lot of hills and hardly any straights. Of all the G.P. circuits, this is the one which metes out the toughest punishment to cars.

When the B.R.M. was successful there in 1966 the H16 car wasn't yet competitive. Consequently, Stewart had to use the 2 litre V8 engine, which may have been low in power compared with the competition, but was high on reliability. By 1967 the H16 version was ready. It had enormous potential power, but it had yet to show any marked staying power. Could it stand up to the rigors of this very difficult tour of the Principality? There were a great many doubts.

Since the advent of the Vanwall and the Cooper back in the late fifties, when British Formula 1 domination began, the B.R.M. has tended to melt into the background. It is regarded as just another racing car. When it's on form it is brilliantly

---

1. With the possible exception of B.R.M. itself. For three years in succession Graham Hill won the United States Grand Prix in one of these cars. In the fourth year Jim Clark won it in a Lotus, but using an H16 B.R.M. engine.

successful. On its off-days it breaks down. In other words, it is very much like any other marque—a beautifully engineered though somewhat capricious machine.

People have short memories. They forget the enormous number of hopes which were pinned on it when it was first announced some eighteen years ago. Other British single-seater racing cars have been constructed, developed and achieved success. But the B.R.M. came first. This was the original serious bid to give the nation a competitive G.P. car.

Raymond Mays, founder of B.R.M., had been extremely successful in motor racing during the years between the wars. At some stage he teamed up with Peter Berthon, a former R.A.F. cadet, who had narrowly escaped death when his aircraft landed upside down.

Between them they designed and built a racing car called the E.R.A. (from English Racing Automobiles Ltd.). It had a $1\frac{1}{2}$ litre engine, but it was essentially a light car and no match in Grands Prix for the thunderous heavyweights which Germany and Italy were racing, though it did very well in less illustrous events.

During the Second World War, Mays went back to Bourne in Lincolnshire to manage his family's wool business. Berthon became involved in aero engine development. They met occasionally, and most of their conversation centred on the possibility of building a car which would do Britain justice in Grand Prix races. By the time the war was over they had produced drawings for it.

Raymond Mays is a tall, erect figure with considerable charm and no less effective powers of persuasion. Furthermore, he is apt to get things done. Having roughed out a plan, he set about enlisting support for it. On March 2nd, 1945, he sent out a letter to motor manufacturers and component manufacturers. The latter included all the firms which had made parts for the E.R.A.

The first two replies came from Oliver Lucas, then managing director of Joseph Lucas Ltd., and Alfred Owen, head of the Owen Organisation. Both sent cheques for £1,000 and offered to provide the components for nothing. Sir John Black of the Standard Motor Company sent a cheque for £5,000, and the funds began to build up. Within a year Mays collected something like £25,000 for his project. A trust was set up to control the funds and direct it.

Among those who volunteered to help were car clubs from all over the country. Those in the Midlands set up a fund to purchase a mobile workshop for the car. Others announced that they were seeking ways in which to be useful.

The Ministry of Supply made vague grunts of approval, but its support was confined to a promise that it wouldn't interfere. As assistance goes, that may sound to be somewhat slender. But in those days non-intervention from a Ministry was something to be cherished.

The first B.R.M. was ready (if that is the right word) by the middle of 1950. It performed a couple of demonstration laps before the King and Queen at the British Grand Prix meeting at Silverstone, and everybody was immensely enthusiastic. Perhaps, in a way, popular enthusiasm was to be its downfall. It was more or less pressed into taking part in the *Daily Express* International Trophy Race on August 26th, when it had no business to be competing in anything. Raymond Sommer was to be at the wheel.

Inevitably, everything went wrong. The car was under-developed, under-prepared, under- just about everything you can think of. As the rest of the field roared away from the starting grid, the B.R.M. jerked forward a couple of yards. There was a dull, metallic crunch, and it came to a sickening standstill. The inner universals of the axle half shafts had broken.

The crowd, who ought to have known better, booed. As the sick car was pushed into the paddock, a few of them mockingly tossed pennies into the cockpit.

The first B.R.M. ought to have been a world-beater. Its massive $1\frac{1}{2}$ litre supercharged V16 engine developed enormous power (by 1952 it was producing 530 b.h.p.). All the famous drivers who tried it—and, in some cases, raced it—admired its design. Even Alfred Neubauer of Mercedes, who once visited the works, praised it. It won fourteen races in five years. None of them was a Grand Prix event.

Furthermore, it suffered from at least one stroke of extremely ill-fortune. In 1952, just when it might have become competitive, Formula 1 was abandoned for the World Championship series. During that year and the following, Formula 2 (2 litres unsupercharged, 500 c.c. supercharged) was used. The B.R.M. was not eligible. Its usefulness was already over.

Let Raymond Mays have the last word on it with his description (from *Competitive Driving*, edited by Peter Roberts) of the V16 starting up.

'It was never a difficult car to start, but one always had to wait a few moments for all sixteen cylinders to hit. When it was fitted with stub pipes a puff of smoke would explode out of one, then another, of the sixteen pipes. Then the rest would catch, and finally the car would scream into vibrant life. The sound and fury of the old car starting up could always guarantee to empty the other parts of the paddock as the crowds thronged round to hear this wonderful noise.'

So far there have been five B.R.M.s. The first had the V16 $1\frac{1}{2}$ litre supercharged engine. Then, resulting from the change in Formula 1 racing regulations, came the $2\frac{1}{2}$ litre 4-cylinder unblown engine. For most of its life the power unit was up front—towards the end, however, it was mounted at the rear. Then (the C.S.I. regulations had changed again) came the $1\frac{1}{2}$ litre V8 unsupercharged; and, finally, the H16.

But back in 1952 there had been trouble in the B.R.M. camp. The method of running things by a trust hadn't worked out well. For one thing, there was a lot of dissatisfaction about the car's apparent inability to win races. And there were obviously a good many other faults—such as the fact that no fewer than 350 different firms were supplying parts.

An extraordinary general meeting of the trust was held at Stratford-on-Avon on September 4th, 1952. After a lot of talk, some of it bitterly acrimonious, it was decided to put the project up for sale. The cars were valued at £500 apiece, and seven offers were received. One of the contenders simply wanted to buy the debts (for tax purposes, one must assume). Another wanted the plant, machinery and motor transport, but not the cars. The only one which included everything came from Sir Alfred Owen. It was thankfully accepted, and the Owen Racing Organisation was formed.

The B.R.M. had been reprieved, but it still had a long way to go.

Superchargers for the original engines had been provided by Rolls-Royce. These were complicated affairs with 124 different components in them. To help the B.R.M. people cope with them, Rolls-Royce seconded a young engineer to Bourne. His name was Tony Rudd.

Tony Rudd has many abilities, and one of them is the gift of total recall. During the war he had been employed on the production of aircraft engines. Nowadays, nearly twenty-five years later, he can still remember the numbers of nearly all the parts.

When he was at school he had to study a Shakespeare play for an examination. He did so by the somewhat original expedient of learning the whole thing off by heart.

He liked things so much at Bourne that he decided to stay there. He resigned from Rolls-Royce, signed on with B.R.M. Presently he was put in charge of the racing shop and the test bed (situated on a disused airfield some miles away from the works at Folkingham). He also carried out engine development work.

In early 1962 there was a dramatic meeting between Rudd and Sir Alfred Owen. The gist of it was that Tony Rudd was offered the post of chief engineer and team manager of B.R.M., but on certain conditions. He had to keep within the budget and within six months he had to win at least two Grand Prix races. If he failed the whole thing would be closed down.

Rudd kept within the budget, and he began to win races. One of them was Graham Hill's victory in the Dutch Grand Prix. By late July he felt confident enough to write Sir Alfred a letter outlining his plans for the following year.

Sir Alfred's reply was posted on August 4th, which was a Saturday. It was a somewhat short note, which pointed out that 'you have not yet won two Grand Prix races'. It reached Bourne on the Monday, but by then the battle was over. On the Sunday, at Nurburgring, Graham Hill had won the German G.P. The end of the year saw Hill as World Champion and B.R.M. winning the Formula 1 Constructors' Championship.

When, in 1965, the new Formula 1 regulations were discussed in Paris, B.R.M. greeted them without much enthusiasm. Motor racing may be a sport, but it is also a business. Like any other enterprise, it is vulnerable to excessive spending, and constructing an entirely new car is a very expensive undertaking indeed.

B.R.M. were in a particularly difficult position, for they only manufacture Formula 1 racing cars. Other teams might be able to adapt sports-car engines. For them it was quite out of the question. They had to build something new.

Like all his colleagues in the sport, Rudd rejected the idea of a supercharged engine immediately. But, having got this out of the way, there still seemed to be an almost infinite number of problems. Solving them was largely a matter of elimination.

The first possibility to be excluded was that of using the V8 engine. It had already been stretched about as far as it could go, and it would certainly never produce enough power ultimately. A V16 engine was considered and turned down, and so was a 24-cylinder unit.

Eventually the choice was narrowed down to a V12 and an H16. The latter configuration had once been used in an aircraft engine, built by Napier for seaplanes intended for the transatlantic run. So far as cars were concerned, it was entirely original.

The V12 was clearly the more simple of the two. It could function with a 5-speed transmission (the H16 needed a 6-speed) and it was lighter. Against this, however, had to be set certain disadvantages. It was inclined to upset the balance of the car which Rudd had in mind, and it hadn't anything like the development potential of the H16.

Admittedly, the H16, being such an entirely new concept, was fraught with unknown quantities. Its weight also argued against it, though it suited the balance of the car. Furthermore, it could use many of the components from the V8 and it was absolutely loaded with development possibilities. Taking the long view, this was the one to have. Tony Rudd and the rest of the Owen Racing Organisation took the long view. The H16 it was.

Nevertheless, the V12 idea was not abandoned. B.R.M. decided to build a number for their customers. One of them was purchased by Bruce McLaren. He told me: 'It's simpler and easier to maintain than the H16. The H16 obviously has more power, but it needs a big set-up like B.R.M.'s to maintain and keep it running.'

There must have been many races which in 1966 B.R.M. would cheerfully have missed. Several of the H16 components had turned out to be much harder to manufacture than anyone could have imagined. It was not until February of that year that the first engine was ready for testing. By May, the car which should have been ready for the Monaco Grand Prix was still in the throes of development. One of them was taken to the race, but it produced so much trouble in practice that it was discarded. Instead, they used a V8.

Indeed such was the problem of fitting development work and testing into an already overcrowded schedule that they used the V8 quite a lot that year. And it was still extremely competitive.

But you can't go on using outdated machinery for ever. In 1967 the H16 engine was to be put to the test for what, in all fairness, was really the first time.

7

Round and Round the Houses

I FLEW out to Monaco in early May of 1967 with one purpose in mind: to follow the fortunes of the B.R.M. team. No other marque had won this Grand Prix so many times in succession.[1] In only needed another victory to put the score up to five. And that would be a record unequalled in any World Championship event.

Perhaps the most extraordinary thing about the Monaco Grand Prix is that it was ever invented. The 1·95-mile circuit is hemmed in by buildings for most of the way. For a brief distance it runs along the harbour wall, where the hazard of colliding with concrete yields to the possibility of pitching into the drink. There are several hills, a tunnel, and hairpins galore.

One can imagine Minis scuttling round it, but as an arena for Formula 1 machines it seems completely impossible.

The first Monaco Grand Prix was held in 1929. The 1967 edition was the twenty-fifth. During this period there have been relatively few changes to the course. One of them has been to shift the starting line. Originally the cars only travelled a matter of yards before they arrived at the first hairpin. It may have suggested a super spectacle but it was highly dangerous.

Apart from this and a few minor modifications the course is just as it was when the old bangers roared round it. And yet the race of 1967 was won at an average speed of 76·34 m.p.h., whilst in 1929 W. Williams in a Bugatti went round at 52·7 m.p.h.

For the winner there's a prize of 10,000 francs, plus the customary item of silverware. Never have francs been more

1. Bugatti won it four times, though not in succession.

arduously earned. The race distance is 195 miles (100 laps), and it takes the best part of 2 hours and 40 minutes, which is the longest time of any World Championship event. The machinery, of course, undergoes most fearful punishment, but before we lavish too much sympathy upon it, let's think of the drivers. To *complete* the race needs enormous stamina. To win it you have to be little less than a superman.

B.R.M.'s headquarters for the event is a garage called the Auto Palace. It is perched up on a hill overlooking the town. For most of the week before the race the team takes over the first floor, which is really a gallery with a rickety rail running along one side and a large lift that wheezes up and down from the ground floor.

From the Auto Palace the cars are towed down to the circuit by the transporter. The route is along steep and twisting roads which make the driver's life a nightmare (though, in all honesty, he never seems perturbed by the experience). And after each practice session they return up the hill, wheeze up in the lift to the gallery, and are promptly taken to pieces and refurbished.

It's not for me to knock motion pictures, but there was one about Grand Prix racing. Everyone was highly emotional in it; and actors, playing the part of drivers, always seemed to be helping themselves to several fingers of Scotch (drivers playing the part of drivers didn't, no doubt because they hardly ever touch the stuff. Overlooking the Monaco circuit is a place called the Tip Top Bar. There's nothing particularly marvellous about it, except that *everybody* goes there on the night of the race. At these Tip Top soirées you can tell the drivers from the non-drivers because they are the only people hitting the fruit juice.). Anyway, in this film there's a lot of shouting and emoting, all of which is very wrong. Whatever turmoils may be seething within, motor-racing people present a somewhat unemotional front to the world. The only time when anyone shouts is when a pack of cars is thundering past, and it's the only way of communicating.

And so it is on the first floor of the Auto Palace. The mechanics go about their work purposefully, seldom talking and then often in whispers. It isn't what you might call a reverent silence, but one of total preoccupation. They work neatly, confidently, with capable movements which are pleasing to watch.

Tony Rudd, manager and chief engineer of the B.R.M. team, is obviously under pressure. The only signs of it, though, are the fact that he is more than usually quiet. He sometimes emits a noise which isn't quite whistling (it's more like steam escaping from a muffled kettle) and has an occasional bout of pressurised finger stretching. He talks slowly. Sometimes he wanders off along the gallery, leans over the rickety rail and looks across at the blank face of the opposite wall. On these occasions his features seem to dissolve into a balloon with the word THINKS written across it. Which is understandable: quite apart from the huge technical problems involved in the race, Rudd is putting on a show in which the performers actually risk their lives.

For this twenty-fifth Monaco Grand Prix he has a further problem. He has to decide which cars to use. He has brought three to the Auto Palace, a pair of H16s and a V8 which was used in the Tasman Series. Jackie Stewart and Mike Spence are driving for him—with Stewart, of course, the favourite. The H16 engine is more powerful, but the V8 has been proven. And this is the eccentric circuit, where top gear is seldom used and very high speeds just aren't possible. Is power more important than reliability? Will a lighter car be more competitive than a heavier one? Which will Stewart feel happiest in? These are the questions and, believe me, they take a lot of answering. Somehow, he has to suck the evidence out of the practice results and then stick it together and make a decision.

There are three practice sessions, and these are rather hairy. It isn't just a question of getting used to the circuit. Nor is it merely a matter of testing the machinery. Like any other motor race, the drivers' positions on the starting grid depend on their lap times. With its somewhat small collection of straights, the Monaco circuit makes overtaking difficult. Whoever gets out in front is liable to stay there (provided he doesn't spin off, or break down. Provided, provided, provided ... the word is always cropping up.). Furthermore, there's a limit to the number of F1 cars which can reasonably take part. Works teams are assured of entries. They take up eleven of the sixteen places which leaves five to be fought for by eight cars. And so, as you can very clearly see, there was a great deal more to practice than practising.

On the Thursday and Friday they took all three cars down to the circuit. Stewart tried the V8 and the H16. Spence drove the H16 all the time. Things went wrong. On Friday Spence's crown wheel and pinion packed up. Stewart's drive shaft (in the V8) broke. He hitched a lift back to the pits on the back of Jim Clark's Lotus.

But that afternoon Rudd arrived at his decision. He decided that Stewart would use the V8 car. He told me: 'I think there are two reasons. The first is that, because it's lighter, the car is less fatiguing to drive on this very fatiguing circuit. That gives Jackie a better chance. The other is that its reliability has already been proven.'

Stewart accepted the news happily enough. That's his way. He is an extremely disciplined driver, with a great deal of faith in Rudd. He drives whatever he's told to drive, though he often argues about it afterwards.

Tim Parnell was there with another V8 B.R.M. driven by Piers Courage. On the Friday practice Courage went into a mild sort of spin and the car was damaged. This added to Rudd's worries. He couldn't see how you can bash a monocoque without distorting it. He drove down to the Parnell garage, looked at the car very, very carefully and asked a good many questions. Afterwards he seemed happier. The monocoque, it appeared, had not been distorted.

In the Auto Palace they worked late on Friday night—just as they had done on the Thursday. There was Mike Spence's gearbox to be taken to pieces and the crown wheel replaced. For the V8 there was another engine which everybody thought would be more powerful. And so the two had to be switched.

Stewart and Spence looked in. Spence, who is a brilliant test driver and takes a most detailed interest in machinery, stayed for quite a long time.

In a mechanic's life before a big race there are two elements: work and sleep. There's a lot of the former and little of the latter. Two of the B.R.M. boys had worked out a system for double-breaking the bank at Monte Carlo. The bank remains unbroken. There was only time to give it one short trial—after the race. (But the Casino should not become too complacent. The trial was considered to be a success. It paid off to the tune of 200 francs.)

Saturday practice was not until late afternoon. They worked on the cars all morning and right up to the time when they went down to the circuit. More drama. The new engine *wasn't* as powerful as Rudd and Stewart had hoped it would be. And a half-shaft was found to be cracked on Spence's H16. They re-changed the engines on the V8 that night and put in a new half-shaft on the H16. And stripped and examined and cleaned up and tuned up and carefully put back just about everything else.

Saturday night was another long one.

Now this is the funny thing about racing cars and their engines. They aren't like horses: you can't breed them. Nature does nothing for them, and nothing can be left to nature. You *invent* them. You build them, you test them, you think about them and re-think about them, you work on them to a degree which would give many less robust minds a nervous breakdown. They are gods and the gods are served with unstinted devotion, and sometimes the gods fail. Now why do they fail? When human skill and effort have been pushed to the absolute limits what the hell goes wrong? And why does metal—which knows about nothing and feels nothing and has no life and yet is everything to the life of an engine—become fatigued and break? Possibly, some time in the future, scientists will find out what a gremlin is. And, equally possibly, they won't. A battle back in history was lost for want of a nail, but racing-car engines want for nothing, and yet they lose far more races than they win.

On the evening of the twenty-fifth Grand Prix of Monaco, nobody in the B.R.M. camp could say with any certainty what might happen on the following day. Stewart had been fastest in practice. Then Surtees went faster, and Bandini went faster, and then Brabham went fastest of all.

So this is race day, and the only thing which need worry nobody is the question of wet weather tyres. Whatever else is going to happen, it obviously isn't going to rain. The grandstands are packed with the kind of people you see at Silverstone and Le Mans and everywhere else. In the seats opposite the Ferrari pits a group of Italian supporters are waving a flag with the *équipe*'s emblem on it. Opposite the B.R.M. pits there's the Royal Box: a sort of pavilion all done in deep red, with chairs which aren't actually thrones, but look pretty much like them.

The pits are an island. On one side the track runs between them and the harbour until it reaches the Gasometer hairpin.

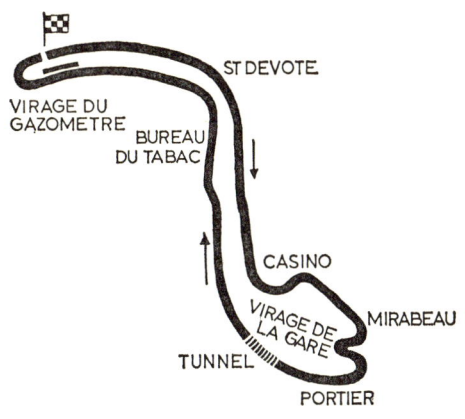

Monaco

Then it bends double and comes back up the other side. On either side of the pits there's a surging unstoppable tide of angry machinery going at almost full bore, and then nearly rupturing itself as it slows to get around Gasometer Bend, and then forcing itself into going flat out again.

Before the race starts there's the customary business of national anthems and the royal arrival, and the Prince and Princess of Monaco make a tour of the circuit in a quite remarkable Lamborghini which seems to have all-glass walls. The yachts in the harbour are crowded with people. The windows and balconies of the apartments overlooking the circuit are crammed. A brace of helicopters swoop over the circuit with surprising agility—whilst down below there is a sweet reek of hot castor oil and rubber, as, with a fearful thunder, the sixteen projectiles are fired from the grid.

And Denis Hulme is in front, and there's Bandin iup there, and Jackie Stewart.

The B.R.M. pits look rather like a ship carrying out an intricate manœuvre. Tony Rudd stands on the counter—large and rather abstracted, with a pair of binoculars slung round his neck. Denis Perkins (known as 'The Sheriff') is busy with the lap chart. Cyril Atkins, the chief mechanic, has settled down with his time sheet on which he records all the signals given to drivers. Helen Stewart has another time sheet and Linda Spence has a third. Pam Rudd (Tony's wife) is also working out times.

The mechanics are watching the race intensely, alert to the slightest sign of trouble as their cars flash by. Racing drivers have unusually quick reactions. So do racing mechanics. And each knows his precise responsibilities. There is virtually no need for any orders to be given. The entire operation is perfectly drilled.

And before the first lap has been completed something most terribly wrong has occurred in Brabham's car. For him the race is over, and the circuit has been made even more perilous from all the oil which has escaped from the ailing engine.

But Stewart—look at Stewart. He is driving at the very top of his form: beautifully, aggressively, like the natural craftsman he is. He has, it seems, almost willed himself to the front of the field, way ahead of everyone else and the V8 is going the way everyone dreamed it might go.

For half an hour.

The V8 engine has been stretched about as far as anyone could stretch it, and all this power seems to be too much for the transmission. The car comes into the pits. Willie Southcott (in charge of the engines) and Alan Challis (Stewart's mechanic) throw down pieces of rag in disgusted, angry, bitterly disappointed gestures. A green tarpaulin is draped over the car, rather suggestive of mourning.

Stewart watches the rest of the race from the pit counter.

One by one, other cars pack up. With Stewart out of the way, Hulme has little to worry him. Bandini is the most serious threat, but Bandini doesn't finish. The story of his disastrous crash, and the fire which followed, has already been told over and over again. I do not propose to re-create that agony.

Mike Spence and the H16 finished. Admittedly, towards the end, the oil pressure was very low, but it soldiered bravely on and passed the chequered flag. The car which had been deemed so unreliable made it.

When the twenty-fifth Grand Prix of Monaco was over, Denis Hulme was the winner. He went to the top of the World Championship table.

And afterwards some people went home. The B.R.M. team and Mike Spence did not. They set off for Monza to do some testing. Jackie Stewart did not. He caught an early flight the next morning on his way to Indianapolis. For that is the thing about Grand Prix motor racing. An event is pushed into history as soon as it is over. What matters is the next. The Monaco Grand Prix of 1967 was naturally a huge disappointment to B.R.M. Nevertheless, it provided a ray of hope for the rest of the year. Possibly the H16 really was a good deal more reliable than most people thought it would be. That was what mattered. Drivers help cars to win races—but the cars always have the last word.

At the end of the Monaco Grand Prix the position of the 1967 World Championship of Drivers was thus:

1. Hulme 12 points
2. Rodriguez 11 points
3. Hill ⎱ 6 points
   Love ⎰
5. Amon ⎱ 4 points
   Surtees ⎰

7. McLaren 3 points
8. Anderson 2 points
9. Brabham ⎱ 1 point
   Spence ⎰

8

Jack Brabham: Man of Two Worlds

With three World Championships to his credit, Jack Brabham has won motor racing's highest honour more times than any other driver apart from Fangio, who won it five times. In one respect, however, Brabham has beaten the Argentine ace. In 1966 he not only became top driver: he also won the Formula 1 Constructors' Championship. And that is a 'double' which had never been pulled off before by one man.

Jack Brabham is an unusual type of celebrity. He enjoys fame, but refuses to work at being famous. He is quiet, shy, and utterly unchanged by all the laurels which have been heaped upon him.

At the time of winning the Championship in 1966 he was forty years old. The Press, seeking any kind of gimmick to bring colour into their stories about him, played on this fact. And then one day Brabham startled everybody. He arrived on the grid wearing a false beard, and hobbling on a stick like an old man.

'It was Jack's own idea,' his manager, Phil Kerr, confesses. 'It was sensational, even exceptional. He doesn't usually have ideas like that.'

Jack Brabham won the World Championship for two years running, in 1959 and 1960, in Coopers. In the following year he set up on his own as a manufacturer of racing cars, and the long struggle through the wilderness began. Between then and 1966 he only won one Grand Prix race. That was the Austrian G.P. of 1963. Dan Gurney, who drove for him in 1963, 1964, and 1965, was scarcely more successful. He won the French and Mexican Grands Prix of 1964. And that, you might say, was the *équipe* Brabham's lot.

Then, dramatically, everything changed. All the teams had new cars at the start of the 1966 season. Brabham, putting his faith in simplicity, took a Repco engine which might have seemed to be underpowered in comparison with others. He mounted it on a reasonably light car which handled exceptionally well, and became more or less unconquerable. He had his first victory in the French Grand Prix, and later won the Dutch, British, and German races, one after the other.

It had to be admitted that his engine lacked the development potential of the others. In the future they might win many more races than he. But the important thing, so far as 1966 was concerned, was that Brabham was winning them *now*.

The fact that he was bound to wear two hats—that of a driver and that of a constructor—should have been apparent fairly early on in his life. His father was a greengrocer in a suburb of Sydney, Australia. He owned a large touring car which he'd bought on April 1st, 1926, the day before Jack was born. He allowed his son to drive it up and down the path at home until by the time he was twelve he was a reasonably accomplished motorist. By the time he was sixteen he was turning out to be a very adequate mechanic.

From secondary school he moved on to trade school, where he did extremely well. He was taught carpentry, metal work, blacksmith's work, mechanical drawing and a little chemistry. Afterwards his career took him by devious routes, and, after a near miss from going to work on the railways as a draughtsman, into a garage. He served his apprenticeship and in 1944 joined the Royal Australian Air Force. He wanted to sign on as a pilot, but there was an air-crew surfeit at the time, and so he became a flight mechanic.

After being demobbed he planned to set up an engineering business. The idea might have progressed a good deal more quickly if he hadn't met an engaging American named Johnny Schonberg.

Schonberg, who'd settled in Australia after serving with the United States Navy during the war, was a midget-car speedway ace. On a trip which the two of them made to Darwin he took Brabham to a meeting. The latter was first amazed, then terrified, and finally hooked. When they got back to Sydney it was agreed that Schonberg should drive the cars and he should act as mechanic.

Brabham is an extremely good engineer. He is also imaginative. When you marry imagination to ability in engineering you usually find an inventor struggling to get out. Before very long he and Schonberg decided to design and build their own car. On its initial outing it tossed a con rod in the first race, and that seemed to be that. However, they'd invested 400 hard-earned Australian pounds in the car, and they decided they'd better do something about it.

With an astounding feat of improvisation they repaired it in time for the last two races, which it won.

He may not have realised it at the time, but during this period Jack Brabham was hammering out certain principles which were to affect all his thinking in years to come. Perhaps the most important one is stated in his *Jack Brabham's Motor Racing Book*. 'Any good basic design', he writes, 'can be improved. Any bad basic design isn't worth troubling with, for the simple reason that drastic changes have to be made time and again and drastic changes, during a season, inevitably end in breakdown and frustration.'

Elsewhere in the book he says: 'No matter how good a driver is, he can get absolutely nowhere unless he has a good, fast car, and a car that is meticulously prepared and reliable.'

Eventually Johnny Schonberg retired from midget racing, and Jack Brabham took over as driver. He won many races and many championships and, in short, did very well indeed.

In 1951 he married. In the same year he decided to give up this type of sport. There were probably two reasons for his decision. One was that it is a somewhat perilous pastime and his wife Betty was against it. The other was that, perfectly naturally, he wanted to branch out into other forms of racing.

By now he'd established a reasonably prosperous garage and engineering business in Sydney. On the motor-racing front he took to road racing, and did very well with an engine which he constructed himself out of salvaged parts and mounted on a Mk IV Cooper 500 chassis. After several victories and a little help from the Redex Company he was able to buy a new Cooper-Bristol. With commendable loyalty to his sponsor, he called it the 'Redex Special'. He raced it in Australia and New Zealand.

At some time in everybody's life there arrives what can only be described as a moment of decision. Brabham could easily have remained in Australia. Business was tolerable, motor racing was going very nicely. A less ambitious man might have settled down very happily.

But Brabham wanted to improve. He was not content to confine his activities to a somewhat local ambience. The world was around him, and he wanted to conquer, in his own quiet way, a part of it.

The Brabhams came to Britain. The stated object was to visit British car plants. As it happened, he managed to fit in some motor racing as well. They stayed in the country for a year, and then went back to Australia. About twelve months later they returned to England, and this time there was no going back. Before very long he'd signed on with Cooper as a works driver in Formula 2 events.

According to the Brabham line, he's tough. 'Any works team keeps its eyes open for talent,' I was told by one of his colleagues. 'We are no exception.' And: 'Jack is helpful to up-and-coming drivers, if he can see that the person has potential. But he must have proved himself.'

Maybe, maybe. But that doesn't alter the fact that he was one of the prime movers in a scheme launched by the New Zealand Grand Prix Association. Known as the 'Driver to Europe' operation, it took the form of a motor-racing scholarship. The winners were given £1,000 each, some letters of introduction to race organisers, and sent off to Europe. The first to win the award was Bruce McLaren. The second was Brabham's team mate Denis Hulme (which seems to prove something about good deeds not going unrewarded and all that sort of thing).

When Brabham won the World Championship in a Cooper he was well pleased—well, who wouldn't be? Nevertheless, Jack Brabham the driver was having an uneasy time with Jack Brabham the engineer. The latter was continually saying: 'Wouldn't it have been better if we'd done it in our own car?' At the end of 1961 the latter won. In the following year the Brabham-Climax, powered by a Coventry Climax V8 engine, made its début on the tracks. The fact that this was the second year of new F1 regulations may not have been entirely coincidental.

And so they raced with no conspicuous success through the $1\frac{1}{2}$ litre Formula 1 years. Dan Gurney, who drove with him for three of them, was almost equally quiet. Mrs. Brabham recalls one evening when they entertained Gurney to dinner at their house. The meal was an excellent one. In terms of conversation, however, the evening was what might be described as a contented flop. Brabham and Gurney scarcely spoke a word the entire time.

Looking back on it, there was something rather unsatisfactory about that period. Any car which had 10 h.p. more than the opposition, and could finish, was almost bound to win. As a driver, Brabham probably felt this more than most people—and not entirely because he wasn't winning anything. In his time he'd driven pretty well everything on wheels. He'd been in Formula 1, Formula 2 and Formula Libre. He'd taken part in the Le Mans 24-Hour Race in an Aston Martin and in a Cooper (once he was teamed with King Hussein of Jordan, but that fell through owing to a spot of bother back at the palace).

But one of his most remarkable undertakings took place in 1961, when he was still struggling to sort out his destiny as a constructor. Armed with a Cooper, he set off for America and competed in the Indianapolis '500'. To the astonishment of pretty well everyone in the United States, he completed the race and finished ninth.

Now this was more than a victory: it was a symbol of things to come. It was the start of the British onslaught, which reached its climax in 1965 and 1966, when Jim Clark and Graham Hill, respectively, took on the motor-racing might of America—and beat it at its own game.

Being Jack Brabham nowadays is a somewhat hectic affair. His racing commitments are sufficient to keep most drivers fully employed. On top of that, he takes a most intimate interest in the design and engineering of the cars he races. And, on top of that, he's by way of being a big-business man.

Fortunately, he has managed to surround himself with some first-rate people. His manager, Phil Kerr, is a New Zealander who has been with him for eight years. His chief designer is a fellow Australian named Ron Tauranac. Tauranac is an admirable person who manages to complement Brabham's own genius. Whilst the latter is essentially a practical engineer who's good with his hands and makes things work, Ron Tauranac is a brilliant theorist. Between the two of them they make an excellent combination—getting the best out of both sides of engineering.

The Brabham empire is divided into four companies. There's

the Brabham Racing Organisation, which looks after his Formula 1 interests; Jack Brabham Conversions Ltd., which does some very clever things with Vauxhall Vivas; Motor Racing Developments Ltd., which builds Formula 2 and 3 cars; and Jack Brabham Motors Ltd., a garage which he owns at Chessington.

When he's in Britain he divides his life between a factory at Guildford and another one at Weybridge. Since, however, he is out of the country motor racing for at least six months of the year, he has to cram about twelve months' work into the other six.

That is the reason why for part of his year as World Champion in 1967 he put an embargo on all press interviews, photography sessions, and so on. He'd nothing against them in principle, there just wasn't enough time.

To save time, and because he enjoys it, he flies his own 7-seater, twin-engined aircraft to all events in Britain and Europe. He also enjoys photography, water ski-ing (inevitably—they all like it), and underwater fishing. He neither drinks alcohol nor smokes (he has gone on record as saying: 'I haven't smoked since I left school'), but he enjoys good food. He makes no conscious effort to keep his weight and waistline down, but, since he is continually on the move, any surplus pounds which are liable to form may be self-liquidated.

The Brabhams have three sons. Mrs. Brabham gets to as many meetings as she can, but she's sometimes frustrated for want of a sitter-in.

Jack Brabham has been racing for longer than any other driver now in Formula 1. If you include his midget-racing days it adds up to a total of about twenty-one years. During all this time he has only once been seriously injured in an accident. This is the kind of statement one hates to make without clinging on to the nearest piece of wood. In Brabham's case, however, it is understandable. He is enormously determined, and any driver who gets a glimpse of him in his mirror knows that he'll be very hard to shake off. He gets tremendous satisfaction out of achieving success and overcoming mechanical barriers. He is, perhaps, happiest when he makes machinery do what he wants it to do.

And this is reflected on the circuit. He admits that he has occasionally lost a race out of sympathy for his car. In his opinion it had taken all the punishment it could reasonably be expected to stand and there was no point in pushing it any more. It is this intelligent understanding of motor racing and its machinery which makes him, in spite of all his will to win, such a paramountly *safe* driver.

One day, one supposes, he'll have to retire—although there are no signs of it happening in the foreseeable future. When it does happen, of course, he will still be very intimately connected with the sport. His F2 and F3 cars are selling very satisfactorily, simply because they are continually winning races. No manufacturer could ask for a better advertisement than that. When the time comes for him to throw away his helmet and goggles one can be tolerably certain that he'll make sure that they go on winning, and that he'll be there to see they do.

Presumably, Jack Brabham suffers from pre-race nerves, just like any other driver. But if he does he never shows it. Like fits of depression, which he regards as a natural weakness existing to be overcome, he keeps everything perfectly under control. He is calm, unflappable, impatient only of inefficiency. That is how he always is at motor-racing meetings: that is how he was before the start of the 1967 Dutch Grand Prix, the story of which I shall tell in the next chapter.

9

Lightness and Simplicity Amid the Sand-dunes

'ZAND' is the Dutch word for sand, and there's plenty of that at Zandvoort. The beach, where visitors (most of them Germans) attempt to sunbathe, has no rocks and no pebbles. It's the same story for a mile or two inland: hundreds and hundreds (nobody's going to count them, there may be thousands) of dunes, thinly covered with tough, whiplike grass. The town itself is a small, reasonably prosperous resort. There's a skyscraper hotel, where you can enjoy the view from the restaurant seventy metres above sea level. If you're not hungry there's a municipal tower which is sixty metres high.

In the days before the last war they used to have motor racing of a kind at Zandvoort. It must have been a strange affair. They shut off the streets and the cars raced round the town. But the streets were not very wide. The general effect, one imagines, must have been either terrifying or fascinating, according to how you view these matters.

They would have liked to build a better circuit, which could be used for Grand Prix racing. There was a lot of talk about it, just as there was discussion on a more national scale about making a G.P. course for Holland, but none of it came to anything.

During the war the German Army moved into Zandvoort. The name means 'the fort on the sands'. Hitherto it had been somewhat inaccurate. The only fortifications were the castles which children made on the beach. The Germans decided that the resort should be made to live up to its name. Before they could build their defences, however, there had to be a lot of blowing up. All told, they destroyed 500 houses and six hotels

This left Zandvoort short of accommodation but rich in rubble. The wartime burgomaster, a man named Van Alphen, had a shrewd idea what to do with it. It could be used as the foundations for a racing circuit.

By 1944 the plans were well under way. The course was laid out and the rubble was rolled in. But there things had to remain for several years. When the fighting stopped there was a lack of road surfacing materials in Holland. It was not until 1948 that the 2·6-mile circuit was finished. In that year the B.R.D.C. held an invitation race there. It was won by Jean Behra in a Maserati.

The straight, which passes the pits, is only a matter of yards away from the sea. The circuit then snakes away inland, going over and round the dunes, and presently returns to the point where it began. It's a nice place for a picnic.

On the whole, it is popular with drivers. It isn't one of the world's fastest, but it's safer than many and it needs plenty of skill. The biggest problem is this question of sand. When the wind blows it on to the track it's as if millions of little balls have been scattered around. This, of course, is somewhat perilous, though the authorities have done much to keep the menace in check. They've planted grass and put black earth down. 'But,' John Hugenholtz, the circuit director, told me, 'we have to think twice about building a new grandstand. That disturbs the sand. There can be no chopping and changing. It's best to leave things alone.' Not that there's any need to build one. The sand-dunes provide all that anyone could want, except that they're not covered in.

I went to Zandvoort in 1967 to watch the race, but I wanted to see it from a particular point of view: Jack Brabham's. He, after all, was the reigning World Champion, and he had won the event the previous year. Brabham's headquarters is a garage in the centre of the town, which also runs the leading taxi service. The proprietor is a man named J. H. Oonk—though, to judge by the sign over the entrance, the firm is better known by its telephone number. Inside the accommodation is not very large. A small parking area leads into a workshop. There's just about room for four racing cars, and that is the number which Brabham brought to Zandvoort in 1967.

The more one sees of Jack Brabham, the more one tries to rationalise his racing outlook into a philosophy. Because he goes straight to the heart of a matter, and because he seems to be unaware of anything which is irrelevant, the answer to every problem is simple. Sometimes it is so obvious that even his own mechanics can't see it. One might describe it as Higher Common Sense.

Dedicated is an extremely overworked word, and it's time people stopped using it so generously. But one simply has to apply it to Brabham. He has no time for small talk, he just isn't interested in anything apart from the job on hand. His far from inconsiderable intelligence is concentrated on one thing: to produce and maintain two competitive cars—one for himself and one for Denis Hulme.

For some of the entrants, motor racing is a big social occasion. They stay in the posh hotels, and it's champagne a-go-go, and racing gossip galore. But you won't find Jack Brabham in this social fish tank. He works with his men. Shy, reserved, reluctant to talk to most people, he seems to be entirely at ease with them. What's more, they seem very contented with him. Three of them are New Zealanders, two are from Australia. There was nothing premeditated about this. They came to England, one at a time, looking for work, and they eventually settled with the Brabham Racing Organisation.

Brabham jokes with them, talks over problems with them, asks their advice and makes suggestions. He does some of the work himself, and the spanner in his hand seems nearly as permanent as the watch on his wrist.

The team which goes racing with him are those five mechanics and Ron Tauranac, his chief designer. At race meetings they all work far into the night, improving the cars. But nobody minds. Brabham is working, too, and he has a lot of driving to do the next day.

One evening Tauranac told me: 'It all depends on what troubles you have. Sometimes you don't have any troubles at all. But we've got a new car this time. We've got to get it all sorted out. We stop when we've finished. It'll probably be about midnight tonight.'

He was over-optimistic. By the time they'd cleared up it was 3 a.m.

Preparing a Formula 1 racing car is a question of working out the ideal combination from several different possibilities. What they actually did that night was to take the second newest engine out of the new car and put it into the old car. But that is almost simple compared with the tyres. Said a mechanic: 'Nobody knows the possible permutations in tyres —even the tyre makers don't really know. Why, the same tyre seems to come out differently every time they make it. Tyres are the biggest headache in the pits today.'

Whatever the problems may be, you won't find any dramatics going on in the Brabham team. Everything is very calm. Possibly Brabham worries enormously, but there is never the slightest sign of it. There's an atmosphere of reliability which seems to affect the cars.

Admittedly, in the Monaco G.P. he lost the race in the first lap, when a con rod broke. Nothing broke in Denis Hulme's car, and he won. Afterwards all the rods were X-rayed for flaws, and a number were rejected. That misfortune is unlikely to be repeated.

Elsewhere at Zandvoort there are plenty of dramatics. They can be labelled Official and Unofficial. In other words, those which are supposed to happen and those which aren't. Into the latter category falls The Case of Richie Ginther. At the eleventh hour a cable arrived from him datelined California. It was addressed to Dan Gurney, for whom he was supposed to be driving. In terse cablese it informed Gurney that his co-driver would not be turning up at Zandvoort: that, indeed, he had retired from motor racing altogether.

Gurney said something rude. Rumours abounded. One suggested that, having failed to qualify for Monaco and then Indianapolis, Ginther had had enough. Another had it that, like some latter-day mystic, he had gone off into the desert to have a long think. Anyway, for whatever reason, Richie Ginther remained on or near the western seaboard of the U.S.A. On the eastern seaboard of Europe, Gurney raced alone.

The Official Dramatics began shortly after the first few minutes of the first practice session. The lap record was jointly shared by Jim Clark and Denis Hulme. It stood at 1 minute 30 seconds. Clark had cut it back to this size while winning the race in 1965. Hulme had done it while failing to win in 1966.

Well now, here comes Hulme in the car which took him to victory a few weeks earlier at Monaco. It isn't a new Repco Brabham—just the same old study in lightness, simplicity and joy, which did so well the year before. And very calmly, with that air of confidence which makes this sort of thing look easy,

LIGHTNESS AND SIMPLICITY AMID THE SAND-DUNES 69

he goes out, and circulates, and tears the old record into shreds.

His time is 1 minute 26.8 seconds.

The objects of practice are twofold. One is to determine who occupies which positions on the starting grid. As such, the sessions become almost a race before another race. The other object, understandably, is to find out a few things about the cars.

Hulme was no doubt very happy about his time, but nobody was under the slightest misapprehension. Said a member of the Brabham team: 'It'll be bettered—without any doubt. The first big lump comes off, and then they nibble at it.' Maybe they nibble, but they take tolerably big mouthfuls. By the end of the final practice session it had come down to 1 minute 24.6 seconds after an exciting duel between Graham Hill (who went fastest) and Dan Gurney (who did it in 1 minute 25.1 seconds). The third man on the front row of the grid was Brabham (1 minute 25.9 seconds).

Denis Hulme had been busy earlier in the week taking part in the Indianapolis '500'. And so had Graham Hill, Jim Clark, Jackie Stewart, Jochen Rindt, and Dan Gurney. The race had been won by Foyt (hotly tipped to take over Ginther's place in the Gurney F1 team) for the very good reason that he was the only driver to finish. The British contingent doubtless covered their expenses and made quite pleasant profits out of the excursion. And then came the mad rush, which is such a feature of the Formula 1 circus, to the next circuit, which was Zandvoort.

As I understood it, Hulme had managed to snatch six hours' sleep in London on the way, and this had more than sufficiently refreshed him. 'I feel fine,' he told me. 'Really fine. Of course the car feels a bit different after the one I drove at Indi. Much slower and not so heavy. The one at Indi produced 500 b.h.p.'

There were seventeen starters in the Dutch Grand Prix, and three of them (Hulme, McLaren and Amon) were New Zealanders. I asked Hulme about this. He said: 'You get a good motoring upbringing out there. You can take out a provisional licence when you're fifteen, and something like 75 per cent of the roads are loose gravel. Everyone can cure a slide—they have to. Even family cars slide on the loose gravel. And then there are back roads with no traffic on them. We all used to race on them.'

Every year, the story goes, Cooper's try to lure Hulme away from Brabham, but without any success. 'I reckon I know when I'm on to a good thing,' he said. He's been on to this particular good thing since 1962, when he joined the staff of Brabham's garage at Chessington. 'I was employed as a mechanic,' he recalls. 'I used to bolt bits on to Alpines and Rapiers—we were doing conversions on them in those days. I had my first race for Jack at the Crystal Palace. It was after Gavin Youl had crashed at Brands Hatch and broken his collar bone. They could mend the car, but they couldn't mend Gavin's collar bone. So I took his place and finished fourth.'

A while later he won the Formula Junior race at the Brands Hatch Boxing Day meeting. It was the first event ever to be won by a Brabham car.

Within the team, Brabham and Hulme get along very well indeed. Possibly it's because Australians and New Zealanders are, in outlook, very close together. 'I'd want any co-driver to be basically the same as me,' Hulme said. 'Of course, this is most important in an event like the Le Mans 24-Hour race, where there are two of you to a car. I tend to have a happy-go-lucky, don't give a stuff, attitude. I'm carefree. I couldn't care less about what happens. Today you try hard, tomorrow has to look after itself.'

One cannot imagine that Brabham, in fact, takes such a light-hearted attitude. He's much too serious. But the two men make a most formidable team, and Hulme's engineering knowledge must endear him to Brabham. He can, for example, take a Formula 1 engine to pieces and reassemble it. Within the team they both have their own cars and their own parts and their own mechanics.

'If Jack blew up an engine there'd be no question of his taking one of mine,' Hulme said, 'and he wouldn't expect me to take one of his.' For the race itself, Hulme elected to use the same car that he drove at Monaco ('I understand it very well. I know what I can do with it. You have to sort out the new one.'). Brabham drove a newer version (the second newest engine in the old car).

Up at the pits and in the paddock there's a lot of chat about old cars and new cars. The old cars are those which were used last year. The new ones result from intellectual exercise which took place during the winter months. The easiest way of identifying them is by their exhaust systems. In the 1967

Zandvoort

version most of them come out of the top.¹ In the earlier one they came out of the sides.

So which is best? The designers, obviously, favour the new. They've been built to generate more power. Power is speed, and speed wins races. But not entirely. There's another aspect, which is called reliability. Some people argue that, since they've already been proven, the older versions have more of it. Some drivers prefer to use last year's cars. They *know* them, whilst the newcomers have still to be sorted out.

But old cars—new cars, practice was pretty sensational. Every driver had done better than the existing lap record but this doesn't really mean such a great deal. There is a vast difference between circulating for a lap or two and covering ninety laps (234 miles), which is the distance of the Dutch Grand Prix. Furthermore, the less fuel you have on board, the lighter your car becomes and the faster you go. Nor do lap times in practice count as official records, for they seldom reflect the average speed of the race. Graham Hill, for instance, did a fabulous 1-24·6 in practice, and the average lap time for the winner was 1-29·39.

It was the first Sunday in June. There was no wind to blow the sand about, and a grey overcast concealed the sun. Raymond Mays, that veteran of Grand Prix driving, said that in his opinion it was a very nice day for such things. 'Not too hot and then, again, not too cold,' he said.

Chris Amon, who was driving one of the three Ferraris, had been worried the night before. It all hinged on tyre wear

1. With the outstanding exception of Lotus. But more of that later on.

which seemed to be excessive. The thing which bothered Amon was that he couldn't blame it on the car, the tyres, or the circuit. The fault, he concluded sadly, must be his. But what, he wanted to know, was he doing wrong? Because he hadn't seemed to do anything wrong, nobody could tell him.

By mid-morning the grandstand and the summits of the dunes began to fill up. Something like 50,000 people were expected. 'You'll see,' an official told me, 'this cloud will keep them off the beach.'

Brabham arrived at the paddock about midday. He studied the cars thoughtfully. 'He probably said, "To hell with this, I'd better go up to the circuit and make a few quid." He's been at this game too long to get butterflies in his stomach,' a friend of his said to me.

Denis Hulme looked relaxed and happy. He said: 'No—I don't get nervous before a race. I like to sit around and watch the opposition. Even though I know who's there, and who is likely to do what, I like to get a picture of the field. I play the race pretty much by ear. If we're up in front, Jack and I don't race against each other, but if we're in the rear, we might have a go.'

It is getting on for half past two. The cars go out on to the dummy grid. Brabham's mechanic winks at him, and Brabham winks at his mechanic.

And so, at 2.30 p.m. on Sunday, June 4th, the Dutch flag is swept downward, and the great mechanical stampede begins. Like a projectile with after-burners blazing, Graham Hill in his Lotus-Ford blasts off into the lead, and the pack streams behind him.

Within a matter of seconds, white flags are waving. They mean that an ambulance or some other service vehicle is out on the track. What has actually happened is that Bruce McLaren has spun off. The car is too bent to continue, but McLaren himself is undamaged. He walks back to the paddock, and watches the rest of the race from the Hunze Rug hairpin. Hill is going like the clappers, way out in front, with Brabham lying second. And so the cars go round and round and nothing changes very much for a while.

There's really no favourite in a motor race, for cars are much less predictable than horses. But Dan Gurney was a very likely winner before his fuel injection pump packed up. He coasts into the pits. Seconds later, he has another go, but it

LIGHTNESS AND SIMPLICITY AMID THE SAND-DUNES 73

isn't any good. That car is not going to race again on this Sabbath by the sand-dunes.

Meee-yow-wah, meee-yow-wah, meee-yow-wah !!!!!!

The cars go by. After ten laps there's another which doesn't go by. It's Hill's Lotus-Ford. He is pushing it towards the pits. Somebody gives him a hand. Hill sees what's happening, and brushes the well-meaning intruder to one side. Help is not allowed. It turns out to be trouble with the valves. What with this, and the man who gave the push, Hill's race is over. He slips on a coat and his tweed cap and wanders off to watch the rest of the race.

'It's never won till the chequered flag comes down,' somebody mutters wisely.

Brabham is travelling very quickly indeed and he's at the front. The car is going like a healthy creature. As he changes down for the Hunze Rug, a jet of flame leaps out of the exhaust pipes. It's rather like a dragon putting its tongue out at the mob trailing behind.

But not all the mob trails behind for long. It's as if Jim Clark has suddenly decided that it's time to stop messing about. He overhauls Brabham, gets out in front and then gets further out in front.

Now this is extraordinary. It confounds some engineering law or other, for Clark's car hasn't even been run-in. Hill's had done, perhaps, thirty laps of testing, but those wheels on Clark's had never turned—right up to the time they arrived at Zandvoort.

And yet it's going as if Old Nick himself is behind it.

And Brabham is in second place and Denis Hulme is in third. And behind Hulme there's Chris Amon, who is now making it abundantly clear that he had no good reason to criticise himself on the eve of the race, and the young hand has lost none of its cunning.

In the B.R.M. pits there had been an air almost of sadness. This was one hell of a time. Nothing, but nothing, was going right. If the engine was producing enough power, then the tyres were wrong. But the engine wasn't producing all that much power, and the tyre situation was the very devil anyway. So what was a man like Tony Rudd who is only human—and can, therefore, work little miracles but not big ones—what was a man like Rudd to do?

And what can a driver, even when he's a natural like Stewart, what can he do? Stewart worked very hard. He drove brilliantly for a lot of laps. Funnily enough, the thing which eventually brought him in was not inability to go fast but inability to slow down. His brakes were fading.

Clark, Brabham, Hulme, Amon. Clark, Brabham, Hulme, Amon. The machinery goes round and round, and the Honda comes out at the pits. Before the race, Yoshio Nakamura, Honda's chief engineer, had told me: 'What we have to get right is the little things.' This particular little thing was a sticking throttle plate.

Clark, Brabham, Hulme, Amon. Clark, Brabham, Hulme, Amon. Meee-yow-wah, meee-yow-wah, meee-yow-wah ! ! ! ! ! !

On and on they go. For a few seconds it looks as if Hulme's third place is in jeopardy. Amon has got right on to his tail. But then, in the Hunze Rug ambiance, Mike Parkes, who's being lapped, does something rather odd. He *might* be trying to block Hulme and let Amon through. He might be doing any damn' thing, but it doesn't work. Hulme keeps on full throttle. Amon has to drop back, and he never again gets so close to his fellow countryman.

Soon afterwards it was all over. Jim Clark was the winner at an average speed of 105·05 m.p.h. Brabham was second. Hulme, third. Amon, fourth. Hulme remained at the top of the World Championship table. Rodriguez stayed in second place. Jim Clark came into third. Brabham went into fourth place and shared it with Amon.

Afterwards everyone was saying how Lotus and Jim Clark were back in business, and wasn't it fantastic, and what a race, see you at Le Mans, at Spa, wherever, good old Jim, and all that sort of thing.

Except Jack Brabham. Back at the transporter he was quietly discussing tyres with one of the mechanics.

10

Lotus: Almost a Legend

Since 1958, when British cars first became a serious threat to foreign competition in the World Championship series, Coopers (in which I include, latterly, Cooper-Maserati) have won 17 Grands Prix, Ferrari have won 16, B.R.M. have won 13, and Lotus have won 30. The results of the others are tiny by comparison. In spite of its considerable promise, the Vanwall only won six of these events, and Brabham only started winning in 1966.

The figures, then, show Lotus a long way out in front, and 1967 promised to be the best year of all. For who could possibly match up to a two-car team in which both drivers were former World Champions and both had won that brutal trial by strength and fury, the Indianapolis '500'?

To a lesser man than Colin Chapman the presence of two such very bright stars in a team might have been an embarrassment. The thing about famous drivers is their determination to win races. To do this they depend enormously on the available machinery. It is difficult enough to produce and prepare one highly competitive car. But two? Wasn't that asking rather a lot?

Chapman was undismayed. 'The Press seemed to think it posed difficulties,' he told me, 'but I don't think so. Each driver has his own cars, his own engines, and his own mechanics. It's been very rare for Jimmy Clark to have any preference, and there can be no question of substituting cars. If his breaks down in practice, he's got a spare one. There's no question of robbing one driver on behalf of the other.'

But, Chapman admitted, the two must work together when they're racing. They are not competing against each other.

Once the race has settled down after one or two laps, whoever's out in front stays there. Other drivers may attempt to overtake him, but not his team mate.[1]

The Lotus factory, where the cars are built, is rather like an essay in surrealism. You drive out of Norwich across the flat Norfolk landscape, and seldom see so much as a cottage. Presently you negotiate a bend in the road, pass a clump of trees and arrive at what looks like a small airport. The buildings are very new. The barriers at the entrance work automatically, and the man gives you a badge, which you have to wear while you're there.

When you go through the immense glass doors into the offices you suddenly seem to find yourself in the midst of the West End, or Manhattan, or wherever. There's an enormous red carpet which contrasts with the rather cold East Anglian colours outside. A couple of Lotus Elans are arranged like cars in a showroom. There are masses of rubber plants and contemporary furniture. It is all very pleasant.

The impression of an airport is not entirely misleading. There happens to be a landing strip and a control tower. The company owns two aircraft, and Clark and Hill each has his own. Around the perimeter there's a $2\frac{1}{2}$-mile test track. Lotus has its own ambulance.

All this was built by the brilliance of Colin Chapman, and it must seem a very far cry from the small workshop in Hornsey, London, where he first began to build racing cars in 1955.

Colin Chapman completed his education at London University, where he took a degree in engineering. He served as a fighter pilot with the R.A.F., and afterwards worked with the British Aluminium Company as a structural engineer. He used to race, but he couldn't afford to spend very much time or money on what was, after all, a hobby.

Presently, however, people began to ask for replicas of his cars. He built them, and sold them, and before very long he was able to resign from the aluminium company and set up on his own. He worked in Hornsey; built a factory at Cheshunt, Hertfordshire, in 1958; and, finally, moved into his Norfolk premises in November, 1966.

Two things made Chapman successful as a racing-car constructor. One was the fact that he always made the cars as light as possible, but gave them perfect road-holding and

[1]. In theory, at any rate.

steering. The other was the simplicity, the beautiful directness, of his thinking. There is, of course, nothing new about power-weight ratios—having the maximum power and the minimum weight, and all that sort of thing. But Chapman got it right. He had to. In those days he had no racing engine, and he was compelled to get the utmost out of the small units available.

Lotus, as it happens, was the nickname of his first special. He has used it ever since.

He is one of those rare people who never stop working. There are some doubts about whether his high-performance mind packs up when he goes to sleep at night. Production is probably shunted off into his sub-conscious, which is left to get on with the job. And yet, in spite of a somewhat daunting programme, he manages to look very fit. It doesn't require much imagination to see him as the young R.A.F. pilot of some twenty-one years ago.

At meetings he considers himself to be less excitable than most people. 'Each is just another motor race,' he told me. 'It doesn't pay to get hot under the collar. I'm not tolerant of stupidity, though.'

Even after one of his cars has won an event it soon becomes 'just another race'. 'You'd be surprised,' he said. 'Winning, really, is an anticlimax. The pleasure lasts for about an hour, and then the problems start all over again. We've got to win the next race. You can never rest on your laurels in this business.'

And, of course, it is a business. He builds two production cars—the Lotus Elan and that magnificent fast-seller in the overseas markets, the Europa. Victories in Formula 1 events help to sell these cars. 'There's another angle, too,' he said. 'Formula 1 involves a tremendous amount of advanced engineering. None of it rubs off directly, but the same engineers get involved in the design of production cars. It also leads to the use of better materials, and gives us a lot of valuable experience. The power of today's cars was unheard of ten years ago.'

The fact that he manages to keep reasonably calm at meetings doesn't mean to say that he hasn't his fair share of worries. The biggest is that some driver may get hurt through a fault of his. 'A new car is exploring the unknown,' he told me. 'It's finding out about the limits of strength and materials. If it's too safe, it will never win a race. And so you try to strike a happy medium. It must be light and small to be effective, and yet it mustn't be dangerous.'

He is entirely responsible for the design of his cars. He works out the basic scheme, and leaves the details to his staff. This involves a great deal of thought; but how do you think when you're running a business, and you're away at the circuits pretty well every weekend?

'It certainly is a problem,' he said. 'It's very difficult to get the time for it. The best time, funnily enough, is at motor-racing meetings. Then you're living motor racing twenty-four hours a day, but you're only actually working for four or five hours. Back in the hotel, in the bath, resting in bed—those are the times to think. I convert my thoughts on to paper when I get home.'

Actually, when he gets back to the factory, there are a thousand and one things to be seen to. The conversion process takes place mostly in the evenings.

He has an unfeigned admiration for both his Formula 1 drivers. He probably admires Jim Clark as much as anybody he's ever known. Of Graham Hill he said: 'Graham and I get on terribly well together. If he and I weren't absolutely confident of each other we'd never work together.'

I asked him what, precisely, he demanded of a driver—other than the rather sweeping generalisation about 'ability to win races'. He said: 'A driver's life has two parts to it. One is how be behaves in his car, the other is how he behaves when he's out of it. Both are equally important. For example, it's important for him to get on well with his mechanics. The driver's job is to convert into success all the dedication which the engineers and mechanics have put into the car. And, of course, he must try to be consistent. He mustn't have any "off days". A driver must always try to maintain the pressure.'

When the 3 litre formula was introduced Chapman was prepared to go along with it, though he didn't necessarily want it. 'I'd hoped they'd limit the number of cylinders,' he said. 'A limit of eight cylinders would have been far more successful. With Honda and B.R.M. going for twelve and sixteen cylinders, I think there's less chance of it being successful—and certainly less chance of the experience rubbing off on to production cars. With an eight-cylinder limit Jaguar and Aston Martin might have been encouraged to come in. The more people there are in motor racing, the better it is.'

Chapman's thoughts are never very far away from production cars. Apart from his own brand, the sales of the Lotus Cortina must be very large indeed. There's no way of telling how much its very successful racing record helped to popularise the less highly developed members of the Cortina breed though it must be quite considerable.

He has already won the Formula 1 Constructors' Championship twice, and so there would be no particular novelty in winning it again. Nevertheless, Colin Chapman does have one ambition left, and one which he feels very strongly about. 'I want my factory to produce the best touring car in the world. I want to make something for people who really appreciate quality. In this respect I think Ferrari's volume is too small. Something like Porsche would be more my mark.'

In some ways he's very patriotic. 'Apart from my personal interest,' he said, 'I'm reluctant to see foreign cars winning more than two or three races a year. That's too much. It might have a very adverse effect on Britain's car exports.'

One of the present problems is the financial aspect. The cost of a Formula 1 racing car is escalating dramatically, and it's very difficult to produce the right projectile with the money available. Ford of America are said to have spent $3 million on developing an engine for Indianapolis. Honda spent a fortune on their motor cycles and are now spending another on their racing cars. Ferrari receives a subsidy from the Italian car industry. If, as seems likely, France makes a come-back into Grand Prix racing, it will almost certainly be with assistance from the state. But British F1 constructors are left to soldier along on their own. With the exception of B.R.M., none of them has a big industrial concern behind it.

So far, Britain has got by through sheer intelligence—by the efforts of a few people sitting and thinking, and then translating their thoughts into action. Chapman's fear is that one day the supply of talent will run out.

He himself has never manufactured an engine. Until the end of the $1\frac{1}{2}$ litre F1 regulations he was allied to Coventry Climax. After Climax withdrew from racing he bought engines from B.R.M. and Ford. His Indianapolis victory of 1965 was won with a Ford engine. In 1967 his Formula 1 cars were using Ford Cosworth units, and Cosworth is a firm for which Chapman has a lot of time. It is run by two men—Keith Duckworth and Mike Costin. Duckworth is a design engineer and Costin a development engineer. Ford of Great Britain offered them £100,000 to carry out motor-racing development on their behalf. Duckworth said, 'Fine—so long as you leave us alone, and let us get on with it.' Ford were intelligent enough to do just that.

The result is that these two men are probably able to squeeze more power out of a given engine than anyone else in the business.

Chapman's own relationship with the larger realms of industry is something which, he finds, needs a fair amount of patience. 'Yes,' he told me, 'I am probably an individualist. Probably the biggest difficulty, when dealing with big corporations, is finding out who to talk to. I believe in talking to the man who makes decisions, but the trouble is finding somebody who'll make them. There are all sorts of committees at work. The director of engineering may say one thing, and then the sales director says something totally different. It can be very frustrating.'

Firstly, and above everything, Colin Chapman goes racing because he enjoys it. He usually flies one of his company aircraft to meetings because he likes flying. 'But', he said, 'so far as the rest of it's concerned, the glamour has worn off. It's the same old road from the airport to the hotel, and then the dusty old autodrome. You never have enough time to stay on and enjoy the place. You have to rush there, and then rush back again.'

His factory is near the small Norfolk town of Wymondham (pronounced Wind-ham), and his home is nearby. He is married, with a son and two daughters.

At the Cheshunt plant they employed about 500 people. When the move to Norfolk was mooted about half of them said they'd come along too—and they came. The rest have been recruited locally. One advertisement brought no fewer than 137 applicants to the factory in a single day. There are no large unemployment statistics for the neighbourhood, and so one has to conclude that quite a lot of the interest was aroused by the possible glamour of being associated with Lotus.

Forty-three people are employed directly by the racing team. The works turns out forty Elans each week, which are afterwards snapped up with praiseworthy avidity.

To watch Team Lotus in action I chose Spa. This is a circuit which Jim Clark has never liked. During his first race there a couple of very nasty accidents occurred, which have probably coloured his thinking. Nevertheless, it is one where he has been particularly successful. Between 1962 and 1965 he won the Belgian Grand Prix four times on the trot.

By contrast, it was one of the few circuits in the 1967 series where his companion Graham Hill had not yet won a Grand Prix. I thought it would be interesting to see how things turned out.

11

The Fastest, Most Dangerous, Circuit

THE Belgians have a rude name for the area around the pits on the Spa-Francorchamps Grand Prix course. The track shoots down into a basin, and then hurriedly leaves it, writhing snakelike up the side of a hill as if impatient to be gone from the buildings and the crowds. When it rains here, which is quite often, the basin seems to fill with water. Said one inveterate Belgian racegoer: 'You can understand how it is—and why we call this the piss-pot of Europe.'

It may be meteorologically correct, but it is a trifle hard on what is, when all is said and done, a very lovely setting. When it doesn't rain, as at the 1967 Belgian G.P., there are few more pleasant places from which to watch motor racing.

When the circuit was first used in 1925 it was mildly revolutionary. Hitherto, the *grandes épreuves* had been fought out over much larger courses, which consisted of lengths of dead straight main road, connected up by a few hairpins. To win, a car simply had to have a very high top speed.

But Spa required new abilities. Braking became important: acceleration was just as vital as frantic maximum speed. It is no doubt significant that of the eight cars which set off on the original Belgian G.P. only two finished. Antonio (father of Alberto) Ascari won it in an Alfa Romeo.

Spa itself is about five miles away from the circuit. It's a somewhat smaller version of Cheltenham or Tunbridge Wells, and, by all accounts, the daddy of them all. It has an atmosphere of genteel respectability—though, to judge by some of the hotels, not many people go there now to take the treatment. What have obviously once been the water holes of wealthy invalids now have a somewhat dejected look. Nevertheless, it is a centre for tourism, and one of the base camps for the Grand Prix course.

There have obviously been modifications to the circuit since those early days of the mid-twenties, but it is substantially much the same as it was. Without a doubt, it is the fastest of all the classic road circuits, with corners which can usually be taken flat out.

Jackie Stewart, who was badly damaged there after a crash in the 1966 race, told me: 'I always enjoy it. It is certainly the most dangerous race in the Grand Prix calendar. It's very challenging. Although it's roughly the same length as the 24-Hour circuit at Le Mans, it isn't really like it. That's smooth, not bumpy. There's an emphasis here on driver ability as well as on car ability.'

The lap distance is 8·76 miles, which is a further hazard, for it is difficult to string out enough marshals over such a large area. When Stewart was trapped in his B.R.M., upside down in a ditch, it was some time before he was discovered. And then it was Graham Hill who saw him, and stopped, and walked to a farm and borrowed a spanner, detached the steering wheel, and got him out. If Stewart's car had caught fire the consequences would have been appalling.[1]

Scenically, the surroundings are terrific. It is right in the midst of the Ardennes—a few miles north of the area in which, during the last war, the Germans launched their final offensive. It is a mass of hills, covered with pine trees; valleys with trout streams bubbling through them; and meadows which, in early summer, become ablaze with buttercups, and where cattle munch contentedly, heedless of the hell-blazing machinery. It has some of the grandeur of Nurburgring, though not so intense.

When Colin Chapman took Team Lotus to Spa-Francorchamps in 1967 he brought with him two cars, two drivers (Jim Clark and Graham Hill), five mechanics, and Keith Duckworth, who designed the engines. Bette Hill was also there to work a stop-watch and keep a record of lap times.

Chapman said: 'Normally we have three mechanics—one per car, plus the chief mechanic and a spare bloke, who works on whichever car needs it most. But this time we've only got two cars. The third one isn't ready yet. Nevertheless,

[1]. Each B.R.M. now has a small spanner taped to its steering wheel—as a precaution.

I've brought along the full team, as there's quite a lot of work to be done. The cars are very new. We're still exploring them.'

This word 'exploring' crops up quite a lot. It's almost as if they've built something and are now trying to find out what, precisely, they've made. This isn't so very far from the truth. They know what's inside it, and they have a tolerably shrewd idea of what it will do. But for how long it will go on *doing* it, and how it will behave under the one hundred and one different conditions of motor racing, these are still imponderables. They have to be discovered by actual experience.

Over and over again one comes up against what seems to be a basic truth about motor-racing machinery. Creatures such as horses are reasonably predictable, which is why there can be a favourite for the Derby, and why the favourite often lives up to its short odds and wins. In motor racing there can be no favourites. Some drivers may be more skilled than others, some cars may seem to be more competitive. Some will go faster and some will go slower. But what will happen during those two hours, when the truth is brutally, often painfully, wrung out is anyone's guess.

It is Friday afternoon, the first of the two practice sessions. I park my car near the entrance to the circuit and walk down towards the grandstands. People are wandering about on the track. From behind the pits comes the screaming, sobbing *gr-grr-grrrrr-gr-gr-gr* . . . of engines being revved up.

The Grand Prix circus has arrived.

How should one think about practice? The best lap times of the various cars will determine their positions on the starting grid. As such, it is competitive. But Chapman is one person who never loses sight of the real purpose. He said to me: 'The normal object of practice is to give the driver a chance to get the feel of things. Grid positions really aren't all that important. If the car is going well, and if the driver gets the feel of it and the circuit, then good grid positions follow automatically. This time, we know we have a problem regarding the fatigue of drive gears, and so the less running we do, the better.'

He looks down to the bottom of the straight where the track bends and starts to wriggle upwards again. 'I'm always pleased when this race is over,' he says. 'It's very fast and very dangerous.'

Brabham is the first driver unofficially to break both lap

records—official and unofficial. He snips 1·1 seconds off the fastest lap time ever made at Spa. Nobody in the Lotus pits is impressed. They know that this is only a beginning. Not long afterwards Gurney shaves 5·7 seconds off Brabham's time, and still nobody's impressed.

There's no reason why they should be. Clark, who has no doubt been getting the 'feel' of things and who has won the Belgian Grand Prix four times on the trot between 1962 and 1965, goes out, circulates the 8·76 miles, and puts up the astonishing time of 3 minutes 29·2 seconds—two seconds less than Gurney.

Now there is an air almost of awe and certainly of jubilation. Chapman laughs: 'We'd better have him in. Otherwise they'll be re-writing the regs and getting us banned.' A mechanic carefully slots an arrow into his board. Clark will see the signal, and know that it's telling him to come in. But then Chapman changes his mind. 'No—take that arrow off,' he says. 'Let him go round again.'

Clark goes round once more. Then he glides into the pits. 'I don't think I'll go out again,' he says. Rather as if he's at the seaside, it's turning a bit cool and he's decided he's done enough bathing for one day.

Actually, he does go out again. This time he snips off 0·2 seconds. Everyone is highly delighted.

On the following day he does some more fast laps, though not quite so fast as on that first afternoon. Chapman observes: 'I remember the times when all we could do was a fast lap. Now we want to win the race. Bring him in.' He is brought in.

On the Friday there was jubilation about so much speed. On the Saturday there is less of it. Depression seems to have set in. Bette Hill voices the general feeling. 'I don't like it,' she says. 'When things go *too* well at practice, it isn't good.'

'Rather like that thing about "fine before seven, rain before eleven",' I suggest. She supposes so. 'A bad dress rehearsal means a good first night?' She nods. I refrain from trotting out any more overworked aphorisms, and query in my notebook: 'motor-racing people superstitious?'

Possibly they are—more than they'd care to admit. When on race day, I bounce into the pits, I bid everyone a very good morning. 'Morale high, everyone feeling confident?' I ask. I am greeted by a thinly veiled look of dislike. Somebody points out that confidence is something that no decent, prudent, intelligent team feels on these occasions.

The hairpin nearest to the grandstands and the pits at Spa-Francorchamps is very reasonably called La Source. It is rather like the source of a river, a point in the side of a hill from which the circuit pours out, splashing madly downwards, tumbling frantically like a beaten-up triangle back to the place whence it began. There are villages at the corners, and it is in these places that the teams have their headquarters. Ferrari is in a Shell garage nearest to the circuit. B.R.M. is in the village of Francorchamps. Lotus and Cooper-Maserati are down in Stavelot, and so on. Actually, Lotus are sharing their garage with Tim Parnell. The former has the service bay, the latter occupies the workshops.

In the service bay a very angry Alsatian dog is caged. Whenever anyone goes too close to the wire it utters a livid cry of rage. Other roars come from the Parnell section as they put the engine together again, switch it on, rev it up, and see if it works.

Friday evening: Clark and Hill are in the garage, talking to their mechanics. A length of cord is stretched across the entrance, rather half-heartedly trying to keep away the crowds which gather outside. Presently a child crosses the cord, and runs up to Jim Clark. She pushes a scrap of paper and a ball point pen at him. Dutifully, he signs. He asks her how old she is. She turns out to be fourteen. Made bold by the success of their one-girl vanguard, other children follow. Soon everyone seems to be signing autographs, Clark, Hill, even Chapman. Some present elegant albums with photographs of star drivers stuck into them. Most have notebooks and grubby bits of paper. It becomes frenzied, but nobody seems to mind.

Autograph hunters and, to a lesser extent, photographers are like flies which are drawn to drivers. They buzz and they push and sometimes they swarm. They get into the pits. After a while, one feels in the midst of a nightmare. One can even imagine them erupting from behind the skirting in the drivers' bedrooms at night.

I wander over and talk with Keith Duckworth who's in between conversations about engines. He's a young man, prematurely grey, with an abstracted look and a deceptively slow, almost vague, way of talking. He graduated at the Imperial College (during which time he used to rebuild

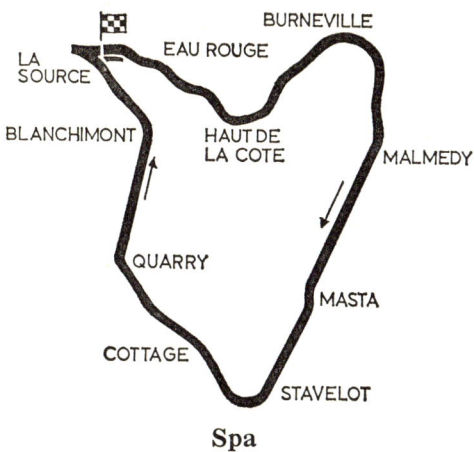

Spa

Climax engines and modify suspensions on racing cars). After a year on the staff of Lotus he formed Cosworth Engineering in 1958. I ask him why he goes motor racing.

'I'll probably go to all the meetings until I get fed up,' he says. 'I go there to look at the engines, to see what's happening to them. I hope I may learn why they did or didn't blow up—and also the circumstances in which they did, or didn't, blow up.'

He agrees that 'if anything's needed, I suppose I'll pick up a spanner and do it.' But, he says: 'I don't go along with major overhauls in the paddock. It's difficult enough to build an engine right under decent circumstances.' Chapman agrees with him. He's another one who doesn't like the idea of keeping his mechanics up all night rebuilding engines. About eighty different items have been changed in the cars since Clark won at Zandvoort. This is not the time to make further alterations. What the mechanics have to do is largely a matter of routine maintenance.

'Mr. Duckworth, when did you start work on designing these engines?'

He tells me: 'April, 1966—that was when we first began thinking about them. Ford commissioned them, so these are Ford engines. They provide us with technical information and research facilities, if we want them.'

'And the Dutch Grand Prix was the first time that Jimmy Clark's had ever been used. And he won. It was pretty good, getting it right first time, wasn't it?'

Mr. Duckworth doesn't appear to think there was any particular virtue in it. After all, they'd been remarkably successful with their Formula 2 units, and the two are basically similar. 'What we've done,' he says, 'is to get the same power as the other constructors get, but out of a lighter, shorter engine, and this enables a small, light car to be built.'

Contrary to the 1967 style of plumbing, the Lotus exhausts do not come out of the top. They come out low down at the sides, and then sweep upwards, almost with a flourish, at the back. 'The reason for this,' says Duckworth, 'is that a very narrow valve angle seemed to be desirable. Also this car doesn't need any body beyond the front of the engine, which leaves plenty of room for them.'

He's about to go back to the cars. Suddenly he says: 'I'm *keen* on engines. Now I come to think of it, I eat, sleep and drink engines.' His wife, who is standing nearby, smiles.

At 3.30 in the afternoon of Sunday, June 18th, the Belgian Grand Prix got under way. Before the start, the drivers processed in front of the grandstands as passengers in open touring cars. One car had no passenger on board. Jack Brabham's. He, presumably, was still busy back in the paddock.

Other people were also busy. The procession was followed by a briefing session for the drivers. When it was over and the group was breaking up, Dan Gurney lumbered up. Somebody said: 'You've missed it, Dan.' And another: 'You're late.' Gurney smiled and hoped it had gone off all right.

The action moved on to the dummy grid. With only a few minutes to go, the Lotus pits were electrified as 'Flash' Gordon, Jim Clark's mechanic, hove in sight at full trot. He was holding a spanner in his hand, which seemed to bode bad tidings. But all he wanted was a bottle of Coca-Cola. Before an event a driver may not seem to have any nerves, but his mouth becomes dry—and it remains dry for all the race.

Between the pits and the track there's a path about a yard wide, hemmed in by the pit counter on one side and a crash barrier on the other. Into this area are crammed all the people with the right passes (such as photographers) and sometimes people without them. At one point during this race a couple was mildly necking to one side of me. Presently, after the customary argument, a marshal sent them packing. An ice-cream salesman who wriggled through the throng was allowed to remain.

This area is overcrowded, and I have to admit that it is not a place where I'd care to be if it was raining, and a car aqua-

Dutch landscape   Scarfiotti (Ferrari)
Stewart (B.R.M.)

German trackscape   Rindt (Cooper-Maserati)
Gurney (Eagle-Weslake)

Urban speedway   Mike Spence (B.R.M.) tours Monaco
Sand-dune spectacular   Mike Parkes (Ferrari) circumnavigates the dunes at Zandvoort

Car passes car Surtees (Honda), foreground, and Rodriguez (Cooper-Maserati), background
Car passes man Spence and pit signal at Monaco

Into the pits   Hulme during the Belgian Grand Prix
Out of the pits   Hill at practice for the German Grand Prix

Ferrariscape   Scarfiotti at Brands Hatch
Towards a conclusion   Amon chases Brabham during the penultimate lap of the German Grand Prix

Bendsmanship Clark at Silverstone
Brabham at Zandvoort

Denis Hulme in his Repco-Brabham (old style)

Jack Brabham in his Repco-Brabham (new style)

planed and spun off along this short, very sharp straight. However, there was no rain this day. The flag of Belgium was swept down. The cars exploded from the grid, and the race began. Except for Graham Hill. His engine did not roar into vibrant life. It was suffering from ignition trouble. He coasted into the pits.

They got it going, only to return soon afterwards. This time it was the transmission. Hill said: 'I can only just get it into fifth, and I can't get it into fourth at all.' A mechanic suggested it was possibly the clutch. Chapman said it must be a question of selectors. Anyway, after another very short circulation it came back again and presently the ailing machine was pushed away into the paddock.

Clark got away to a tremendous start and was well out in front, with Stewart behind him and Gurney behind Stewart. Presently an ambulance was seen to depart and the white flags were waving. Then the helicopter took off.

The commentator informed us that Mike Parkes had crashed on one of the bends, but it wasn't serious. 'I repeat,' he said, 'it is not at all serious.' (Actually, he said it in French, but that's what it amounted to.) The departure of the chopper did nothing to reassure anyone, and presently it became known that Parkes had broken his left wrist and suffered a compound fracture of his right leg. He was also suffering from shock.

'Mike's been a bit too hairy. He can be very hairy indeed,' somebody said.

The race continued.

Clark's mechanic was just putting out a signal to him when to everyone's astonishment the Lotus came in. While they got busy at the back, Clark shouted for something to drink. He was offered a choice between Coke and mineral water. He chose the latter. Graham Hill opened the bottle, and passed it to him.

With the delicacy of a dentist taking out a tooth, the mechanic was extracting a plug from the engine. 'It's exploded,' he said. 'This plug has e-x-p-l-o-d-e-d.' He put another one in. Clark set off once more. Before very long he was back again. More trouble. His first stop had already cost him the race. There was little more to lose.

Bette Hill said to me: 'Richard, you didn't keep your fingers crossed.' I said that they'd been crossed all the time, but it didn't seem to work.

Eventually, with a slightly ailing car, Dan Gurney won the event. With a sicker car Jackie Stewart came second. Chris Amon came third. The leading places in the World Championship table now stood thus:

1. Denis Hulme, still with 16 points (neither he nor Brabham finished in the Belgian G.P.).
2. Chris Amon and Pedro Rodriguez, both with 11 points.
3. Jim Clark 10 points.
4. Dan Gurney 9 points.
5. Jack Brabham 7 points.

12

Honda: The Sun Will Eventually Rise

In a white-walled workshop at Slough, a pair of Hondas are contentedly grazing. A team of Japanese mechanics, immaculately dressed as seems to be their custom, is preparing to carry out some reasonably complicated mechanical surgery on them. As befits such an operation, the room is immaculately clean. The instruments, of course, *shine*.

Hovering on the fringe, seeing everything but saying very little, is Yoshio Nakamura. He is dressed in a brown sports shirt and a pair of slacks. Through his heavy horn-rimmed spectacles his eyes suggest a mixture of deference and defiance, humility and too much knowledge to justify being humble. As a director of Honda's research and development company, Nakamura is concerned with the evolution of engines, production cars, and Formula 1 racing cars.

They are between races and very busy. Intruders are not likely to be welcomed. However, as one's calling compels, one intrudes.

Nakamura is, as always, the very soul of politeness. 'You wanted . . . ?' he breathes.

'To begin with, a brief history—a sort of outline,' one says.

'Honda was established, I think, in 1947. The object was to manufacture motor cycles, cultivators, petrol and diesel stationary engines. Mr. Honda is in his early sixties. He used to manufacture castings. In the last war he made piston rings for aircraft.'

Like all Nakamura's explanations, it is simple, and concise.

One thanks him for this information. 'After Honda had been in motor-cycle racing for two years the machines were already winning championships . . .'

'Forgive me,' he politely corrects. 'It was three years.'

'After three years, then—but after three years in motor racing you've only had one victory. Isn't this rather disappointing for you?'

He smiles, gestures, tilts his head from side to side. 'I am not so unhappy about it,' he says. 'And then, again, I am not so happy. But I think it is important to remember that we have not been in many races, and one must know why we do it in the first place.'

In the late forties the roads of Japan were in a mess. They were narrow and overcrowded. Only relatively few of them were surfaced. The situation didn't encourage the building of motor cars. What people needed for personal transport was something swift, small and economical. The finger pointed at motor cycles, and the two-wheeled boom began.

Everybody seemed to be trying to get on to the bandwagon. At one time no fewer than thirty firms were turning out machines. Some—such as Suzuki, Yamaha, and Honda—had a sufficiency of capital and facilities. Most of them did not. One by one, the small outfits went bankrupt. In the end, only the big and the strong and the brilliant survived.

Eventually, the highway mess was sorted out. The demand for cars grew. A number of firms, including Honda, decided to build them. But there was one commodity which the up-and coming industry was desperately short of. Experience. They knew all there was to know about building trucks. They had mastered motor-cycle manufacturing and were beating most of the world at it. Aircraft they could construct without any bother at all. But the collective engineering might of Nippon was stuck for expertise on car-making. When it came to producing high-performance cars they were even more stuck.

The firms sought truth in their various ways. Mr. Honda and Mr. Nakamura discussed the problem at length. When the talking had to stop they decided that the quickest way was to take up motor racing. There are, of course, all manner of types of racing, and who could have blamed them if they had elected to try something small and modest.

But caution was cast to the East Wind. Basing their decision on the philosophy that it's a good thing to start at the top, they opted for Formula 1. Their original idea was to build the engines themselves, and to get somebody like Jack Brabham to make the chassis.[1] But the object was to study high-speed techniques. It is all very well to create power, but power must have something to drive. There has to be suspension and steering and braking and all the other things. Mr. Honda and Mr. Nakamura, ever courageous, said that they would build a complete racing car.

If the original plan had been adopted today's Honda racing car would no doubt be different. It is a large vehicle. An opposition driver, describing the problems of overtaking it, once likened it to a double-decker corporation bus. It is a theory of B.R.M.'s Tony Rudd that works which construct cars, engines and all, tend to build bigger projectiles than those which buy in their power units from outside. I put this point of view to Nakamura.

'I think Tony may be right,' he said. 'The first purpose of our car is to study high-speed techniques. The second purpose is to win races. If winning races came first, I think we should probably make something smaller and lighter.'

Research, then, is everything. The logic behind Honda's first year in motor racing is a little hard to follow. Since they lacked experience as constructors, they reasoned, the sensible thing was to employ a driver who was equally inexperienced. And so they chose Ronnie Bucknum, who is talented and had driven all manner of cars, but never a Formula 1.

Also, it seems, in Bucknum's favour was the fact that he had practically no knowledge of mono-post cars.

That first year, which was 1964, was nothing to write home about. The Honda and Bucknum took part in few races and won none of them. When the season was over, the Honda hierarchy took a solemn look at things. 'They decided they'd learned something,' Nakamura said. 'They thought they'd got some potential.'

For 1965 they elected to race two cars, and to buy in some experience in the form of Richie Ginther, who also happens to be very good on the technical side. The arrangement was concluded triumphantly at the end of the year, when Ginther won the Mexican G.P. This was his first Grand Prix victory —and Honda's first, too.

---

1. They did this in Formula 2. During the 1966 season Brabham used Honda engines and beat nearly all comers. When the Formula 2 regulations were changed, however, the Brabham-Honda *entente* came to an end, and the former went back to Cosworth.

In that year, with Ginther and Bucknum driving, they raced two cars. Since then they have kept it down to one. As Nakamura very reasonably points out: 'To race two cars you must have at least three—and at least five engines. That is too much for us, especially as all the construction has to be carried out in the prototype factory. It would hinder the development of new production cars.'

From Honda's point of view, the New Formula 1 regulations might have seemed to be catastrophic. There they were, with only two seasons behind them, having won their first race. They had conceived and delivered a racing car. They were still smarting from the birth pains, and then their child, the child which had been begotten with sweat and disappointment, lay dead. It was killed at a conference in Paris, far away on the other side of the world.

Said Nakamura: 'We had joined the Formula 1 Constructors' Association. I discussed the new regulations with Mr. Honda, and we decided to obey any decision agreed by the European constructors. Mr. Honda and I never put an opinion forward.' He sighed. 'If I could stay in Europe all the year round, you know, it would be easier. In Tokio one can only see what's happening from the newspapers. There is not so much information.'

And so they scrapped the car which had only won this one race, and set about designing and building another. Of course, the exercise was not entirely wasted. They had learned many things from it. Not least of all, it had taught them about suspension.

'I think,' Mr. Nakamura said, 'that we had found out all we needed to. We had exhausted the subject.'

If motor racing were an operation governed entirely by economic prudence one might have questioned the wisdom of entering the sport when the current regulations had only two more years to go. But this is usually one of the least considerations, and it certainly doesn't seem to have bothered the people at Honda. They wanted knowledge, and they wanted it quickly. There could be no question of waiting a couple of years. Whatever feelings they may have about their $1\frac{1}{2}$ litre experiences, regret is not among them.

The new car wasn't ready until late in 1966. For most of the season Ginther was loaned to Cooper. He drove Hondas in the Italian, United States and Mexican Grands Prix. There were no victories.

HONDA: THE SUN WILL EVENTUALLY RISE 95

And then came Surtees.

Nakamura is commendably frank about it. When, at the end of 1964 they revised their ideas about the kind of driver they needed they'd have liked John Surtees. He wasn't available. He had just won the World Championship in a Ferrari. Enzo Ferrari was pleased with him, and one had to assume that he was pleased with Enzo Ferrari. Whatever strife was building up, swelling to the point at which it erupted at the Le Mans 24-Hour Race of 1966, certainly did not show. The ace had not yet been involved in his very nearly calamitous accident at Mosport. (His injuries included two fractures and a dislocation of the hip, four fractured vertebrae in the lower part of his back, concussion, a ruptured kidney and a broken pelvis. Nobody thought he'd live—except, perhaps, Surtees himself.) He seemed to be content with life, but, since he is no great conversationalist and is certainly not given to offloading his troubles on to other people, that was about all anyone could tell.

By contrast, Ginther was suspected of wanting a change from B.R.M. Closer inspection confirmed his availability, and he was signed on.

And so to Le Mans.

There's no point in digging up the debris of past feuds. The Surtees-Dragoni contretemps has been more than adequately reported. The last angry words had scarcely been uttered when the Press picked up the pieces and assembled them into news stories which travelled all over the world. Among the papers which printed them were those delivered at the Honda plant.

The row took place in June. For the rest of that year Surtees drove for Cooper-Maserati and rewarded them by winning the Mexican Grand Prix. Back in August, however, Honda began negotiations with him. The months dragged by. They were concluded in December.

'There was this thing about it,' Nakamura told me. 'John had come from motor-cycle racing into car racing. We were doing the same thing.' But there was obviously a lot more to it.

Surtees is thirty-four years old. His hair is prematurely grey. His complexion is pale. At first sight he looks delicate, even fragile. This is entirely misleading. If he had not been stupendously fit he couldn't possibly have survived the Mosport disaster.

Furthermore, on closer examination, he turns out to be well

built, with powerful shoulders and strong arms. He used to be fond of football, and one can imagine that he'd have made a very good soccer player. However, his father—who owned a garage—was a well-known motor-cyclist, and that was the way things went. John Surtees won seven World Championships on two wheels before going over to car racing.

If the colour of his complexion is misleading, the expression he habitually wears on his face is not. He looks withdrawn, reticent, as if he is preoccupied with a lot of complicated thoughts and doesn't welcome intruders. There is something of the solitary about him: the apparently lonely figure, who isn't really lonely at all, who goes his own way—preferably alone.

He looks preoccupied because he invariably is. As a driver, he takes a tough, get-out-of-the-way-I'm-coming-through, attitude. All the top racing drivers are reasonably dedicated to their profession, but Surtees brings a new dimension to dedication. He is completely single-minded about the sport. He lives in a delightful house in Kent and his wife Pat is a very beautiful woman. But there is no room for anything else. He has built his own, extremely successful, sports-racing car (driving it in the Can-Am series, he is pretty well invincible). In European sports-car events he now drives a Lola Aston Martin (the herald of a British renaissance in this field?). He is an above-average engineer, and he isn't fussy about what he undertakes. I can, for example, recall the occasion at Silverstone when he was up until 2 a.m. on the eve of a British Grand Prix, doing a welding job on his car.

So there he is: withdrawn, a loner, a brilliant driver and a scarcely less talented engineer. This is what Honda bought when they signed on John Surtees.

They could not possibly have done better. I suppose one could look up the distance between Tokio and the nearest European circuit, but the statistic would not be very important. It's enough to say that it's thousands of miles. The cars are built in Japan, but when they're not racing they spend most of their time in this factory at Slough. Three Honda mechanics are in residence there. Nakamura tries to come over about once in every two months, but he's a very busy man. For major modification the cars, or the engines, are flown to Tokio. They can go there and come back in a week, but this is extremely expensive.

This Honda outpost in Britain is divorced by immense distance from the works and governed by somewhat remote control. When they signed on Surtees they not only acquired a crack driver but also an engineer capable of supervising the work, of thinking creatively about the cars—a perfectionist who is happy in isolation.

Nothing could have been more in Honda's interest—and nor, for that matter, in that of John Surtees. One might, perhaps, have wondered whether Honda's apparent indifference to winning, their overwhelming concern for research, would have conflicted with the Surtees proposition, which is that races are for winning regardless of anything else. However, before we put too much importance on to it, let us not forget that Honda are now turning out large numbers of production cars. They are past masters of the art of exporting, and every time there's a Honda victory the sales shoot upwards. It does not take much imagining to conclude that they will want to win races very badly.

Surtees himself enjoys a lot of freedom. By May of 1967 he had made four trips to Tokio. He is also more or less continually in touch with Nakamura by telephone, telex, letters and during the latter's visits to Europe. Nevertheless, there is no rule about his consulting Honda before he does anything, or tries anything out. It is enough that he shall tell them what he has done.

Said Nakamura: 'We're all going the same way—in the same *direction*. I'm not pretending that distance makes no difficulties in our relationship, but it doesn't make too many.'

The three Honda mechanics who live in a flat at Slough are less to be envied. Japanese personnel used to be employed there on a temporary basis. Nowadays, however, there is a degree of permanency about such appointments. Quite apart from their understandable reluctance to be parted from their families, the mechanics find the question of language difficult. None of them can speak very much English.

The Honda research and development company employs about 400 engineers. Between February and May, some of them work on the Formula 1 racing cars. Then that project is pushed to one side, and they are assigned to something else. Thereafter, three engineers work on the engines, and another three on the chassis.

When considering possibilities for the 3 litre engine, they

H

looked at V12, V16 and V24 arrangements. The V12 won—largely because it could use the same pistons as those in the 4-cylinder Formula 2 engines.

You can tell when the Formula 1 Honda goes by because it seems to do something rather nasty to your eardrums. Some misguided souls prefer to call this 'the Honda music'. It is, Nakamura points out, a sign of how beautifully the engine is breathing, and consequently developing more power. His rivals, on the other hand, consider that he is unreasonably optimistic. As one of them told me: 'An internal combustion engine uses up the thermal energy from petrol in three ways: by pushing the pistons up and down, by heating the water, and in the gases which escape through the exhaust system. The more that gets away through the exhaust pipes, the less there is for pushing the pistons. That's why a noisy engine is not necessarily an efficient one.'

Nakamura counters this by saying that the undue noise is due to exhaust pulsation, and it's easier for the gases to escape. 'It certainly doesn't mean heat-loss,' he protests. The argument could probably go on all night. Certainly the Honda does not appear to suffer from lack of power. At its first outing, in the Monaco G.P. of 1967, it was forced out of the race by a fractured water pipe. For five laps Surtees was driving with no water in the system at all. Afterwards, when the engine was stripped down, the damage was found to be comparatively small.

'But that is our aim for 1967,' Nakamura told me. 'To get the details right. To overcome these little things, like a leak in a tube, which are very small, but which lose races.'

Nobody can deny that nationalism of a kind infects motor racing. One day, beyond any reasonable doubt, Honda will win the Formula 1 Constructors' Championship. Obviously, they would like it to happen with a Japanese driver behind the wheel. That really would be a resounding victory for Nippon.

'But,' said Nakamura, 'that will take a long time—maybe five, six or seven years. A Japanese World Champion may come one day, but not soon. You can learn engineering techniques. You can build and rebuild and modify cars until they work. You can do all this in one season. But a driver is a human being, and that is very different. If a nation takes two or three years to build a competitive car, it takes much longer to produce a competitive driver.'

And so, in the meanwhile, there is John Surtees and there is Honda. And there, too, to judge from their misfortune in 1967, are a lot of problems. But, make no mistake about it—the sun will eventually rise.

13

And So To Le Mans

IF a German named Gottlieb Daimler invented the petrol-driven automobile the French invented motor racing. The first event took place in 1894, when a motley collection of twenty-one cars set off from Paris on an 80-mile trip to Rouen. Some of them were powered by internal combustion engines, others chugged along under steam. It was somewhat euphemistically called a 'reliability run'. To the terror of peasants, poultry, and anyone else in the vicinity of the highway, a few of them actually completed the course. The winner was Count de Dion, who took 6 hours and 48 minutes, travelling at an average speed of just over 11 m.p.h.

The oldest race in the present motor racing calendar is the Targa Florio, named after Count Florio, who established it in 1906. Fifty days later France—or, to be more precise, the Automobile Club de l'Ouest at Le Mans—presented the first national Grand Prix.

A 65-mile circuit was mapped out for the event. It was roughly in the shape of a triangle. Two of the sides were main roads. The third was a wooden road, built to link them up and to keep the competing cars away from the towns. Part of it ran past a horse-racing course where, in 1908, the Wright brothers were to give Europe its first glimpse of a flying machine.

The race was run over two days. The drivers had to complete six laps on each of them, making a total of 780 miles. Somewhat rudimentary rules governed the cars: there was, for example, a weight limit of 2,240 lb, and they had to be able to cover at least 9·4 miles per gallon. So far as the engines were concerned, it was a delightful free for all. They ranged from the massive 18 litre units of the Panhards and the de Dietrichs, down to a 7½ litre unit which was considered to be somewhat on the small side. The race was won by a Frenchman with the almost totally unpronounceable name of François Szisz, who had once been Louis Renault's mechanic. Appropriately enough, he drove a 13 litre Renault car. His speed was something in the region of 65 m.p.h.

Having carved its name into motor-racing history for the first time, Le Mans lapsed into obscurity for the next fifteen years. In 1921, after an hiatus of seven years, the Grand Prix circus made a fresh start. True to tradition, the first post-war race was a French one. The original intention was to hold it near Strasbourg to celebrate the return of Alsace-Lorraine to French rule.

However, the local authorities in Strasbourg seem to have followed a pattern favoured by their colleagues in most other parts of the world. They shillied and shallied, they talked about 'on the one hand . . . but, on the other . . .' and so it went on. It was not until 1922 that they eventually got around to making a race possible. In the meanwhile the extremely reactive Automoile Club de l'Ouest had taken the 1921 event over.

Those huge engines of the 1906 days were rather like the brontosaurus: impressive to look at, but somewhat ineffectual in performance. Their enormous crankshafts rumbled round at about 1,200 r.p.m. producing a paltry 100-120 b.h.p. By 1921, however, the designers had discovered that size is not necessarily synonymous with power, and that a unit which seems big enough to propel a battleship may fall a long way short of being perfect for a racing car.

Most of the 1921 engines were 3 litre straight-8 affairs, turning at between 3,500 and 4,200 r.p.m.—at which speed they developed between 115 and 120 b.h.p. The event, run over a 10·6 mile circuit, was won by Jimmy Murphy in a heavily Bugatti-influenced Duesenburg. His average speed was about 80 m.p.h. Murphy won in spite of a fractured radiator and some broken ribs. In the latter respect he was possibly more fortunate than one mechanic, who was knocked unconscious by a flying stone.

Among the more original features of his car were hydraulically operated brakes, H.T. coil ignition, three overhead valves per cylinder, and a three-speed gearbox with a central gear lever.

Conceivably there would have been more Grands Prix

races at Le Mans had not, in 1923, the circuit been shot into fame for its endurance race. It all began when Emile Coquille, a discerning business man who introduced the Rudge wheel to France, made an offer to the Automobile Club de l'Ouest. He was prepared to hand over francs to the value of about £4,000 if it organised a new kind of race. M. Coquille made his proposal on the Rudge-Whitworth stand at the 1922 Paris salon. Among those present were Charles Durand, secretary of the club, and Charles Faroux, an extremely articulate elder statesman of motor racing.

Out of the trio's deliberations the Le Mans 24-Hour Race was born. The first event was held in pouring rain at the end of May, 1923. The Grand Prix course of 1921 was used, but there were a number of other attractions which had nothing to do with motor racing.

It was, the organisers not unreasonably decided, asking rather a lot of spectators to imagine that they would contentedly watch cars circulating, no matter how excitingly, for twenty-four hours on the trot. There was to be a fireworks display, but unfortunately that had to be cancelled owing to the rain. More successful were jazz bands and a cinema.

Albeit in somewhat reduced circumstances, the 24-Hour Race began as it was clearly meant to continue. Since then, a portion of the circuit has been snipped off, cutting the lap distance to 8·41 miles. The track has been widened and given a much better surface, and since the fatal crash which killed so many spectators in 1955 a good deal has been done to improve the safety and facilities of the grandstands and pits.

But the 24-Hour Race is much more than an event in the motor-sport calendar. The man who worked the projector in the small electric palace of 1923, the jazzmen whose melodies competed with the snarl of sports cars, were starting something very big indeed. Today Le Mans has become larger than Battersea Pleasure Gardens, more popular than any other motor race in Europe, better attended than the Derby or the English Cup Final, in short a French national custom of the greatest magnitude. Some people go there to watch motor racing. Others go to shop in the village, to eat and drink, to lark about in the seemingly innumerable funfairs, to camp, to picnic, to wander along dusty paths for hours on end, looking for something and never seeming to find it. It is an occasion when firms connected, however directly or in-

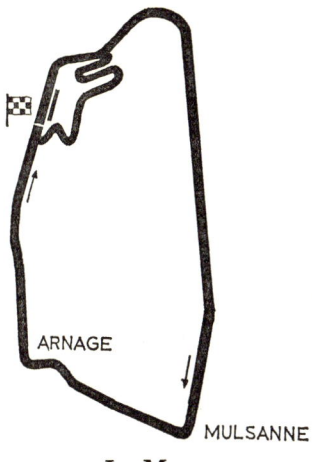

Le Mans

directly, with the motor industry, entertain their customers; when lap records are, to use a word much favoured by the local press, 'pulverised', when people from all over Europe come to pay homage to the mechanical deity; and when hundreds of gendarmes (they call them 'poulets' in that part of the world) are unmercifully catcalled by the crowd.

That is the Le Mans 24-Hour Race; and, believe me, in the minds of most of the spectators it is a long way removed from the more dedicated atmosphere of a Formula 1 Grand Prix.

Since the World Championship was introduced in 1950 the French Grand Prix has been held at Rheims, Rouen and (once, in 1965) at Clermont-Ferrand. All these, like the one used for the Le Mans 24-Hour Race and the Belgian G.P. course at Spa-Francorchamps, are road circuits. In other words, when there's no racing they become part of the normal highway system. Furthermore, since they are part of that system, there is a limit to the amount of use which can be made of them. After all, the traffic must flow.

The only closed circuit in France which existed in isolation was at Montlhery near Paris. It is small, bumpy, and far from ideal. The last time it was used for a Grand Prix was back in 1937.

Clearly, then, with Montlhery inadequate, France needed a substitute: something which could be used for training young drivers, for testing cars, and for other functional purposes. And this is what they built at Le Mans. It was completed in 1966.

The new circuit is 2·7 miles long. It includes the straight which goes past the pits on the 24-Hour course and then, just before the Esses, it turns right. Thereafter it takes the shape of a hand with forefinger and thumb extended, before returning to the pit straight. There are six fairly slow corners.

They called it the Bugatti Circuit and it was there on the first Sunday in July that the 1967 French G.P. was held.

If the 1967 French Grand Prix were regarded by show-business standards it would probably be considered disappointing. The audience was small. The performers were a good deal less than enthusiastic about the course—and out of the sixteen starters only seven finished. Lotus, Eagle-Weslake, Ferrari, the H16 B.R.M.s, they all packed up. After eighty laps, or 216 miles, the race was won by Jack Brabham —with Denis Hulme (also in a Repco Brabham) coming second. Jackie Stewart, driving (of all things) a V8 Tasman B.R.M., was third.

One can't help feeling that, in some respects, the race suffered from comparisons. It took place only three weeks after the 24-Hour Race, which was won by Dan Gurney and A. J. Foyt in a 7 litre Ford, and which was watched by over half a million people. Perhaps it seemed to be an anticlimax. Perhaps not enough of the spectators felt like returning to Le Mans so soon. Had it been held at one of the other circuits, the turn-out might well have been better.

Graham Hill described the Bugatti Circuit as 'a Mickey Mouse' affair. Somebody else suggested that it might be better for karting. Most of the drivers seemed to feel that it was too small for Formula 1 cars. But were they being fair? Admittedly it is smaller than Rheims (lap distance 5·15 miles) and Rouen (lap distance 4·08 miles). On the other hand it is larger than Monaco (1·95 miles), Watkins Glen (2·30 miles), and Brands Hatch and Zandvoort (both 2·65) miles. Possibly it just seemed to be small by comparison with the huge 24-Hour Race circuit.

The French Grand Prix was the fifth in the series—in other words, very nearly half time. It continued an interesting trend in which every race was won by a different driver. Rodriguez in a Cooper Maserati won the South African G.P., Denny Hulme in a Brabham won at Monaco, Jim Clark in a Lotus won in Holland, and Dan Gurney in an Eagle-Weslake won at Spa. But this time it was no longer a different car. Brabham Repcos now had two races to their credit, which put them (for the time being, at any rate) at the top of the constructors' table. It looked as if the lightness-and-simplicity theory might very well pay off for the second year running.

In the case of at least two of the retirements, certain characteristics became evident. The Lotus-Fords of Jim Clark and Graham Hill were going with remarkable speed before they packed in. Nothing, but nothing, could touch them. It was pretty obvious that the Lotus-Ford engine, when it was turning the wheels of the car, was unbeatable. The trouble occurred in that complex department, where the power is transferred from the engine to the road. Once again, unable to stand up to such force, the transmission failed. This was the weakness. This was the problem which had to be overcome before the Lotus-Fords could be relied upon to win all the races which, if Chapman could find a solution, they undoubtedly would.

Gurney's car was another which ought to have tanned the hide off most of the others. But here—and, once again, it was a recurring weakness—the trouble was fuel starvation. The engine had all the vigour that anyone could possibly ask of it. The transmission left nothing to be desired. It was just a question of getting the petrol into the system, which sounds easy, but isn't.

In some respects the most interesting features of the 1967 French Grand Prix were the things which didn't happen. For example, the Honda and John Surtees were not there. Having failed to finish in any Grand Prix event since the South African G.P. back in January, they had stayed at home. Yoshio Nakamura—the technical master-mind behind the car—was trying to improve its reliability.

When the European season began there were three Ferraris competing. At Le Mans there was only Chris Amon, and he had to retire after the throttle cable broke. Bandini—that brilliant young driver, who was so gentle and courteous away from the track, and so determinedly competitive on it—had died after his smash at Monaco. Mike Parkes was still in hospital recovering from his injuries at Spa. That left only Amon and Scarfiotti. Ferrari was running short of drivers—and of cars.

During the 24-Hour Race Scarfiotti was teamed with Parkes. They had driven an extremely powerful P4 sports prototype, which had it in its power to lick the hairy Fords. But on the second day Scarfiotti was a very tired and, it seemed at a casual glance, sick man. He turned up at Spa, but was not particularly competitive. Now, it appeared, Enzo Ferrari had ordered him to rest.

Ludivico Scarfiotti is a wealthy young man, who can obviously afford to retire from motor racing whenever he feels like it. He looks tough, and he gives an enormous amount of thought to his profession. He once told me: 'Now I can understand a bit about it all. Now I drive a little with my heart and a little with my head. It is very dangerous to drive only with the heart, as I used to. You are reckless. You always want to win, and you can't know properly what you are doing.

'Since I started using my head as well, I know what I'm doing. I can see the other drivers and know what they're doing, too. The heart and the head are complementary.'

He also appeared to enjoy what he was doing. Later that day he told me: 'I am always relaxed when I am driving. All my problems are finished when I am in a race.'

That was at the start of the season. Since then one of his team mates had been killed and another injured. Scarfiotti's heart, conceivably, was taking over from his head. A friend of his told me after the French G.P. that it might be some while before he raced again.[1]

Bruce McLaren's transporter was not at the French G.P. Instead of driving his own car, this very able New Zealander, who never seems to become excited, drove an Eagle-Weslake for Dan Gurney.

Bruce McLaren had a wretchedly unsuccessful season in 1966. It was his first year as a Formula 1 constructor. He had some very convincing ideas, but he didn't have an engine worth the name. As a sports car constructor he had been relatively successful. His record in the Can-Am was a good one, putting him second only to John Surtees. Driving a Ford—for which firm he does a lot of testing—he had won the 1966 Le Mans 24-Hour Race in company with his fellow countryman, Chris Amon. It was only the Formula 1 prizes which seemed to elude him.

At the beginning of 1967 he was more optimistic about his chances. He had done a deal with B.R.M. He was to start the year with a V8 engine, pending the arrival of the much more competitive V12. But the months went by, and the V12 showed no signs of turning up.

1. After a bad smash at Rheims some years ago Scarfiotti retired from motor racing for a time.

Until it arrived there was little point in going on. He stayed away from the Belgian Grand Prix, and then came this news that he had signed on with Dan Gurney. Richie Ginther's sudden retirement from the sport had left Gurney short of a driver. There was talk of Foyt's coming over from America, and Foyt's name was down on the list of potential drivers for the Belgian G.P. But he never arrived. Now, it seemed, McLaren was to be Gurney's second driver in the European events, whilst Foyt was to drive for him in North America.

The situation must have been somewhat galling for McLaren, but he would be the last person to let it show. He once told me: 'I guess I worry enormously, but I try not to. One oughtn't to worry, ought one?'

People show signs of stress in innumerable ways. McLaren's is simply to smile a little bit less.

Alas, even the Eagle was to betray him. After twenty-six laps, when he was lying seventh, his car came to a halt with ignition trouble. He was left to consider Jackie Stewart's third place, and ask whether, after all, he might not have done better go stick to his own car.

After the French Grand Prix Denis Hulme was still at the top of the World Championship table with 22 points. Brabham went up into second place. Rodriguez held on to third place, Amon slipped back into fourth, and Jackie Stewart shared fifth place with Jim Clark.

Everyone went home to prepare for the British Grand Prix at Silverstone on July 15th.

14

A.A.R.: or the Dream of Daniel Sexton Gurney

WHEN Dan Gurney won the 1967 Belgian Grand Prix the crowd roared and went on roaring. This enthusiasm was partly due to Gurney's engaging personality, and partly to the fact that people admire courage. Motor racing is never a pushover. For Gurney a lot of it has been very tough going indeed.

If you mention bad luck to his colleagues, however, you are unlikely to find pity bubbling to the surface. Not unreasonably, they point out that, now and then, everyone has to retire from a race. That is the way things go. If there's no lack of skill and endeavour, ill-fortune's about the only hazard left. Furthermore, they are determined, whenever possible, to look on the bright side of things. Possibly he *was* compelled to retire from a number of races through mechanical faults. Nevertheless, they explain, he won two out of six races during the first half of the year—or, to look at it another way, whenever he finished he won.

Dan Gurney is 6 ft. 2 in. tall. He is thirty-seven years old, and looks like an elongated version of Lawrence of Arabia. He has a reputation, which is not entirely justified, for being one of the silent men of motor racing. As Bill Dunne, who manages the U.K. end of his business, points out: 'Sure—he's shy, and he doesn't talk much. He listens to what people have to say. When he's considered everything, and gets around to saying something—well, after that, there's not much left to add.'

Nor, in any case, can there be very much time for talking. As president of All American Racers Inc., a company he owns on a fifty-fifty shareholding basis with Carroll Shelby, his year's programme reads like a travel agent's nightmare.

The headquarters of A.A.R. are at Santa Ana in California, where they manufacture Indianapolis cars and monocoque hulls for the Formula 1 vehicles. The latter are dispatched to Rye in England, where the suspension is hung on and the engines installed. This outpost, officially known as 'All American Racing Inc. trading as Anglo American Racers', is managed by Dunne. Nevertheless, Gurney cannot be regarded as an absentee employer. He looks in there whenever his time allows, and often when it doesn't.

Gurney was born in New York City on April 13th, 1931. His father was an opera singer, and a very good one, too. He frequently appeared at the Met, made a number of records which are still in circulation, but never quite reached the status of an international star. His mother was a competent performer in opera chorus. Their gifts seem to have been short on heredity. People who have been treated to the rare experience of hearing Dan sing, recall it with a certain amount of pain.

After leaving school he studied liberal arts at college and took a particular interest in psychology. He still takes it. Says Bill Dunne: 'When he's getting ready for a race he's one of the most demanding people in the world. But when he's the company president, and can see a problem from different aspects, I've never known a more understanding person. There's nobody who can see another person's viewpoint quicker. That's Dan's psychology paying off.'

When he was fifteen he went down with his first bout of racing fever. It must have been a powerful attack, for the germ has remained in his system ever since. It wasn't just a question of wouldn't-it-be-fun-to-drive-fast-cars: at the age of sixteen he took a Ford V8 engine to pieces. That, given the right tools, is within most people's ability. In Gurney's case, however, he made a number of modifications, and then reassembled it. Afterwards it performed a good deal better than the average Ford V8.

During the Korean war he served as an army anti-aircraft gunner. Coincidentally, two other mainstays of A.A.R., Bill Dunne and Richie Ginther, were also out there. Dunne was working as a U.S. Navy demolitions expert, Ginther as a helicopter mechanic.

Gurney got back from the war, moved to California, and presently bought a TR2. The year was 1955. In his first race he finished third in his class. Later, he replaced the Triumph by a Porsche. He took part in a lot of events, and people began to notice him. One of them was Luigi Chinetti, Ferrari's concessionaire in North America and master-mind behind the North American Racing Team. Chinetti invited him to co-drive with Bruce Kessler at Le Mans in 1958. It was the young driver's first trip to Europe.

The 24-Hour Race was disappointing. His companion crashed the car early on and was seriously injured. Gurney never got a drive. He did better in the 1,000-km. race at Nurburgring, in which he came first in his class and sixth overall. Otherwise, largely due to cars crashed by his co-drivers, the trip was unsuccessful. When the season was over he went back to America with plenty of ambition and not very much money.

Looking back on it, that first trip was less of a failure than the stark facts suggest. By devious means it had brought him to the attention of Enzo Ferrari. The Master beckoned, and Gurney went off to Italy. After a few tests on the autodrome at Modena somebody produced a contract. In 1959, a bare four years after his first race, he was taking part in G.P. events at the wheel of an F1 Ferrari.

The Ferrari-Gurney *entente* lasted for one year. Gurney is not given to complaining, but one can't help feeling that it was not an entirely happy relationship. Some people are born organisation men, and some are natural free-lances. Gurney belongs to the latter. In spite of his quiet manner, he brings a strong stamp of individualism to everything he undertakes. When, after a reasonably successful year, his contract came up for renewal, he made no effort to remain on the Ferrari payroll.

During the next few years he drove for B.R.M., Porsche and Brabham. For Porsche he won the French Grand Prix of 1962; for Brabham he won the French and Mexican Grands Prix of 1964. Meanwhile, however, he had been planning to set up as a constructor in his own right.

Perhaps the crucial occasion was a taxi ride in London one day in 1962. Carroll Shelby and he were both over there on business. At some point they met, found that they were going in the same direction, and shared a cab for the journey.

Talking things over, they discovered that they were both thinking, more or less, the same thoughts. They agreed, tentatively, to go into business together, building racing cars.

Spasmodically, over the next three years, they worked out a plan. By the middle of 1965 it was sufficiently well advanced for them to move into 2334 South Broadway, Santa Ana, California. The sign said, briefly, 'A.A.R.' All American Racing Inc. was in business.

Gurney never had any formal training as an engineer. He just picked it up as he went along, gathering fragments here and there, and turning them over in his high performance mind.

When in 1966 the original American Eagle F1 car took to the circuits it seemed to be a rather nasty mistake. The first problem was to get the 2·7 Climax engine functioning in such a manner that it stopped shaking the chassis and the driver to bits. The second was to produce something which handled properly. As he confessed after the Belgian Grand Prix of 1966, driving this under-powered, under-steering machine in the very wet conditions of the race was one of the hardest jobs he'd ever done.

That was about all he said, but he was doing a good deal of thinking. He spent hours looking at drawings and the chassis itself, trying to deduce what was wrong. Presently, rather like a detective working out a mystery, he narrowed things down to the suspension geometry. After scratching his short fair hair, chewing the ends of innumerable pencils and frowning rather a lot, he got it. He promptly stopped chewing pencils and began to use them. Within a very short time he had sketched out the necessary changes. And, what's more, they worked.

Talking to Dan Gurney invariably brings up the question of his preoccupation with Formula 1 events. As a very able exponent of those two peculiarly American pastimes, stock-car racing and racing on oval circuits, why should he bother himself with trips to Europe? Surely, as many another American driver has made abundantly clear, it isn't worth the price of a plane ticket?

Asking this question does Gurney a great deal less than justice. It suggests that he is only in the game for whatever loot can be got out of it. That is very far from the case. He runs a business and is a competent business man. Nevertheless, he's something of an artist. One can't help feeling sometimes that he is more concerned with perfection of engineering and driving than he is with the balance sheets.

He believes very strongly that Formula 1 is the ultimate in motor sport. 'As constructors,' he will explain, 'the best way to prove ourselves is to win F1 races. Events like Indianapolis and Le Mans are more spectacles than they are races. It's the guy who becomes World Champion that really matters.'

And so at Santa Ana they build Indianapolis cars (which are for sale) and Formula 1 machines (which aren't). Annual output amounts to about eleven of the former and four of the latter. At Rye, apart from bringing about the sacred union of monocoque hull, suspension and engine, they are also equipped to repair cars. 'But,' Bill Dunne hastens to say, 'we've never had call to do it. We don't employ crashers.'

The first product of A.A.R. was an Indianapolis car for 1966. By the time that project was in train there wasn't a great deal of time left to build a Formula 1 car. For the first part of the season they soldiered bravely on with the antique Climax engine, playing, as you might say, for time.

At this point in the story Harry Weslake comes on to the scene. Weslake is a man of about seventy, who looks as if he's in his mid-fifties. He has always been a brilliant engineer, and age certainly hasn't withered his ability. The genesis of the Gurney-Weslake relationship began back in 1960, when the former was driving for B.R.M. On the B.R.M. staff at the time was a young engineer named F. Aubrey Woods, who was responsible for the famous V8 engine. He and Gurney became friends.

In 1962 Woods left B.R.M. and joined Weslake. Later in the year he invited Gurney down to Rye to meet his new employer. The quiet young American and the English engineer got along famously. Out of this early conversation came a number of modifications to Ford engines, which served Gurney extremely well in the Indianapolis '500' and the dozen other oval circuit events which take place in America each year.

When the question of a 3 litre F1 engine cropped up the obvious place to look for ideas was the Weslake plant. It was also, as things turned out, the place to seek accommodation for Anglo American Racers.

The premises are just outside the town, beside a private road which leads to Rye harbour. Over to the right, Camber Castle tries to hide its ancient bulk behind a line of trees. All around are swampy meadows, where sheep graze. A few yards further along, the road ends abruptly at the harbour.

There's a large collection of dinghies, some cabin cruisers and a pub.

Weslake Engineering occupies premises alongside the road. Behind them, tucked away out of view, is the A.A.R. set-up. What it really amounts to is a large garage, a yard, and a few pleasantly furnished offices. It may look simple, but it once prompted Juan Manuel Fangio (no less), who happens to be a Gurney fan, to remark that it housed one of the most professional Formula 1 organisations he'd ever seen.

Producing the V12 3 litre Weslake-Eagle engine for the F1 car was a fight against the clock. Nevertheless, ten months after Weslake's pencil had made its first tentative scratches, a unit was ready. It took part in three races at the end of 1966, revealed untold promise, and broke down each time. Not that this surprised anyone. The pressure of racing was so frantic that it was not until these races were over than anyone could get down to circuit testing. That got right to the heart of the problem, for the difficulty had been that faults (mostly to do with fuel, oil and water) which occurred in races were not appearing on the test bed.

Dan Gurney is an easy-going man. He eats well before a race, and sleeps without any difficulty. He gave up smoking because he believed it was affecting his stamina. His drinking habits are nothing if not moderate.

This doesn't mean to say that they left out the nerves when they built the man. In fact, he worries as much as anyone else. His strength lies in a stock of self-control which seems to be endless. Certainly, during the first part of 1967 he needed every scrap of it. On top of the normal occupational hazards of motor racing came a spate of business worries.

A.A.R., like most other constructors, relies on three sources for its income: development contracts from suppliers of oil, tyres and so on, the sale of cars (in this case, the Indi vehicles), and the rewards of racing itself—starting money, prize money, etc. To keep A.A.R. going in Formula 1 events costs about £100,000 a year.

All was well enough before Mobil retired from motor racing. When this happened one of the economic supports of A.A.R. was suddenly taken away. For the first six months of 1967 Shell helped by the supply of free fuel and lubricants. Unfortunately, however, Shell's racing budget was stretched to the full. There could be no talk of any retainer.

The situation seemed a crazy one. Here was one of the stars of Grand Prix racing, a set-up which was a formidable contender for both the drivers' and constructors' championships, with no oil company to back it. The solution came on the eve of the British Grand Prix at Silverstone when, after weeks of negotiation, Gurney signed with Castrol. What was even more encouraging was the fact that the door was left open for renewal in 1968.

Another thing which must have disappointed him at the time was the retirement of his friend Richie Ginther from motor racing on the eve of the 1967 Dutch Grand Prix. This, Gurney stresses, was predictable—he had seen it coming ever since the Indianapolis race of that year. At the time, as I've already related, rumours abounded. In fact, the whole episode had a reasonably happy ending. Ginther is still employed by A.A.R. as the executive responsible for the development of titanium and magnesium for motor racing applications.

Soon afterwards his place in European events was taken by Bruce McLaren. Who asked whom first is a matter of conjecture. 'But,' recalls Bill Dunne, 'if Bruce didn't ask us we'd most certainly have asked him.' He also says, 'I'd like to have Bruce McLaren driving for us full time—though I guess that's impossible.'

Possibly because his parents were in show biz and spent a lot of time travelling, the nomadic life of motor racing seems to suit Dan Gurney very well. Indeed, if you ask him about other ambitions he talks about the possibility of trips behind the Iron Curtain and to Scandinavia.

Dan and Arleo Gurney were married in 1952, when he was only twenty. They met when they were both in their teens, and after that he never looked at another girl—at any rate, seriously. Mrs. Gurney, to quote one of their friends, 'is strong, intelligent and beautiful'. She is a director and company secretary of All American Racing Inc. As mother of four children, with their ages ranging from six to thirteen, she can't get away to the circuits very often.

In 1967 they bought a house near Santa Ana overlooking the Pacific Ocean, with a splendid view of the island of Santa Catalina. This, strangely enough, is the first home the Gurneys have ever owned. It is pretty much a dream house, and Dan's one regret is that with his hectic programme of transatlantic commuting he can't see more of it.

Gurney's relaxed manner (he has the build and movements of motion-picture star James Stewart) suggests that he might be reasonably good at taking things easy. In fact, to judge from his favourite pastime, this doesn't seem to be the case. When he isn't snared up with the pre-occupation of motor racing he likes to race off into the mountains on his motor cycle. Bill Dunne told me: 'I used to take part in motor-cycle events. Dan has never raced on two wheels, and yet when we go out together I can't keep up with him.'

The personnel at Rye are a pretty cosmopolitan team. Dunne, who majored in journalism, worked as public-relations man for airlines, and is still a contributing editor to a motor-racing magazine, was born in new York City, within five miles of Gurney's own birth place.[1] Chief mechanic is Australian Tim Wall, formerly a Brabham man. The other mechanics are Mike Lowman (also ex-Brabham), Joaquin Ramirez—a Mexican, who has worked for Lamborghini, Maserati and Ferrari, and Rouem Haffenden—who actually comes from Rye.

But they all have one thing in common: devotion for Gurney. Indeed, the more one thinks about quiet, shy, very determined Dan Gurney, the more one comes to the conclusion that he's the type of person legends are made of.

---

1. *Quick fashion note:* Bill Dunne is easily recognisable at circuits by the African bush hat he wears. Actually, he receives supplies (at the time of writing he is halfway through his third) from an outfitter in San Francisco.

15

The Anatomy of a Grand Prix

AT 3 p.m. on July 15th, 1967, R.A.C. Competitions Manager Dean Delamont swished down the Union Jack, and twenty starters in the twentieth British Grand Prix took off from the grid at Silverstone. Just under two hours later the race was won by Jim Clark. Denis Hulme came second and Chris Amon third. The drama, for the time being, was over. A feat of organisation, which had been in preparation for the better part of a year, disintegrated into lorry loads of litter, and long lines of spectators' cars crawling to get back on to the main roads.

Before World War II there had been only two British Grands Prix (in 1926 and 1927). Both were held at Brooklands and both, as it happens, were won by drivers using Delages. If you had mentioned the name Silverstone to anyone in those days he'd probably have said it meant nothing. For it was still just a village in Northamptonshire, surrounded by agricultural land and a few miles from Towcester on the A5.

During the war the Ministry of Defence built an aerodrome near the village. It was used for the training of Lancaster bomber pilots. Afterwards the R.A.F. moved off and the airfield was left to its own devices. The familiar process of decay began. Weeds began to prise open the concrete runways. The paint started to peel off the hangars.

But the greatest days of the old airfield were yet to come. It was, in almost every way, ideal for a motor-racing circuit. By no means the least of its advantages was its location. It was within reasonable driving distance from London, and equally handy for the large population centres in the Midlands. When, after a lot of talk and a certain amount of acrimony, it was decided that Brooklands would never be used for racing again, the R.A.C. approached the Ministry of Defence. The outcome was that the ministry agreed to lease the Silverstone airfield for motor sport.

The first British Grand Prix was held there in 1949. Between 1955 and 1962, the race took place at Aintree and Silverstone on alternate years. In 1964, the Grand Prix circuit was completed at Brands Hatch. Since then, the British G.P. has gone to Brands on even years (e.g. 1966) and to Silverstone on odd ones—as in 1967. All told, it has been held at Silverstone on twelve occasions.

Nowadays the lease of Silverstone is held by the British Racing Drivers' Club, which also runs the farm at the circuit. On behalf of the club, a versatile gentleman named J. W. Brown combines the duties of track manager and farmer.

When the Grand Prix is held at Silverstone the organisation is shared between the B.R.D.C. and the R.A.C. The former is responsible for everything to do with spectators—the latter with running the race itself. Dean Delamont assumes the duties of clerk of the course, which is tantamount to being commander-in chief. 'Another way of putting it,' he told me, 'is to think of a managing director. I am responsible to the stewards, who are rather like the board of directors.' They are, as a matter of fact, a somewhat distinguished body, for they include the Marquess Camden, Lord Chesham, the Hon. Gerald Lascelles and Prince Metternich-Wineberg (recalling the fact, perhaps, that motor racing was once the sport of the noble and wealthy).

Also in the select company of stewards is John Gott, M.B.E., G.M., the Chief Constable of Northamptonshire and vice-chairman of the R.A.C. Competitions Committee.

The task of organising a British Grand Prix begins soon after the previous one is over. The race invariably takes place in July. The people concerned then depart on their holidays. In early September they all meet in London. 'We hold an inquest on the race,' Delamont told me. 'After that we meet once a month.' As one of the R.A.C.'s two delegates to the F.I.A. (the other is Harold Parker), he reckons that about half his life is spent in committee meetings.

He is stocky, invariably wears a brown trilby hat, and looks relaxed. During the race he spends most of his time in a caravan near the starting grid. Telephones and radio link him to key points around the circuit. 'Yes,' he said, 'I do have the power

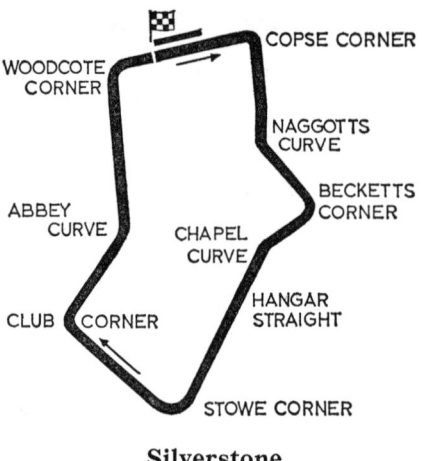

Silverstone

to stop the race—and it once was stopped owing to a cloudburst. But that is exceptional. The possibility of the track being blocked is unthinkable.'

Once the race has got under way, his biggest problem is that of looking after important guests. There are pretty well foolproof standing orders for the conduct of a Grand Prix, and the organisation is a masterpiece of decentralisation. Responsibilities are clearly defined. At every corner on the circuit there's a unit consisting of a flag marshal, an observer, a doctor, and somebody responsible for fire fighting. A team of incident officers is based on the paddock. Each has his own car with a white flag mounted on it and is ready to depart at a moment's notice if somebody crashes.

Something like 1,000 people are involved in the running of a Grand Prix—and, of them, about half are concerned with the actual conduct of the race. They vary from people who are just interested in motor racing to professional men whose skills may be needed in an emergency. For example, at Silverstone in 1967 there were thirty-three doctors plus fifteen medical students from St. Mary's Hospital Motor Club. There were nine timekeepers, four commentators, seven scrutineers, and so on. Since most of the readers of this book were probably there, I won't bother to give the complete list. It appears on pages 12 and 13 of the official programme, and there are a great many names.

All of them are volunteers, glad to work in return for the privilege of seeing a day's first-class motor sport from exceptionally good vantage points. The marshals are recruited from

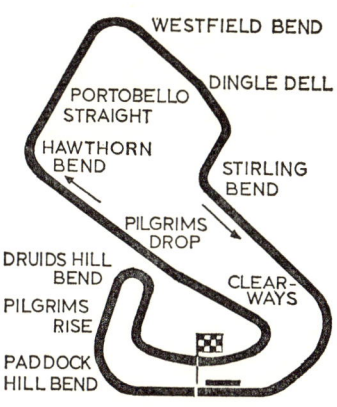

Brands Hatch

seventeen motor clubs—ranging from the Bentley Drivers' Club (who work the score boards) to the Bath Karting Club. Some of the marshals spend summer weekends touring from one circuit to another. A number of them, at Silverstone, pass the time under somewhat rough circumstances. Those who are there for the full three days (which includes the two days of practice) are accommodated in those huge hangars which once housed the bombers. It's probably a lot of fun, but it's nobody's dream of a luxury weekend.

A British Grand Prix meeting differs from those on the Continent in at least two things. The first is the richness of the programme. On the Continent there is a minor event (touring cars or, more recently, Formula Ve) as a curtain raiser, and the big event. That is usually all. In the U.K., however, people have been educated to expect more for their money. They get a full day's racing, made up of four events, plus a sideshow in the way of skydivers, or aerobatics, or whatever.

It certainly seems to attract the crowds. At the 1967 British G.P. there were over 120,000 spectators.

The other difference is the question of crowd control. Circuits on the Continent use policemen for this purpose. They aren't popular, but they're accepted. 'But,' Niel Eason Gibson of the B.R.D.C. told me, 'we wouldn't dare to use policemen over here—it would upset the public. People in this country are easy to deal with. If you started using policemen they'd begin to get uppity.'

A newcomer to the G.P. scene in 1967 was the Grand Prix Hospital Unit. This is a massive vehicle—so big, indeed, that its creator, Louis Stanley, had to get special dispensation from the Minister of Transport to run it on British roads. Antiseptically sealed off from the rest of the world, its interior is equipped with X-ray apparatus, operating facilities, and so on. Often, in the treatment of serious injuries, promptness is vital. It may be a question of life or death. This is where the hospital unit comes into its own.

Some circuits are better equipped by nature in this respect than others. The Mountain Circuit on the Isle of Man, where the motor-cycle T.T. races are held, is a bad one. There used to be places where, if a rider came off and damaged himself, he had to wait until the race was over before receiving treatment. This difficulty was overcome in 1962 by one of the oil companies,[1] which chartered a helicopter from B.E.A., stationed it near the paddock, and put it at the disposal of the T.T. organisers. During its first visit the chopper saved one life. It has since become a permanent feature of the T.T. and Manx G.P. events.

At Brands Hatch a helicopter was on duty for the 1966 British Grand Prix, but it was never used. Silverstone, by contrast, has no need for such devices. The circuit is entirely accessible, and the worst that could happen is that those fine fields of ripening corn might become rather trampled. Since they are farmed by the very people who own the circuit, nobody is likely to worry very much. And, as Dean Delamont admitted, having the Chief Constable of the county as one of the stewards helps to get casualties away swiftly by road.

There they were, then, those thousand workers, doing everything from manning first-aid posts to selling hot-dogs, and the 120,000 spectators, all in their appointed places for the British Grand Prix. Before the race there had been several worries among those taking part. The new Cooper-Maserati was making its début. It wasn't entirely new, as a matter of fact. They kept to the old nose for fear of overheating. The new design, which is more tweaked-in and streamlined, might not have admitted enough air.

In motor racing everyone tries to make sure of everything, which is a somewhat vain endeavour. Cooper's had hoped to have the new engine ready in time, but it would have been foolhardy to have depended on it. Consequently, they allowed

1. Shell-Mex and B.P. Ltd.

for the possibility that the older, larger unit might have to be used. To make room for it, they'd fitted fuel tanks which were rather smaller than they'd otherwise have been. It was one of the reasons why Cooper-Maserati—in company, it must be confessed, with most of the other teams—indulged in a spot of frantic topping-up between the warming-up lap and the start.[1]

Chris Amon was worried about the performance of his Ferrari on the straight. He said it felt 'slow and heavy', and looked forward to the next race (the German G.P.), when they'd have sliced 50 lb. off the weight of gearbox and engine. B.R.M. had worries left, right and centre, but mostly to do with the suspension on Jackie Stewart's new car. Honda were discovering a lot of difficulty in tuning the fuel injection system to the new camshaft, and at practice the car handled like a pig. Both the Eagle-Weslakes (of Dan Gurney and Bruce McLaren) were suffering from oil leaks.

By the Friday night havoc still reigned on at least two fronts. McLaren took his Eagle out for a final, unofficial, lap or two when practice was over. Presently it came to a grinding and far from silent halt. The engine had packed up.

They put the ailing car back on the transporter, and took it to the garage at Brackley, where A.A.R. had established their headquarters. Mechanics worked through the night, fitting a replacement engine.

In the Lotus-Ford camp the tension was even greater. At practice on the Friday morning Graham Hill was approaching the pit road at about 70 m.p.h. when one of those tiny items which are so insignificant to look at and yet so important broke in the rear suspension. The car went out of control. A wheel came off. The front end slammed into the safety wall, smashing the front suspension and damaging the monocoque hull.

Hill, mercifully, was unhurt. All he said—in public, at any rate—was that the car had felt 'a little bit snaky on braking'.

The action moved to Norwich. Working non-stop for fourteen hours, a team of mechanics built what was very nearly a new car. They salvaged bits from the old, and took other components from another vehicle which was still under construction. Hill made two airlifts from Silverstone to Norwich

1. In fact, the new engine was ready.

in his plane.[1] By noon on the Saturday, a car was at Silverstone—which, if untried, was at least something for Hill to go racing in.

There was little let-up to the drama during the race itself. Mike Spence brought his B.R.M. into the pits early on, with smoke trailing astern. When he stopped, flames leapt from the transistor black box in the ignition system, and the fire extinguishers went into action. Amazingly enough, the fault was put right, and Spence went back into the race.

Rindt returned to the pits with a bad oil leak. It was patched up. After two more pit-stops his Cooper-Maserati (the new one) finally expired from total lack of oil pressure on lap 26.

Meanwhile, Graham Hill's somewhat improvised car had been displaying excellent form. Both Lotus-Fords were proving what everybody suspected already: that they were the most potent machines on the track. Soon after the race had settled down Hill overtook Clark and shot into the lead. He remained there until the fifty-fifth lap. Then he went missing. It was the old trouble, more or less, all over again. A bolt had fallen out of the rear suspension. With tremendous skill he kept the car under control and somehow got it back to the pits. The bolt was replaced. He went back again, now in seventh place behind John Surtees. For another ten laps he motored on, cutting the gap between himself and the leaders by four seconds a lap. But there was more trouble in store. As he was approaching Copse Corner, the engine gave up.

'It was making,' he recalled afterwards, 'a very expensive sounding noise.'

With Hill out of the way, Clark won easily. Denis Hulme —who, earlier on, had cut back his lap record to 1 min. 27·0 sec. (121·12 m.p.h.)—came second. Chris Amon, after a magnificent race in which, after a long fight, he overtook Jack Brabham, came third.

The first half of the 1967 World Championship struggle was over. Hulme was in first place—where he'd been ever since his victory at Monaco. Clark and Brabham now shared second place. Amon was third, Rodriguez fourth and Gurney

1. The Graham Hill airlift is becoming a feature of the British Grand Prix. During practice for the 1966 event he made several flights between Brands Hatch and Bourne, ferrying in parts with which to repair damaged suspension on Jackie Stewart's B.R.M. At the time Hill was Stewart's team mate.

fifth. The circus now had three weeks in which to get ready for the German G.P. at Nurburgring. As one constructor said to me: 'By heaven, we need it!'

There was certainly much to be done. Both the Eagle-Weslakes had succumbed during the race, leaving the team with enough cars but no engines. Brabham was doubtless wondering about the Lotus-Fords and their power, whilst Chapman was probably thinking about Brabham and his reliability. Honda must have been happy that, at last, the car had finished in an event—albeit in sixth place. And Cooper-Maserati were going through all the teething troubles to which new cars and engines are prone. The three-week gap between the British and German Grands Prix may have been a long one as these things go, but nobody was likely to be able to take it easy.

16

Cooper-Maserati: Keeping a Name Out in Front

THE reason why the Cooper Car Company goes motor racing is simple. It is: to keep the group's name before the public. To those hard-headed men Jonathan Sieff and David Blackburn, who guide the group's fortunes, motor racing is very much a business. It has to pay off in terms of favourable publicity, and it must keep within a reasonable budget. If it fails in either particular—woe betide it.

David Blackburn used to be responsible for the distribution of Mercedes Benz cars in Britain, and so he knows all there is to know about publicity. Jonathan Sieff, coming from Marks and Spencer, is hardly likely to be short on business acumen. Nevertheless, of the two, he is most likely to regard motor racing with sentiment. He used to go racing himself. A promising career was brought to an abrupt conclusion in the Le Mans 24-Hour Race. While roaring along the Mulsanne Straight his car suddenly, and for no apparent reason, flew off the road. It smashed through a wall, into a house, and nearly killed its driver. In hospital afterwards the doctors gave him a 20 per cent chance of recovery (usually they shake their heads solemnly, and put the odds at 50). Happily, Sieff had an extremely good constitution and a great will to live. He recovered.

The Cooper group has many interests. It owns a number of garages in the Home Counties. Among its merchandise are such automobile exotics as Maseratis, the Moskvitch, Alfa Romeos, Lancias, and the B.M.W. There is, of course, also the Mini-Cooper 'S', which is put together at, and raced from the group's factory at Byfleet. This side of things comes under the command of John Cooper.

'Cooper' is a name which in motor-racing circles is justly regarded with a certain amount of reverence. When the Formula 1 Constructors' Championship was introduced in 1958 it was won by a Vanwall. And then for the next two years running it was won by Coopers. All this was tremendously significant. It meant that the iron grip of Italy on motor racing had been prised loose. Britain, after what seemed like centuries in outer darkness, was on top at last.

Technically, Cooper could fairly claim to be responsible for the racing car as it is today. Following the practice of their little '500' (and what a lot of famous drivers, including Stirling Moss, began their careers in *them*), they put the engine where it really belonged—at the back. Within a very short space of time all the other constructors were following the Cooper example.

History has an uncanny way of asserting itself—of repeating, you might say, a pattern. The original Cooper set-up began with Charles Cooper and his son John turning out 500 c.c cars in a Surbiton garage. Later it moved victoriously into the Formula 1 arena. It may not be without significance that the present operation began with a swarm of Minis scuttling round circuits, like Davids furiously seeking Goliaths to throw stones at. And then, with assistance from Maserati, came Formula 1 again. If the circle was to complete itself it seemed (at the start of the 1967 season) that the victories must follow. This was a possibility about which the present Cooper management was understandably optimistic. After all, had they not already won the last race of 1966 (in Mexico) and the first race of 1967 (in South Africa)? Furthermore, if *all* the points scored in 1966 had counted towards the constructors' championship Cooper-Maserati would have come second in the table—beating Ferrari by one point.

The present company used to be called the Chipstead group. It owned a chain of garages and wanted, from an image-building point of view, to get into motor racing. This is a sport in which people and teams and cars get to the top, stay there for a few brief hours of glory, and then come tumbling down. It is full of peaks and depressions, and few people remain in one or the other for very long.

In 1965 Cooper's were in one of the depressions. They hadn't produced a competitive car for some time. Charles Cooper had died, and the situation was somewhat unhappy.

But then, like a fairy godmother inhabiting an executive suite, along came Chipstead. They took Cooper's over, eventually changed their own name to the Cooper Car Company, and (in a manner of speaking) pinned up notices saying 'Think SUCCESS'.

Earlier on the group had purchased a couple of garages from motor-racing ace Roy Salvadori. Within a fairly short time of the Cooper take-over the management was on the telephone to Salvadori. 'Come and talk to us,' they said. When the conversation ended Salvadori found himself appointed to take charge of the group's Formula 1 interests.

The bother about the new Formula 1 regulations was that there didn't seem to be enough engines to go round. In September, 1965, Salvadori went out to the Maserati plant in Italy. After a good deal of rummaging around they discovered a very old $2\frac{1}{2}$ litre engine. It had last been used in a car driven by Fangio in 1956. Many of the parts, indeed, were a lot older than that. The crankshaft and the con rods were all of eighteen years old, and it even had hairpin valve springs.

It may not have been perfect, but at least it was something to go racing with. The engine was crated up and presently shipped to England.

Now this was a very remarkable engine. Once they'd put it into a car, they subjected it to 2,000 miles of circuit testing. In spite of its age, it performed faultlessly. Since then they have naturally fitted new and improved parts. The 1967 engine had a three-valve head and the car had an entirely new chassis. Nevertheless, Cooper-Maserati owe a good deal to that ancient engine, which got them out of trouble at a time when, as Roy Salvadori says, 'you couldn't get them for love nor money.'

To build a car to fit it, Derek White left Jaguar's and became chief designer. Tony Robinson of British Racing Partnership, who's a monocoque expert, was seconded for three months to impart some of his know-how. The Cooper-Maserati was in business.

Coopers still depend on Maserati for their engines, and all the development work is carried out in Modena. Ford of Great Britain put something like £100,000 into the small firm of Cosworth, and left them to get on with the job of developing racing engines. The arrangement has served Lotus more than well. It is tempting to think that Maserati might do a similar thing, but if you put this question to Roy Salvadori he'll answer blandly, 'There's been no such decision.' Nevertheless, one can't help thinking that one day there might be.

Roy Salvadori is an interesting and extremely effective choice of team manager. His own motor-racing career was long and distinguished. In his time he won over 100 races—including, with Carroll Shelby, the Le Mans 24-Hour Race of 1959. The fact that he never won a *grande épreuve* is of no great significance. Since the World Championship was introduced in 1950 over 150 events have supplied points towards it, and a mere thirty individuals have actually won the races. If you eliminate the drivers who only gained one victory in a World Championship event the figure slumps down into the mid-twenties.

On top of his considerable experience as a driver, Salvadori supplies a marked administrative flair, a great deal of charm, and (naturally) a considerable insight into and understanding of the way a driver's mind works.

Tony Rudd of B.R.M. has sometimes talked to me about the agony of watching motor races, the fearful anxiety which grips him if a driver doesn't pass the pits when he's expected. Rudd has never been—at least, not seriously—a driver. For Salvadori one might imagine that the experience would be even worse. Like a doctor, who knows the meaning of the pains and twinges he suffers, you might imagine that he dies a thousand deaths every time he goes near a circuit.

He admits that, if he went as a spectator, that would probably be the case. 'I think I'd be very disturbed,' he said. 'But as a manager there's too much to do. When you're involved you don't give a thought to the dangers—though, of course, I'm terribly keyed up.'

Not that he normally looks it, but that is part of the Salvadori technique. Writing about him in *Men at the Wheel*, Peter Miller suggested that: '... when he is driving fast, he becomes more relaxed than he ever could sitting still. When he is doing 100 m.p.h. and more it is just like lying back in a hot bath.' But Salvadori says: 'If you're too relaxed the thought is are you just driving for the starting money? Possibly there are times when you drive better if you're relaxed; but it has to be a very long distance race like Le Mans, when you start off in this condition. Certainly not in a Grand Prix, where you have to drive hard the whole time to be competitive.'

By no means the least of his difficulties is keeping track of his drivers. He employs two: Jochen Rindt and Pedro Rodriguez. The former is apt to be anywhere in the world at any given moment, and the only sure thing is that he won't be wherever he is for very long. During a not untypical fortnight he planned to be in Paris, at Nurburgring, Indianapolis, and Monaco. As Salvadori quite reasonably asks: 'How the hell do you even *write* to a chap under such circumstances?'

Rodriguez, of course, is either at home in Mexico, or else at his apartment in Paris, and that doesn't assist communications either.

Roy Salvadori criticises the furious pace of a modern racing driver's career. 'He should be continually driving,' he told me, 'without becoming *too* caught up with his commitments. Some programmes nowadays are too heavy to be taken on by one driver.' (He looks sadly at the ceiling.) 'There's *so* much money involved. It's a commercial business, but it's too heavy. Somebody should cut down these drivers' activities to reasonable proportions.'

His ambition is to form a compact team. Cooper-Maserati treat their drivers well. They receive a retainer out of the team's payments from the oil and tyre companies, plus starting money.[1] Following motor-racing tradition, 10 per cent of prize money goes to the mechanics, the rest is split fifty-fifty between Cooper-Maserati and the driver who wins it.

Said Salvadori: 'Drivers shouldn't have to compete for places in a team. Some of them just have the odd drive for an entrant, but that isn't right. The team should stay with the driver, even if he's having a bad run. There have been so many occasions when drivers had had spells of bad luck, and then things have picked up again. One should be loyal to a driver within reason—provided he's trying. He should have an element of security.'

So far as picking drivers is concerned, he likes to go as near to the top as he can. The idea of untried talent doesn't appeal to him at all. He points to John Surtees and says: 'He *make* a car go. He makes it a better car, and he makes a good car superb.' And: 'The present Formula F2 is a wonderful opportunity to train drivers for the 3 litre F1 cars. But at present, when considering a driver on his 1966 performances, I'd prefer to look for a G.T. driver, who has had experience of 180–200

1. Based on their World Championship points in 1966, Rindt received about £440 a race in 1967—Rodriquez, about £200.

m.p.h.—and, of course, the kind of power one expects from an F1 car.'

Happily, he seems to be very content with Rindt and Rodriguez. Of the former, he says: 'Jochen's only sort of measurement is ten-tenths.' Of Rodriguez: 'He's very fit and tough. He's terribly impressive—has a very intelligent approach. He's very contained, and he'll be there all through the race—rather like Graham Hill.'

The drivers, for their part, seem to like Cooper-Maseratis. They say they handle as well as any Grand Prix car. And that, from drivers, is a lot of praise.

As a driver, Salvadori has definitely retired, and he says he has no regrets. 'You can't do my job and drive,' he told me. 'Brabham seems to manage it, but he's the exception.' In 1966 he used to do quite a lot of testing, but he has since given that up, too. Since Rindt and Rodriguez are nearly always busy somewhere else, he used Richard Attwood, Frank Gardner and Alan Rees for this work.

Asked whether he considers it possible that Cooper-Maseratis might go in for other forms of motor racing, Salvadori admits that Formula 2 is a possibility. As for the rest, 'I can't quite see how we'd handle it. There's so much work to be done in Formula 1, if we want to remain competitive.'

At the beginning of the 1967 season it was Salvadori's opinion that, as in 1966, 'a good, reliable car will count. By 1968, it'll be different. Everybody will be so well sorted out that maximum power will be the thing.'

In his driving days Salvadori was never happy when he was racing in heavy rain. 'I would also worry about a race if there were any indifferent drivers taking part. I'd also have a tough time if I was on the front row of the grid. Funnily enough, I drove better if I'd had a bad time in practice. I suppose I hadn't so much to lose. I'd also drive more quickly after I'd had a spin. Again, I think it was because I hadn't so much to lose.'

But Roy Salvadori may now very well be faced with the greatest challenge that has ever confronted him. As he himself says: 'In motor racing you don't necessarily make a financial loss, if you keep it within bounds. It depends entirely upon being successful.' It is an opinion with which his directors would no doubt devoutly agree.

How, then, does he set about making it successful? And how

K

does the race-time attitude of Roy Salvadori, the team manager, differ from that of Roy Salvadori, the driver? These were two questions which were going round inside my head as I set off for Nurburgring and the German Grand Prix.

17

The Biggest Switchback in the World

FRIDAY, *August 4th, 1967:* The Grand Prix circus had arrived at Nurburgring ahead of me. After a long and very tedious drive across northern France and southern Belgium (don't *ever* go to Nurburgring *that* way) I presented myself at the circuit in a condition which can only be described as lacklustrous. By contrast, I'd expect the Formula 1 fraternity to be looking all pink and healthy and dedicated, as they lapped up the vinous air of the Eifel Mountains.

As a matter of fact, it wasn't quite like that. The big overspill of troubles was biding its time, waiting for Saturday practice. Even so, there was no lack of problems, and anyone who couldn't find something to worry about was either very fortunate or else extremely tough.

The Eifel Mountains lie along the western edge of Germany, between the Rhine and the Belgian frontier. Actually, 'mountains' is a somewhat grandiose term for them. They aren't nearly as craggy and big as the Scottish highlands, and even a lesser Alp would sneer at them. There are thick forests, expansive upland meadows, and hills galore. But if you went there loaded with ropes and pitons, and walked leaden footed in climbing boots, the locals would probably think you were mildly eccentric.

Nurburg itself is a tiny village which lives off tourism and is overlooked by the ruins of a twelfth-century schloss. It is, indeed, a rather fine ruined schloss, with a tall and sinister tower and lots of bits and pieces of crumbling Gothic. It's the kind of thing old suck-a-blood Count Dracula himself might have designed as a residence.

When the Nurburgring track was built in the mid-twenties

one of the objects was to provide jobs for the mass of unemployed workers in the Koblenz-Cologne area. Understandably, the project was made as big as possible. The result was a rugged brute of a circuit, over fourteen miles long, with 172 corners (eighty-eight of them left-handers), some quite fantastic switchbacks, and those battalions of pine trees generating an atmosphere of Wagnerian doom. It was ready for the second German Grand Prix in 1927 (the first was held on the Berlin Avus circuit in the previous year), and has been doing its fiendish work as a car-killer ever since. Its only redeeming feature in this respect is the fact that between races it is used as a test track for the motor industry.

You can, if you're lucky, soldier along with Nurburgring, but you can't beat it. For example, before the 1967 German G.P. Pedro Rodriguez had a quiet word with veteran ace Fangio, who happened to be there. With his customary humility and eagerness to learn the young Mexican asked the middle-aged Argentinian for advice. The latter pointed out a particular section and described in detail how to cope with it.

On the first day of practice Rodriguez carried out this advice to the letter. Unfortunately, and to his enormous dismay, he found that he and his car had not only jumped about two feet into the air but, to add to the complications, the latter was banking at an alarming angle—rather like an aircraft making a tight turn.

With a lot of skill he made a perfect landing. 'But,' he said afterwards, 'I'd forgotten that it was ten years since Fangio had driven at Nurburgring. Cars have changed. Everything becomes different. Little trees have become big trees.'

Watching the Cooper-Maserati team at work is an extremely enjoyable experience. They are very anxious to win races and they have as many (probably more) problems as anyone else. Somehow, however, they managed to maintain an impression that even in these febrile times of brutal competition and ultra-professionalism going motor racing can still be fun.

They take about ten people with them. Starting at the top, there's Jonathan Sieff—one of the firm's two managing directors. Sieff, as I've already explained, used to be a racing driver. He's well built, young-looking and presumably has the constitution of an exceptionally healthy ox (he needed it to survive that smash at Le Mans). As managing directors go, he's remarkably adaptable. He is happy enough to perform such menial chores as helping to push a car through the paddock to the scrutineers. He will also—though, one imagines, with less relish—spend endless hours at a frontier, arguing with Customs men who are holding up the delivery of an engine.

Salvadori, as racing manager, looks after all the administration, soothes the drivers, gets the cars to and from the circuits, and wrangles with the race organisers. Quite apart from his not inconsiderable charm, he commands a good deal of respect. As one of the few who wear the red armband of the Club Internationale des Ancien Pilotes de Grands Prix, he is one of the sport's nobility.

John Cooper, technical director of Cooper-Maserati, father figure of the Mini-Cooper movement, was also there at Nurburgring. He has many gifts. One of them's a quick sense of humour. Another is of knowing just about everything that's happening in the G.P. ambience at any given moment.

And then there's Derek White, designer of the Cooper F1 cars, a quiet-spoken South African who, like everyone else in the team, is never flustered. No doubt he believes in that old, what-was-it?, axiom about troubles being things to be overcome or something. If he does he has plenty to play with.

These are the Cooper motor-racing hierarchy. Jochen Rindt and Pedro Rodriguez do the driving. Six mechanics look after the cars. At some time during my first evening at the hotel in Nurburg, Roy Salvadori said to me rather sadly: 'We're the hardest-worked team in the business. But people get tired.'

Good mechanics somehow manage not to show it. Going for nights without sleep, putting in effort which is liable to evaporate in a cloud of despair after the race has begun, these are part of the deal. They seldom see their homes, make better bachelors than husbands—for how can they possibly compete in the domestic mouse race?—and are sometimes tormented by odd apprehensions. One of them said to me: 'I get this queer thing about whether I've tightened the wheels, just when he's on the first lap. I know I've done it O.K., in fact it's just about the last mistake I'm likely to make. But, just the same, I worry about it.'

And from another: 'It's the hell of a responsibility. In what other walk of life do you have a man's life in your hands?'

At the time of the 1967 German G.P. the current Cooper-Maserati anxiety had mostly to do with engines. Maserati's plant is at Modena, in northern Italy. The Cooper plant is in Surrey. It's a long way. The arrangement is strictly a business one. Maserati's people don't go motor racing. They had dreamed up a new engine which is 30 lb. lighter than the old and is a three-valve effort instead of a two. But engines are like children. You have to bring them up carefully. You have to sweat a bit developing them. The difficulties are huge.

'But,' Jonathan Sieff told me, 'we haven't done badly, really. One would have liked to win more races. The competition, of course, is very tough, though I wouldn't have it any other way. Perhaps we've under-estimated on engine development. Perhaps we've under-budgeted.'

Obviously it would suit everybody a lot better if the business of building the Cooper F1 engines were hauled home to England. That way, there'd be no umpteen hundred miles between the two sides of the operation. There would also be no frontiers, and they are by no means the least of the bothers. It is a strange fact of life that you can drive around Europe in a road car. All you have to do is to flash your passport and green insurance document at the authorites and they wave you into the next nation with a genial flip of the hand. But try to get a Formula 1 engine across and there may be a delay of anything up to three days. Heaven knows what the Customs men think happens. Possibly they imagine the cylinders are packed with 'pot'—or that the funny cylindrical object is not really a starter motor but a cunning nesting place for a batch of wrist watches. No hazarded explanation can be utterly absurd, for the whole business takes folly a lot higher than the tallest hill in the Eifel range.

The brunt of all this falls on a young German named Heini Mader, who is Cooper-Maserati's man at Modena, engineer, racing mechanic, transporter of engines, and goodness knows what all else. Mader, quite possibly, has the patience of a saint. He needs it. But the only alternative, that of making the engines in Britain, would cost a fortune. As every entrant in the business will tell you, nobody, apart from a few top drivers, makes a fortune out of motor racing.

Saturday, August 5th, 1967: The German Grand Prix is an odd one, for it is two races run as one. Formula 1 cars erupt from the front rows of the grid, with Formula 2 projectiles screaming on their heels from the rear rows like a pack of frenzied terriers.

THE BIGGEST SWITCHBACK IN THE WORLD 135

Practice for Formulae 1 and 2 on the Saturday was from 11 a.m. until 1 p.m. There were one or two clouds in the sky, which looked as if they meant business, but didn't do anything about it. The huge grandstands craned their necks above the surrounding pine trees, and there was a tolerably big scattering of spectators.

The pits are like a long, thin island with the track on either side and a couple of tunnels connecting them to what might roughly be described as the mainland. Like most pits, they are usually overcrowded—especially at practice.

Nurburgring itself is more than just one circuit. It is virtually a kit, from which you can build an assortment. The main one, of course, is the whacking great 14·25-mile effort that is used for the race. But by the artful use of link roads joining the straights on either side of the pits, there's a very much shorter affair which comes in very handy for bedding in brakes, seeing the effect of minor adjustments, and so on.

At this stage in the book it's probably stating the obvious to observe that one of the objects of practice is to find things out. As a matter of fact, in the somewhat excitable atmosphere of timing the laps and seeing who's going to get pole position on the grid, it's an aspect which tends to be overlooked—at any rate, by the public.

Certainly there were a number of things which the Cooper team wanted to discover. They had brought three cars with them to Nurburgring. Two of them were the old ones, pretty well unchanged since the victories at Mexico City in the last race of 1966 and in South Africa at the beginning of 1967. The third was the new car. The newcomer was a damnable enigma. It seemed to be underpowered. Its handling characteristics were not calculated to send any driver into frenzies of delight. And because it was so new nobody completely understood it.

One of the uncertain quantities was its petrol consumption. This is never unimportant, but at Nurburgring it has to be judged to the nth degree. The track is such that if a car's hull is too close to the ground it won't be long before the bottom has been ripped to pieces. Adjustments to the suspension and fitting larger wheels can cope with part of this problem. Even so, if it is weighed down with too much fuel on board it is still asking for trouble. Too little fuel, of course, means that it will run dry, and nobody ever won a motor race that way.

Roy Salvadori told me: 'What you really need to check the petrol consumption is to run for about thirty miles flat out, but that isn't easy.' As things turned out, it was downright impossible. At eleven o'clock that morning they clearly didn't intend to use the new car at all. And who could blame them? The old ones had already revealed certain, not unimpressive, evidence of reliability. At Nurburgring speed alone conquers nothing. A car must also have guts of fantastic toughness.

I don't know what strange furies rule at Nurburgring. Nor do I know whether the brothers Grimm ever went there, though I can't help feeling they did. It's that kind of place. There could be ogres in the forest and witches casting down spells from the crumbling walls of the castle. And at practice on that Saturday morning that old monster of a circuit really showed its hand.

The day before, a bolt in Brabham's rear suspension parted company with the rest of the assembly. The car shed a wheel, and Brabham could count himself fortunate that he didn't lose a lot more. As it was, he saved the car and himself and repaired the former.

On the Saturday Graham Hill got into an awful lot of trouble. His Lotus-Ford went flying off and ended up in the grass with three wheels torn off and looking the father and mother of all messes. Hill was unhurt.

And then there was the case of Jochen Rindt. Towards the end of the practice session he went missing. Eventually he was located at the fast right-hander, which leads into the Karussel.[1] Time passed, and there was no sign of him. John Cooper jokingly remarked that he'd probably gone into a house for a cup of tea. The only certain thing was that he wasn't injured.

The Automobilclub von Deutschland is far from parsimonious in its offering at the Grand Prix meeting. There are also races for G.T. cars, sports cars, and those single-seater weirdies known as Formula 'Ve'. Because of this packed programme the track was used continually on the Saturday, and there could be no question of the Cooper van setting out by the most direct route in search of Rindt, who might or might not be in unfortunate circumstances.

Eventually he turned up at the pits after receiving a lift along

[1]. So-called, not because there's an actual merry-go-round there, but because the track is heavily banked and rather gives the impression of one. As drivers will tell you, there's nothing merry about the Karussel.

Nurburgring

one of the roads from a press photobrapher. He said there'd been an explosion at the rear. 'It sounded,' he explained, 'as if the starter motor had blown up.'

Eventually Jonathan Sieff got the car back. The mechanics briskly took it to pieces and found a multitude of troubles.

You can never tell exactly what causes something to blow up at high speed, for it inevitably damages other parts, and there's no knowing which of the calamities happened first. After all, the whole eruption begins and ends in the fraction of a second. Furthermore, at these speeds and at such tremendously high vibration, fatigue (which is the cause of so many troubles) is speeded up to an impossible degree. An hitherto flawless component can suddenly develop a crack and disintegrate in less time than it takes to write this particular sentence.

The effect on Rindt's car was as if a hand-grenade had gone off at the back. The starter motor had been sheered off and made a nasty mess of the rear chassis. Fragments of flying metal, rather like shrapnel, had caused other damage. The cause, probably, was the flywheel. In some fiendish millisecond it had succumbed to fatigue and exploded.

For this car the German G.P. was over before it had even begun. There was also trouble with Rodriguez's car. Most of it had to do with the brake pads, which were showing traces of copper where no copper had any right to be.

It would be wrong to pretend that anyone in the *équipe* Cooper slept easily that night. The mechanics who were working on the Rodriguez car hardly slept at all.

Sunday, August 6th, 1967: According to a statistic which was handed to me by a public relations man over a quarter of a million people came to the Nurburgring to witness the German Grand Prix of 1967, and I must say that it looked like it. The clouds had gone away: a pale gold sun burned down on to the circuit, and if all the beer bottles were laid end to end I shouldn't wonder if they'd have extended for 213·84 miles (which happens to be the distance of the race).

At 2 p.m. the cars—seventeen Formula 1 and eight Formula 2—set off on a journey which, for some, ended sadly swiftly, and for others went on until five past four. Dan Gurney nearly won the race, except that on the thirteenth lap (out of the prescribed fifteen) a half-shaft on his Eagle broke and, to add to the mess, fractured the sump. Denis Hulme did win it, and Jack Brabham came second.

Havoc is an attendant devil of motor racing. On this occasion it turned up pretty punctually. As soon as the first lap was over, a sorry stream of distressed cars began coming into the pits. Others never made it and had to be abandoned by the track. The Lotuses, still unquestionably the fastest, succumbed from suspension ailments. The B.R.M.s went down with (in Mike Spence's case) gearbox trouble and (in Jackie Stewart's) a broken crown wheel and pinion. Bruce McLaren gave everyone a nasty moment when it looked as if his car had caught fire. Actually, it hadn't. The illusion was caused by escaping oil.

Nobody in the Cooper team had been at all happy about the new car which, after the bother on the previous day, Rindt had to drive. They were right. It gave up its automotive ghost a hundred yards or so away from the pits with: (a) An oil leak. (b) A water leak. (c) Damage to the ratchet in the steering mechanism. Later, Pedro Rodriguez brought his car in with a rose joint in the rear suspension adrift. Breaking some record or other, a mechanic streaked away to the garage in the paddock, came back with a replacement, and fitted it. Rodriguez went on racing, though he'd already lost far too much time. Later on he was seen to travel with one of the exhaust pipes stuck in the air. The effect was rather like a miniature traction engine belting round in reverse. As soon as he realised what had happened, he stopped and ripped off the damaged pipe. 'I was frightened it would fall off on to the track,' he told me afterwards. 'That would have been very dangerous for the other drivers.'

It was all rather depressing. The last question I asked Roy

Salvadori before going back to England was: 'What happens next?' He said: 'We go testing at Goodwood on Wednesday and get the damn' thing right.' Possibly that is another thing about motor racing: most people get another chance. But, so far as the 1966 World Championship was concerned, there couldn't be another chance for Rindt and Rodriguez. Denis Hulme, who now had 37 points, was going to take the hell of an effort to beat. If anyone could do it the most likely candidate would be Brabham (25 points)—with Clark and Amon (who finished third at Nurburgring) sharing 19 points. At the best they could be regarded as outsiders with tolerably long odds. It looked as if the Brabham-Repco brew was going to triumph for the second year running. Still—there were four more races to go, and a lot of things can happen in four races.

For the meanwhile, I was left to consider the remarks which Roy Salvadori had made to me earlier in the year, and which I reported in the previous chapter. 'In 1967,' he said, 'a good reliable car will count. By 1968 it'll be different. Everybody will be so well sorted out, that maximum power will be the thing.' The 1967 season was already more than half-finished. Was everybody really so well sorted out? Brabham appeared to be, but who else? Even Lotus-Ford, which certainly had power, seemed to lack stamina. I couldn't help wondering whether, as things were now turning out, Salvadori's forecast was not about one year out. But that is the nature of Grand Prix racing. That old devil fortune which governs sophisticated machinery has made a nonsense of many predictions before now. And, if I'm any judge, it will go on doing so for as long as there's motor racing. Perhaps that's what makes it all so exciting.

18

Enzo Ferrari: Ride a Prancing Black Horse

COMMENDATORE (a title he doesn't particularly like—he much prefers to be addressed as Engineer—but people persist in using it) Enzo Ferrari has been responsible for winning the following:

The World Championship of Drivers—6 times.

The Mille Miglia—8 times (between 1948 and 1953, six times in a row).

The Le Mans 24-Hour Race—8 times (between 1960 and 1965 six times in a row).

The Automobile Tour de France—9 times running.

Grand Prix races—51.

That was at the time of writing. Quite possibly some of the figures will be larger by the time this book comes out. With Ferrari, winning things is a continuous process. It goes on all the time.

His cars have, of course, won many other races, but if we go into all the details we're going to have trouble with this chapter. It will become a compile-it-yourself Appendix kit, not the fast-moving narrative stuff readers are supposed to want from my sort of writer.

Enzo Ferrari is seventy years old. He looks younger. He is tall, erect, with a fine mane of white hair. He regards the world through tinted glasses, which ought to make him appear enigmatic. They do, up to a point. Nevertheless, he leaves people in little doubt about his emotional state. He can convey benevolence, impatience, power, humility, friendliness, loneliness, naivety and wisdom, and he can ring the changes quickly. At his factory at Maranello in the north of Italy his power is absolute.

ENZO FERRARI: RIDE A PRANCING BLACK HORSE 141

He inhabits an office which is furnished with a simplicity that almost amounts to austerity. There are no rugs on the parquet floor. Nothing clutters the top of his desk. The walls are painted dark blue. There is only one picture, a large photograph of his son Dino, which faces the desk.

It is in this room that he awaits the results of motor races. He doesn't like being asked why he never goes to watch them. His public relations officer shrugs the question off with 'Surely —everybody knows about that?' You take the hint and don't bring it up.[1]

Apart from this he considers questions courteously and answers them at quite a lot of length. He doesn't speak English, but can talk fluently in French.

He works prodigiously long hours. He invariably drives himself, although an engaging gentleman named Pepino has been his chauffeur for the past forty years. At the Maranello plant they point out with amusement that 'chauffeur' in French literally means 'heater', and that seems to be Pepino's main job. Half an hour before Ferrari is due to depart, Pepino is rung up. 'Warm up the car,' he is told. When his master arrives Pepino moves obediently into the passenger seat.

Ferrari has four cars in all. A Mini-Cooper 'S', which he uses for town driving, a Peugeot 404, a Fiat 850 coupé, and a Berlinetta 2-plus-2. The Berlinetta is all that you might expect it to be. The others have been, as they put it, 'Maranello-tuned'—which means that they display considerably more panache than you might expect, even from such normally far-from-sluggish motor cars.

The factory itself is large. It is kept immaculately clean, and, like Ferrari's own office, is a very quiet place. The workers seem to be very serious. They radiate an atmosphere of intense dedication. When, in a big British car plant, you take photographs there is amusement spiced with frequently Rabelaisian wit. At Maranello they don't seem to notice you.

In his memoirs Ferrari recalls that he can celebrate two birthdays. The happy event occurred on February 18th, 1898, in a village near Modena. A severe snowstorm was raging at the time, and it was not until two days later that his father was able to get into town and record the new arrival. Thus, if

---

1. In *The Enzo Ferrari Memoirs* he headed a chapter 'Though I don't attend Races', but never told us precisely why.

you look up the records, you'll see Enzo's birth registered on February 20th of that year.

This business of two birthdays is, of course, a characteristic which he shares with royalty. The coincidence is amusing and not entirely inappropriate. At Maranello he enjoys something extremely close to regal status.

Ferrari, Snr, was a structural engineer. Enzo's own ambitions seem to have encompassed three possible occupations: opera singer, sports writer, and racing driver. His voice was nothing to sing about and he had no ear for music. That disposed of the first. He did become a journalist for a while, and was managing director of the *Corriere dello Sport* before it moved its headquarters from Bologna to Rome. And that left motor racing.

He took part in his first events for an organisation known as C.M.N. (Costruzioni Meccaniche Nazionali), which had originally built four-wheel-drive tractors for towing guns. It went racing with a 3 litre 4-cylinder Isotta Fraschini engine. As well as competing for them, Ferrari also acted as a test driver. Among the races in which he took part was the Targa Florio. To reach the Sicilian circuit he had to drive his car down to Naples and then catch a ship. Somewhere along the way he found himself being chased by a pack of hungry wolves as he struggled through a blizzard.

It was only after he had fired revolver shots at them that the animals were put to flight.

Later he joined Alfa Romeo. He went there as a driver and presently became the *équipe*'s racing manager.

In the late 1920s Alfa Romeo decided to close down its racing department. Ferrari wasn't at all happy about this. It seemed tremendously wrong that the triumphant red of Italy should be removed from motor racing by the stroke of a boardroom pen. He retired thoughtfully to Modena. Within a relatively short time he had rented a workshop and was preparing Alfas for racing. Although he depended on the big manufacturer for cars and certain services, this was, in every other way, his own enterprise.

During the First World War an Italian fighter ace named Francesco Baracca always flew with a black rampant horse painted on his aircraft. On his last mission Baracca was shot down and killed. Years later, after a motor race at Ravenna, Ferrari met the young flier's father. This led to an introduction to his mother, who said: 'Ferrari, why don't you put my son's rampant horse on your car? It will bring you luck.'

Ferrari thanked her for the suggestion. He mounted the horse on a gold field, for gold is the colour of Modena, and it has been his emblem ever since.

Scuderia Ferrari saw that Alfa went on winning races, and that Italy retained her place at the top of Grand Prix racing. So successful were the later cars that when motor racing returned after the last war Alfas were still winning races with the famous 158, which had originally been commissioned by Ferrari.

But by then he had cut off his connection with the firm and was working on cars of his own. The actual break came in 1939, due, as Ferrari describes it, to a 'crisis of conscience'. The substance of it was mostly technical. He may be prepared to compromise on some things but never on anything which offends his engineering principles.

A Ferrari took part in its first event at Piacenza in May, 1947. It led for two laps and then the fuel pump seized. 'It was,' he recalls, 'at least a promising failure.'

Ferrari has many talents: one of the greatest, it might be argued, is that of attracting talent. There are very few outstanding drivers who have not, at one time or another, driven for him. Similarly with designers: his plans depend on brilliance, and brilliance is what he normally receives.

Of the drivers who have been employed by him, he still considers Nuvolari to be the greatest. Fangio was the one with whom he was obviously least at ease. Stirling Moss may very well be the one he would have liked most to employ, but never did.

Nowadays Ferrari is the only Formula 1 constructor in Europe who also builds complete production cars (Colin Chapman of Lotus doesn't manufacture engines). The factory turns out about 1,000 of these a year, and each takes something like 2,000 man hours to build. Five hundred men are employed on this side of things, and a further 120 in the racing shop, which occupies one wing of the works.

This is a pretty considerable undertaking, and it needs to be. In 1967, for example, Ferraris were fighting for victories on no fewer than four fronts, There were Formula 1, Formula 2, sports prototypes (represented by the P4), and sports cars (the 2 litre Dino). After every event a meeting is held in

Ferrari's office and attended by all the departmental heads. The object is to chew over the lessons of the race, to explore any way in which they can rub off on to the production cars.

Make no mistake about it: although Ferrari himself no longer goes to the circuits, he is still very much the master of his team's destiny. His chief engineer on the racing side is a brilliant young man named Mauro Foghieri, who graduated at Bologna University and joined the Ferrari plant—where his father is in charge of maintaining the machine tools. The racing manager is Franco Lini.

Franco Lini was a motoring journalist. He was Italian correspondent for the French sporting daily *L'Équipe*, sports editor of an Italian motoring magazine, and he contributed to several others. Before agreeing to take over the duties of sports editor he had insisted that he be allowed to travel with no restrictions on distance. Thus his reports came in from as far away as Mexico and Japan. Not only did they help to sell the paper: these experiences gave Lini an almost unique knowledge of the drivers.

One day towards the end of 1966, when he was covering a rally in Spain, he found a message from the *L'Équipe* waiting at his hotel office. It seemed that somebody wanted to see him in Milan. He made a vague note of it, and went back to his work. Later, his wife telephoned him. 'Mr. Ferrari wants to see you,' she said. 'It's very urgent.' Unfortunately, you cannot just drop an assignment, even if one of the biggest names in motoring wants to see you urgently. 'Tell him I'll come on Monday,' Lini said.

On the Monday he arrived at Ferrari's office. Ferrari went over and locked the door. Then, speaking in a conspiratorial whisper, he offered Lini the job of racing manager.

Franco Lini recalls: 'I never was so surprised. I had never considered such a possibility, and I told him so.'

When I went to see him about three months later Lini told me: 'The job is good for me. I like it at this moment. Fortunately we started the year by winning the race at Daytona. That made me very happy. It helped my morale a lot. I am a lucky man, and I think my luck is continuing.'

After every race Franco Lini submits a long confidential report to his employer. Between them, he and Ferrari choose the drivers for the next event. There are various problems which have to be taken into consideration. For example, Mike

Parkes is getting on for 6 ft. 4 in. tall, and so he had to have a special car made for him. Furthermore, he held an important executive position on the production car side. As he told me: 'I often think Ferrari would like to see me doing more project engineering and less motor racing, whilst I'd like to do less project engineering and more motor racing.'

Enzo Ferrari gave up driving in motor races for two reasons. One was ill-health. The other was the birth of his son Dino. He considered that the dangers of the sport and the responsibilities of parenthood made poor allies. This was something about which he knew only too much. Many of the drivers whom he knew well were killed. Once, when the President of Italy visited the works, he said: 'They tell me, Ferrari, that you spend the whole of your day here, staying on late in the evening. I suppose you'll be making a long day of it today, too.'

Ferrari replied: 'Perhaps it's better like that. It's only by working without a moment's rest that one can avoid thinking of death.'

But death still managed to intrude. One tragedy, from which he'll never recover, was the death of Dino in 1956. The young man had charm and talent, but his health was poor. Ferrari was left without an heir.

Look through the current batch of rumours and it's almost certain that you'll find one about the future of the Ferrari plant. Ford once made an offer for it, which was turned down. The Italian motor industry helps to subsidise the racing activities and Fiat is known to be a staunch ally.

Ferrari, when he wants to be, can be extremely direct. He makes his decisions clearly, with no 'ifs' and 'buts' and similar hesitations. On the other hand, when it suits him he can be no less vague.

When I asked him about the future of his plant he told me: 'Everything is possible, and this subject has already been discussed—a great deal has been spoken and written about it. The future of Ferrari must be assured. This is definitely not the last of my thoughts—but, rather, a goal to be achieved.'

You can make of that whatever you like.

Ferrari also told me: 'When I wake up each morning I always have something new to achieve, and this pleases me. If it were not so it would mean that I had given up living.'

In 1966 one of Ferrari's achievements had been the winning of the Italian Grand Prix. Ludovico Scarfiotti had been at the wheel, and this was the kind of thing which sent the huge Italian crowd of spectators into transports of delight. Could Ferrari repeat this success in 1967? On September 7th I caught a plane to Milan *en route* to Monza. Three days later I was to know the answer.

19

A Funny Thing Happened on the Way to the Chequered Flag

At Mosport, on August 27th, 1967, Canada held a Grand Prix as part of its centenary hi-jinks. One couldn't help wondering whether packing yet another World Championship event into an already overcrowded calendar was a good idea. Consider, if you will, the case of Graham Hill. After competing at Mosport on the Sunday he had to catch a night flight back to London. At Heathrow he was hurried over to another part of the airport. He climbed on board his own aircraft, took off and headed for Brands Hatch, where he was due to take part in a saloon-car race. Unfortunately, the landing strip at Brands was hidden by early mist. He was diverted to Biggin Hill. A car picked him up there, took him to the circuit, and by mid-afternoon he was back on yet another starting grid. Rindt, Stewart, Brabham and Irwin made similar breakneck dashes from circuit (Canada) to circuit (England). Even allowing for the fact that racing drivers are somewhat tough, it seems rather a lot to ask of flesh and blood and muscles and mind.

The outcome of the Mosport spree was that Denis Hulme remained at the top of the World Championship table (he came second in the race). Jack Brabham, who won it, made his second place in the table considerably more secure. With 34 points to Hulme's 43, he was now a fairly substantial threat to his team mate. Not that this made any difference to the Constructor's Championship. With Brabhams way ahead of all the other cars, it was already in the bag.

None of this was particularly dramatic, and yet drama was

something of which this particular August produced far too much. Bob Anderson was killed while testing his car at Silverstone on the 14th. Shortly afterwards BP announced its intention to withdraw its support from motor racing at the end of the year. And, in a Formula 2 race at Enna in Sicily on the 24th. Pedro Rodriguez was involved in a very nasty smash. He was trying to take the lead from Beltoise at the time. The two cars touched wheels. Rodriguez, who was travelling at about 140 m.p.h., was deflected on to the barrier. His car broke in half. He was dragged along the track for several yards. When, at last, they got him to hospital he was suffering from cuts, bruises and a broken bone in his ankle. At the very earliest he could hope to be back in business at the Mexican Grand Prix on October 22nd. But even that needed a certain amount of luck.

For Cooper-Maserati this was extremely unfortunate. In company with Honda and Rob Walker they were affected by the BP decision. Now, to make matters even worse, the Enna episode had robbed them of a crack driver. Richard Attwood took Rodriguez's place at Mosport. In the Italian Grand Prix at Monza they used that brilliant young Belgian Jackie Ickx (of whom Ken Tyrrell—for whom he drove in F2 events—once said: 'He's outstanding. He's a very fine young driver. He's going to bring a lot of fame to Belgium.')

And then there was Monza.

I arrived at Milan airport at lunchtime on the Friday, picked up a Fiat 850 from the Hertz organisation, and set off for the circuit. I was just in time for the first afternoon's practice.

At this rather pleasant little town in northern Italy there's a palace surrounded by an enormous park. It used to belong to the Italian royal family. In 1900, however, an anarchist slew King Umberto I in the palace garden. Understandably, perhaps, this episode put the rest of the royal family off the idea of living there. They departed and never went back. The park and palace were turned over to the public. Among the attractions of the latter are a horse-racing course and the autodrome.

They built the autodrome in 1922, and a pretty impressive task it was, too. Within six months of the first slice of earth being turned, cars were racing there. Three thousand, five hundred labourers were employed on the job, 200 lorries, thirty light trucks, and they even constructed a special length of railway track, five kilometres long, over which a locomotive and eighty wagons hauled supplies to the workers.

The Grand Prix circuit is 3·56 miles long. The race is run over sixty-eight laps (242·08 miles). It is one of the fastest in the calendar and was disposed of (in 1967) in 1 hour 43 minutes and 45 seconds.

I have to admit that I like Monza very much indeed. There are masses of trees, the pits and the paddock are extremely well appointed, and in some ways it's rather like a mini Le Mans. There is, for example, an excellent restaurant, a motor museum, and all sorts of other diversions in the way of funfairs and a children's playground for anyone who wearies of motor racing.

Over 80,000 people turned up to the Italian G.P. of 1967.[1] The crowd is excitable, and so are the commentators. You hear a somewhat frenzied babble of words. Suddenly everyone cheers and waves, and you think that Something Big has occurred. Actually, it probably only means that driver A has overtaken driver B and the whole happening has been predictable for the last several seconds. Nevertheless it's all rather more fun than the calm, somewhat deadpan attitude with which people go motor racing in Britain.

The people at Monza have three heroes. One is Enzo Ferrari, another is Scarfiotti, and the third is anyone else who happens to be driving a Ferrari car. Since 1949 Ferraris have won the race seven times, which is considerably more than any other marque. When in 1966 Scarfiotti-plus-Ferrari was the victor, the huge Italian crowd was transported into a seventh heaven of delight.

If you are a car constructor and you want to be sure of victory you cannot do better than to study the Ford strategy for the Le Mans 24-hour race. You build the biggest, most rumbustious engine that the regulations allow. You sign on as many crack drivers as you can get. You invest enough money to keep the economy of some lesser South American republic happy for the next decade. And you turn up with masses of cars.

The idea is that all but a few are expendable. They can wrench their guts apart, wearing out the opposition, but some will inevitably survive. One of them, unless you are very unfortunate indeed, will win.

1. In 1967 it carried the title of European Grand Prix.

Ferrari has employed similar tactics (though, it has to be admitted, on a more modest scale) from time to time. At the Italian G.P., for example, there has usually been a tidy scattering of scarlet on the grid. There have, furthermore, mostly been highly experienced giants of the Formula 1 profession behind the steering wheels.

But 1967 had been an unhappy year for the prancing black horse of Maranello. It began with four top drivers: Lorenzo Bandini, Mike Parkes, Ludovico Scarfiotti and Chris Amon. Bandini was killed at Monaco. Parkes was badly injured at Spa and, at the time of writing, it seems unlikely that he will race again in Formula 1. There was a good deal of indication that Scarfiotti was pulling out of F1 racing after Parkes's smash at Spa, and that left Amon. As a matter of fact, the young New Zealander did extremely well. For most of the season he hung on to third place in the World Championship table, and nobody could complain about that.

But Amon was alone. Two Italian drivers actually took part in the Italian race. Neither of them drove a Ferrari. Baghetti was there with a Lotus and Scarfiotti (surprise, surprise!) was at the wheel of the second Eagle-Weslake.

Before we go any further we'd better try to shed a little light on the Scarfiotti situation. He is a very rich man. He comes from one of Italy's leading families. He could give up motor racing at any time and scarcely notice the drop in income. In Italy his family makes him an exceedingly hot property. As a public relations man told me before the race: 'If he were killed here it'd be like the assassination of an American president. A professional driver's death would make about thirty lines in the papers—maybe less. But Scarfiotti...' He shrugged his shoulders and turned his eyes to heaven.

After the Le Mans 24-Hour Race in June he had been uncertain about his future. Several forces, plus a number of whispering doubts in his own mind, seemed intent that he should give up single-seater racing. He is said to have talked the situation over with Enzo Ferrari, who suggested that he should concentrate on hill climbs and sports-car events and opt out of Formula 1. At the time Scarfiotti seemed relieved that somebody, at last, had made up his mind for him.

A certain amount of this is hearsay. Nevertheless, in an interview with a correspondent from the magazine *Car* (issue September, 1967) Ferrari's racing manager Franco Lini said:

'Ludovico Scarfiotti—well, is not his job Formula 1.' And: 'I suggest Scarfiotti to stop the F1.'

Certainly, at this time, the Ferrari team was very preoccupied with professionalism. Because there are relatively few circuits in Italy, and no opportunities for a young aspirant to go club racing every weekend (like in England), the country scarcely turns out any professionals. In 1967 the ouput was nil.

Considering, presumably, that Scarfiotti had heeded his advice, Enzo Ferrari was shopping for drivers at the time of the 1967 Italian Grand Prix. Two whom he was known to have approached were Jackie Stewart and Jackie Ickx. Whilst neither turned his offer down, they didn't accept it either. They had other suggestions to consider.

Meanwhile, back in the Gurney camp, Bruce McLaren had departed. After Ginther's retirement earlier in the year he had driven Eagle-Weslakes at Silverstone and Nurburgring. But this could only be a temporary arrangement. McLaren is a constructor in his own right. He was simply waiting until the V12 B.R.M. engine he'd ordered became available. It arrived in time for the Canadian G.P. and showed plenty of promise. So Gurney had a vacancy, and who should we find filling it at Monza but none other than Ludovico Scarfiotti.

It is difficult to discover what, precisely, happened. Bill Dunne, Gurney's racing manager in Britain, merely told me that the Scarfiotti arrangement was on a race-to-race basis, but he and Gurney were very happy about his approach to things. The truth, of course, lies in Scarfiotti's own mind. Somewhere along the line he had done a rethink. Was it the memory of his triumph at Monza in 1966? The sweet sensation of success which, here, is sweeter than anywhere else: the sheer adulation of the Italian crowd? One can't help feeling that this is possible, and one cannot possibly blame Scarfiotti for succumbing to it.

None of this was any help to Ferrari and Chris Amon. The only consolation may have been the fact that they had a new car and one that, in theory at any rate, was very well capable of winning the race.

It is a well-known fact that up to the time of the Le Mans 24-Hour Race each year the brunt of Ferrari's technical resources—and, indeed, his own thinking—are devoted to the prototypes. Afterwards, with that out of the way, they get down to serious thinking about Formula 1. During the summer they had succeeded in getting a fair amount of weight off the existing car and increasing its power. They were also busy devising a new one.

The engine of the newcomer was run for the first time on the Sunday before the Italian G.P. On the Wednesday it had done about ten laps of the diminutive circuit at Modena, which proved little more than the fact that it would actually go. The moment of truth (actually, there's no single moment—it's a stretched-out business, but the phrase will have to serve), the discovery of what, precisely, they had conceived and built, would have to wait until the race itself.

During the latter phases of the car's construction Enzo Ferrari had been more or less commuting between his villa near Rimini and the works at Maranello. He had worked fantastically long hours and he spent a good many of them in the racing shop.

The main difference between the new car and the others was that the former had four valves per cylinder (two inlet and two exhaust) as opposed to three (two inlet and *one* exhaust). It was considerably lighter. Indeed, they proudly told me, it was the lightest car in the race.

There is nothing particularly new about completing a new car within a matter of days before an important race. Jim Clark had shown that the outcome could be satisfactory when he won at Zandvoort that year. Earlier, in March, Bandini proved something similar when he took second place in the 'Race of Champions' at Brands Hatch with a brand-new Ferrari.

But would it work this time, on the home ground, where that crowd of 80,000 people was more or less solidly behind Ferrari, and where the honour of Italy seemed to depend on one young New Zealander and one unproven red car?

On the first day of practice I came upon Chris Amon behind the pits. He seemed to be stalking the car like a hunter. It looked as if he was trying to catch it unawares, and, by doing so, to discover some sort of truth about it.

Me: Do you like it?

Amon (worried): I don't know. It's not yet as fast as the old one. We've got to get one or two things sorted out.

Me: Do you like the circuit here at Monza?

Amon (still worried): Well—I've got to like it. It's all right. It's very fast.

Arrival

Chris Amon

Departure

Richie Ginther

Those responsible

Left
Colin Chapman
Enzo Ferrari
Tony Rudd

This page
Above Yoshio Nakamura
Right Roy Salvadori
Below Rob Walker

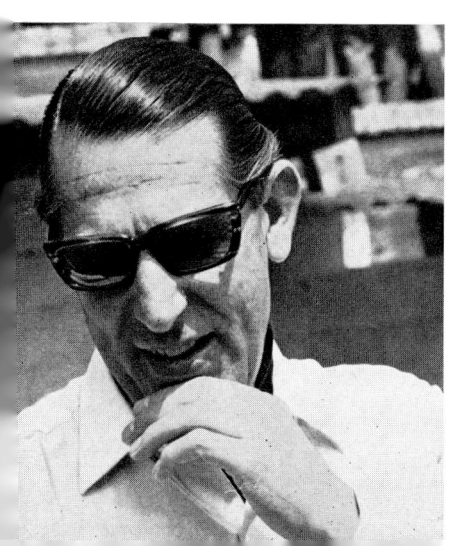

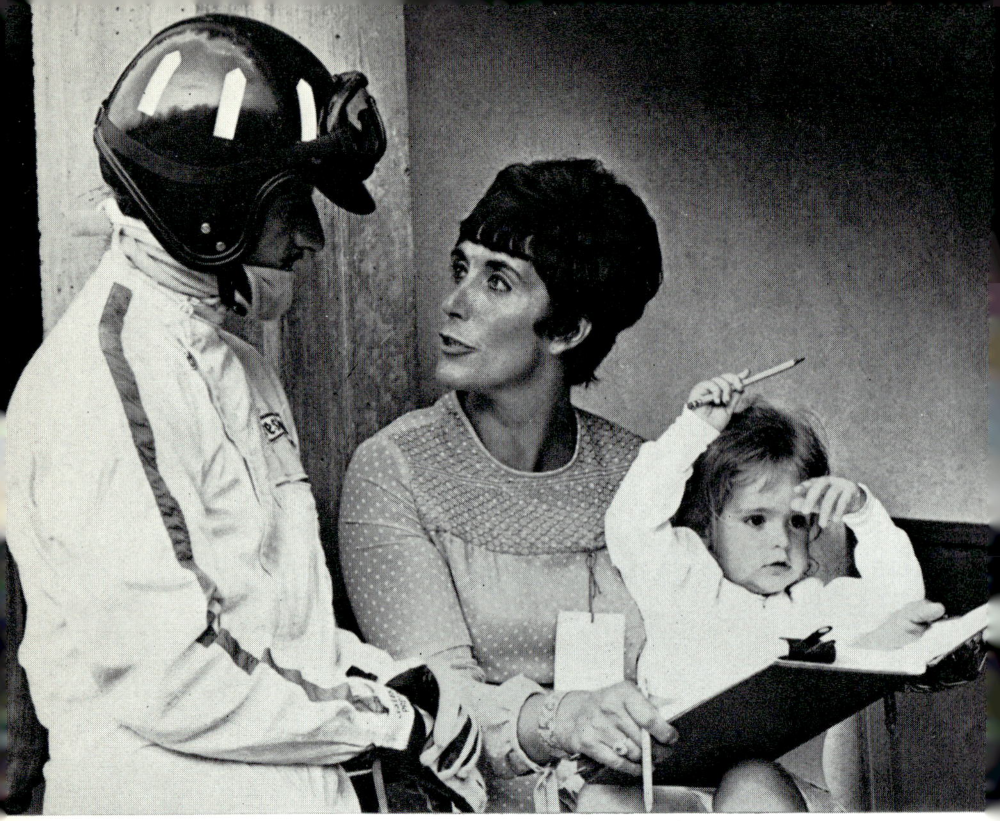

Stopwatch wives

Opposite
Bette Hill (with time chart, husband Graham, and daughter Samantha)
Pat Surtees

This page
Angela Rodriguez
Pat McLaren

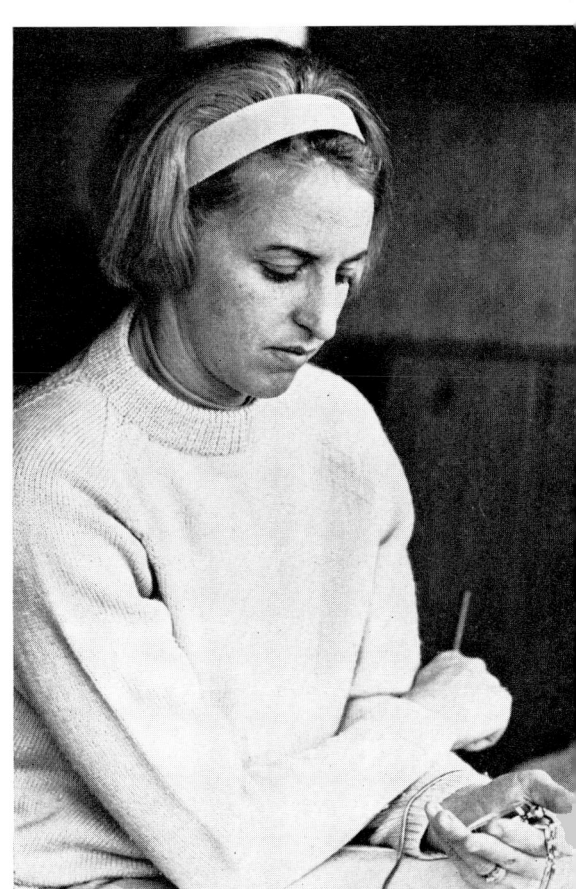

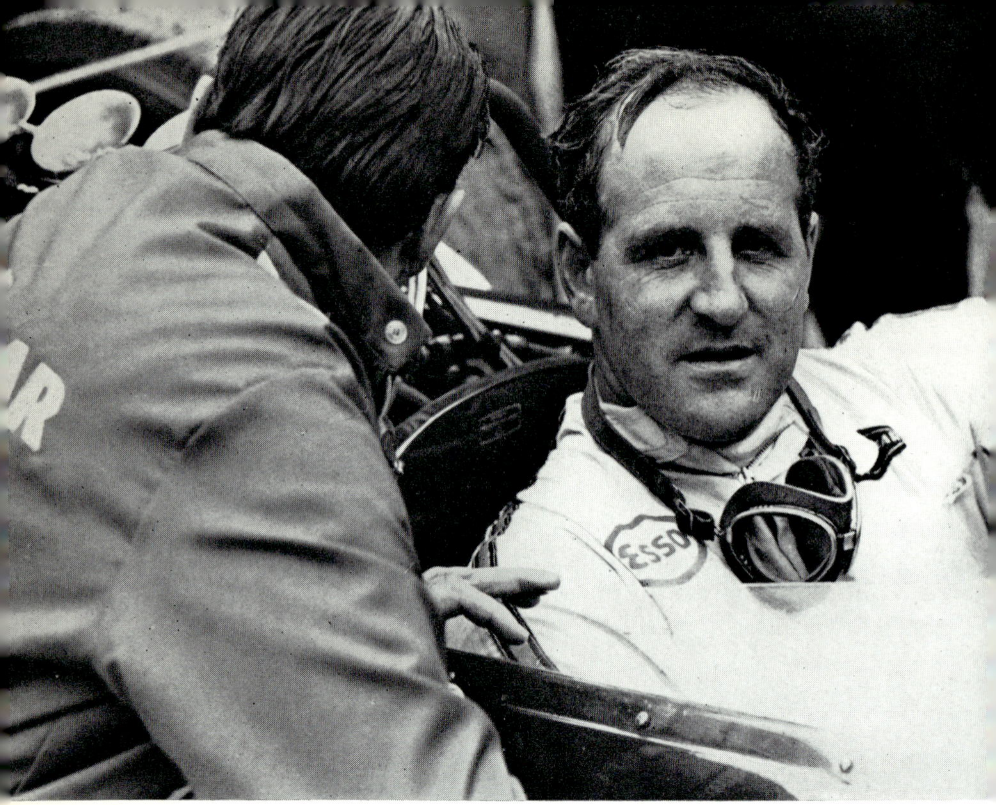

Conversation pieces

Denis Hulme half-attending Brabham and Tauranac—strictly technical

Clark and pressmen
Hill and friend

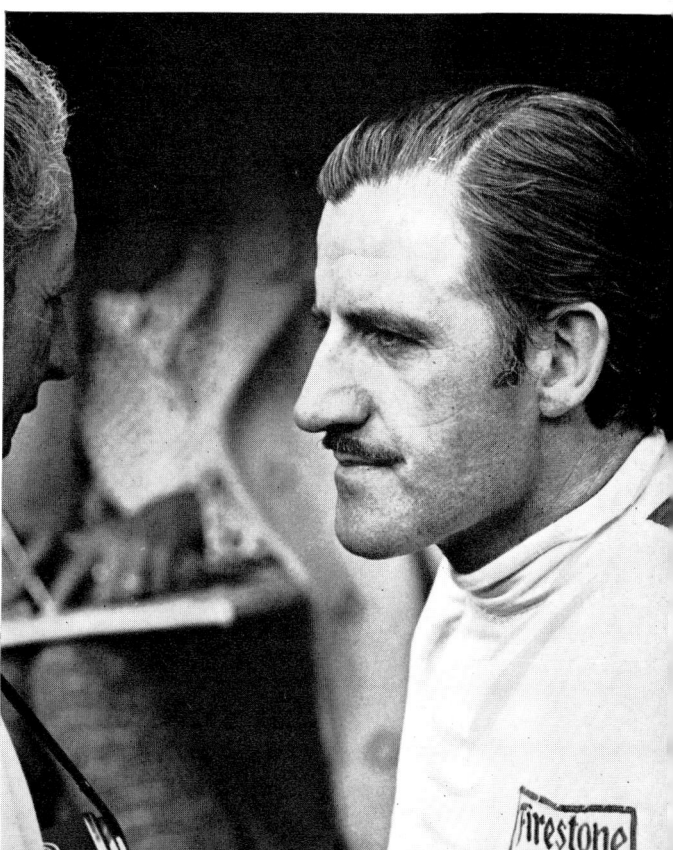

Tribute to Bandini

Lorenzo Bandini died from the result of injuries received when his car crashed at the chicane in the Monaco Grand Prix of 1967 and caught fire. The picture to the left was taken just before the start of this ill-fated race. The shot below shows Lorenzo with his wife in the office of the garage they owned in Milan

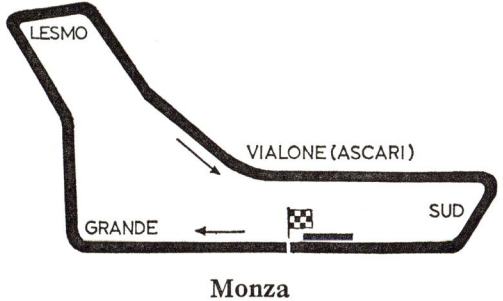

Monza

Enzo Ferrari never goes to races, but he does go to see practice at Monza. He stations himself at the end of the pits, a regal, rather withdrawn figure who manages to convey a terrific presence. Wherever he is, he holds the centre of the stage. People pay court to him. He treats them politely, even graciously. Now and then old cronies come up and he seems to enjoy this. He talks to them with a certain amount of animation, and sometimes laughs. A lot of people ask him for autographs, and he obliges. It is impossible not to be impressed by him.

At the circuit he leaves everything to Franco Lini and his chief technician Mauro Foghieri. Nevertheless, whenever Amon brings the car into the pits, Ferrari hurries over to it. He asks Amon a few crisp questions, smiles, and looks, looks, looks at the car. His scrutiny differs from Amon's. It's as if his eyes are trying to penetrate the very molecules of the metal itself, scooping up every vestige of detail.

The first day of practice produced little interest, except one moment when Amon, coming up behind two other cars, poured through the gap like teeth sinking through melting chocolate. It was still not entirely certain whether they'd use the new car for the race. The old car was also at the circuit, and Amon was doing a lap or two in the one, and then a lap or two in the other. For the race they might use either, or they could mount the new engine into the old car. As I've probably already suggested, racing cars are rather like Meccano. If you've a big enough set you can build all sorts of things from it.

On the second day, as on the first, there was practice from 3 to 6 p.m. The first day had been brilliantly fine. Now there were some clouds in the sky. From time to time the rumble of thunder came from somewhere over the horizon. It was rather like sitting on a bomb which was giving friendly mur-

murs just to show it was charged. As the clouds grew bigger, an atmosphere of depression settled on the Ferrari camp.

A Ferrari Spokesman: If it rains we could retire the car and all go home.

Me: Why?

A Ferrari Spokesman: Because of the driver.

Me: What's wrong with the driver?

A Ferrari Spokesman: The driver doesn't like rain.

Me: Who does?

A huge grey cloud, which obviously had a lot of fire in its belly, came over the trees, not giving a damn about what havoc it might cause. Everybody became more depressed. Just after four o'clock it unzipped itself and pitched its contents down on to the track. For about an hour it hammered the circuit with a quickfire deluge. Then it pushed off towards the Alps. Practice was extended for an hour—until seven. Sometime during the storm Enzo Ferrari, Mrs. Ferrari, the poodle which goes around with them, and Ferrari's public relations officer, had slipped off to Modena—where, in his apartment next day, Enzo would watch the race on TV. He might experience a few moments of pride during the session. He would undoubtedly die a thousand deaths. But nobody can really say, for these moments are strictly private. Nor, in any case, would Ferrari betray anything to an onlooker. He is far too much the master of his emotions to do that.

During the second day of practice the new car went rather better than it had gone on the first.

Race day, and a brilliantly blue sky, and 80,000 Italians certain that Ferrari could never be wrong, and one team manager saying, 'We'll have it all sorted out by the Spanish Grand Prix next year', and an American voice enunciating with great deliberation to an unseen audience: 'There are, in motor racing, once and again, occasional moments of calm.' At that particular moment we didn't seem to be in the midst of one, which was just as well. Calm was about the last thing that huge audience wanted.

You notice all kinds of things. Big things and silly little details. One of the details was in the paddock. Elsewhere, photographers in these places keep their lenses strictly for recording racing cars. At Monza there was something like one 35 mm camera taking pictures of perambulating birds in miniskirts for every two sucking up machinery through their shutters. Perhaps the Italians have a better sense of proportion than other nations.

Round about eleven o'clock I went to see Foghieri.

Me: Have you decided which car you're going to use?

Foghieri (with a curious gesture of crossing fingers and extending both elbows simultaneously): The new car—we hope.

Me: You hope?

Foghieri (now nodding his head affirmatively): Altogether we are hoping very hard indeed.

At two o'clock, just before they went down to the circuit, a Ferrari mechanic unrolled a large poster in front of the new car (the old one had been locked away in one of the garages). On it was the Ferrari emblem and a chequered flag. It was, presumably, for the benefit of photographers. It seemed to be a little optimistic. At half past three the race began. Now this was a somewhat strange start. Several versions of what may have happened have since been recounted. I can only tell you how it seemed to me, and precisely the same story was told to me by Foghieri afterwards. So far as this book is concerned, it's official.

There are, let us say, two stages to this start. Stage one begins on the dummy grid. They get all the photographers and mechanics and what-not away off the track. Then a man lowers a green flag. This signals the beginning of stage two. The idea is that the cars shall proceed at a walking pace to the starting grid. Once they have assembled, the Italian national flag is to be lowered. When this happens the cars blast off and that's it.

However at this, the thirty-eighth Italian Grand Prix, somebody (or somebodies) blundered. When the green flag went down a sizable proportion of the pack shot forward and got on with the business of racing. Others (Jim Clark, for example) did what they were supposed to do, crept forward and stopped. Some over-revved their engines, and I believe that one or two stalled them. The result was mayhem. It was reminiscent of that bit in *Lays of Ancient Rome*, where Macaulay wrote: 'But those behind cried "Forward!" and those before cried "Back!"'

It had all manner of kick-backs on the race which followed. One way of attempting to win at Monza is to tuck your car neatly in behind the leader's and get a tow. This particular circuit is singularly good for slipstreaming. There must have been several drivers who had their eyes optimistically focussed on the rear end of Clark's Ford Lotus. As a matter of fact, the Clark technique is to tear away at full bore, when everybody else is taking things a little bit carefully. By the time they're in a suitable mood to get up behind him, he's far away over the horizon.

But anything like this was completely out of the question in the confusion, and perhaps the marvel is that some sort of order was restored, and that nobody and no car got hurt.

The race itself was a perfect example of how every spectator would like this sort of thing to be and which, in Grands Prix, it unfortunately so seldom is. Early on, the lead was constantly changing. There were some marvellous dices: Amon dicing with Surtees, Surtees dicing with Brabham, and so on. There were also some colossal disappointments as Fate, in a mood either of malice or frivolity, toppled the leaders. Hulme at one time seemed to have everything nicely sewn up. But then his engine pegged out. Gurney's threw a con rod early on, and that fixed him. Timing gear in the other Eagle fixed Scarfiotti. Hill seemed certain to win (for a while). A broken crankshaft put paid to that idea. Clark lost 90 seconds owing to a puncture, but he got out again, sliced through the field and got into the lead. He was still leading when the official concerned was carefully unfurling his chequered flag. But then his car ran out of petrol. It-actually-ran-out-of-petrol. Spent, empty, cheated by the fiends which haunt motor racing, it slipped back and coasted home in third place.[1]

The Brabham-Surtees fight went on to the end. Surtees had very neatly been slip-streaming the reigning champion. At precisely the right moment he shot out and overtook. He won by 0·12 of a second or approximately a car's length. But it was beautifully done, and let nobody talk about luck. Running out of petrol was Clark's misfortune. Winning the race was Surtees's skill. It was the master touch of which, due to a certain malaise which had made the Honda rather less than competitive, we had seen far too little from him that year.

From the crowd: ecstasy. Everything, everywhere in the

1. It happens. In 1964 Dan Gurney ran out of petrol on the last lap of the Belgian G.P., having led throughout the race.

world, was forgiven. They lifted John Surtees out of his car. They carried him to the platform, where Mrs. Bandini (and what a nice touch *that* was) presented him with the trophy.

And Ferrari?

We are in a room not far from the pits, and the race is over. Drinks are being served. At the far end Foghieri is leaning against the wall. I go over to him.

Me: How do you feel now?

Foghieri (emphatically): Very bad!

He recalls the ill-starred start. He talks about trouble with the rear shock-absorbers, which caused Amon to make two pit-stops and thereby to lose the battle which, at one time, he'd been having with Surtees for third place (Amon finished seventh). He speaks of unspeakable brakes, and generally makes it clear that, wherever happiness may be at this particular moment, it isn't anywhere near him.

Time passes. I drift over to Amon, who is reclining in a chair, thoughtfully considering a Campari-and-soda.

Me: How do you feel now? (By now, you'll have noticed that this is one of my standard opening gambits.)

Amon: Oh—quite happy. (Corrects himself quickly.) No, really, I'm very disappointed. There's been no real chance lately. In Canada, it rained you know. And in the starting mix-up here, I over-revved it at 2,000 over the top. That's why there wasn't more power. The car's basically more competitive than any of the others.

Me: The first time we met was in an aircraft. You were flying out to Italy to join Ferrari. That was about nine months ago. Do you think you've changed at all during this period?

Amon (smiling): I think I'm a little bit harder. I've learned a good many things.

Me: Do you like living in Italy?

Amon: Yes—I do now. I like it more than I thought I would at first. I've got an apartment now.

Me: Has it been a worry, carrying the whole weight of Ferrari's Formula 1 interests for so much of the season?

Amon: No—I haven't minded. In Italy, though, in this race, it was very much a strain. So many people are looking at you. If it had been anywhere else, I might not have over-revved it at the start.

Amon is the hell of a nice person. He's tired now, and I'm

not going to worry him any more. He's obviously got enough on his mind, without having to answer questions. I drift off into the crowd. Anyway, the Italian Grand Prix, 1967 edition, is over.

20

The Last of the Lone Wolves

THERE is still, thank goodness, a place in motor racing for the weekend enthusiast, the talented amateur who regards it as a sport and simply wants to have a go. There are clubs all over the country which cater for this sort of thing—no matter what is going on at the top.

At the top there are about seventeen drivers and a handful of teams, engaged in what one driver has described as 'no longer a sport, but a profession'. Every year the cost of being competitive at this level mounts, and it becomes more and more difficult for the lone wolf to take part in Grands Prix. Nevertheless, there were two individuals who tenaciously kept on trying. One is Rob Walker. The other, until his tragic death at Silverstone, was Bob Anderson. In spite of monumental difficulties, they hardly ever missed a race.

Rob Walker: Patron of an Art

Pippbrooke Garage is a large, modern-looking place beside a dual carriageway on the edge of Dorking. It all appears very efficient, and the chaps who sell petrol are most affable. One imagines that Rob Walker, the proprietor, must occupy a sumptuous office on the first floor.

'But no,' the petrol vendors say, 'you won't find him here. He's down at the racing shop.' And they give you rather intricate instructions about how to get there.

You peel off from the road, drive uncertainly past a body-building workshop, and then find yourself in a courtyard. You feel you might be forgiven if you mistook the racing shop for a barn. It's that kind of a building.

There's a Formula 1 car in a state of partial construction.

A big red near-historic sports car, which is being restored, and something that looks exciting, but which is concealed under a dust sheet. Actually, it's a Delage and it is insured for £10,000.

From behind a half-open door a voice says 'Did you want me?' You say 'Yes' and step inside.

The room couldn't possibly be described as large, and it is certainly not the kind of place you see tycoons inhabiting in the colour supplements. Nevertheless, it is entirely fascinating. The walls are crowded with posters advertising motor races. There are other souvenirs, such as a narrow yellow armband with something written on it in German. One supposes it admitted somebody to something once upon a time. There are masses of papers and magazines, and some very fine models of old racing cars. Behind a desk at one end sits a secretary who is extremely nice-looking. At the other end is Rob Walker. He is tall, looks younger than fifty (which he is), and is wearing a light check coat and dark grey trousers.

R. R. C. Walker (to spell out his initials) has been at Formula 1 motor racing for longer than any other entrant with the exception of Ferrari. He has seen it emerge from the sport of gentlemen to a mass-spectator industry involving millions of pounds. He has also seen it change from the days when to take part in many top events the prime consideration was whether you could afford to buy a car, to the time when, to stand a chance of winning anything big, you more or less have to belong to a works team.

All these things he has seen; and yet, with splendid determination, he has retained his independence. He is still the private entrance *par excellence*, the patron of the art. He admits that, one day, even he will have to give up. But one thing is certain—it's going to take a great deal to make this happen.

It is not revealing anything to say that Rob Walker is a very wealthy man. His great-great-grandfather was Johnny Walker. An uncle of his was head of the firm, until he retired ten years ago. Nevertheless, it takes a lot more than money to make a success out of being an independent in motor racing. Everything has to be purchased from outside, and no racing organisation is going to part with its best machinery. Unless people like Rob Walker are very careful they're likely to get whatever's left over when the needs of the works teams have been satisfied.

Rob Walker must have been careful. His cars have won

eight World Championship events in their time, and in one season they won five out of the seven events in the Tasman series. Stirling Moss drove for him for five years, Tony Rolt for six. Jack Brabham had a drive or two in a Walker-entered car during his first Grand Prix season. Graham Hill, Jo Bonnier, most of the big names have driven for him at one time or another.

This remarkable record really began one day in 1924. Young Rob Walker, aged seven, was on holiday at Boulogne with his mother. There was a Grand Prix of some sort arranged, and Mrs. Walker took her son to see it. If there ever was an act of destiny this was it.

There were Darracqs and Bugattis and thundering great cars in the main event. To add spice to it all, he sat next to the wife of one of the drivers. Afterwards the Walkers, mother and son, hired a taxi and were driven round the circuit.

Back in their Wiltshire home, the Walker family had a very long drive. At a somewhat precocious age Rob Walker was given a bull-nosed Morris by his mother, and he used to belt this up and down it. Then came the Baby Austin and the almost inevitable intention to turn it into something potent for hill-climb events. In fact, Rob Walker has no very marked mechanical ability, but the second chauffeur had all that was needed. The latter's job was mostly to take people to and from the station. Since the inhabitants of the house and their guests were not continually catching trains, he had plenty of time to spare. The transformation of the Baby Austin came along very nicely.

After attending a prep school and then Sherborne, Rob Walker went up to Cambridge. His academic record is a little confusing. In his first year he read history. In the second it was English. And in the third it was something called 'general'.

Towards the end of his last term he received an invitation to dinner from the master of his college. It looked harmless enough—until he reached the small print. There was some reference to 'after you've taken your degree', or something like that. Since Rob Walker assessed his chances of getting a degree as somewhat slight, he politely declined. Actually, he did himself less than justice. When the examination results were published he was listed among those who'd passed. But by then he was busy motor racing.

He was walking down Park Lane, enjoying the sunshine.
M

There was no hint of drama in the air—just an ordinary, rather pleasant, day. Presently he came to a car showroom and, as was his wont, he stopped and looked in the window.

On display, a thing of huge magnificence, was a 3·6 litre Delahaye. There had, admittedly, been one previous owner; but, since he was Prince Bira of Siam, the famous racing driver, nobody was likely to quibble about it. The price was £400 (note for comparison: the price of the cheapest Rolls-Royce in those days was £1,100).

Now it happened that Rob Walker didn't have £400 on him at the time, and there was no likelihood of his acquiring so much currency in the foreseeable future. With the determined optimism which has influenced so many of his decisions he went inside and bought the car on hire purchase.

In company with Ian Connell, he raced it in the Le Mans 24-Hour Race of 1939. It was a very fast race that year—the winner's speed was 86·85 m.p.h. compared with 82·35 in the previous year, and 82·27 when the event was resumed in 1949 and won by a Ferrari.

Nevertheless, they managed to come eighth, which was particularly creditable in the light of a certain misfortune. Just after midnight, when Connell was at the wheel, the exhaust gasket blew. This caused a stream of very hot gas to come pouring up into the cockpit. It burnt Connell's foot and when he came into the pits at 4 a.m. he said that he couldn't continue.

For the next twelve hours Rob Walker drove on and on and on. He overcame the heat by drenching his rope-soled shoes in cold water. On one occasion he stopped to revive his energies with a glass of champagne. Otherwise he just kept at it.

It is, perhaps, an interesting glimpse of fashion to note what he was wearing on this occasion. At night he wore an immaculate navy-blue pin-stripe suit. For the daytime he changed into a check suit.

Those were wonderful days, when people raced at Brooklands, and the only qualification for a licence was to complete ten laps without getting into trouble. If during a race you did something wrong, the stewards were pretty tough. They either took the licence away or else entered your name in a sinister Black Book.

Rob Walker nearly got into trouble once when his car spun off and went into the bank. Since he had no reverse gear, the problem of getting back into the race was rather difficult. He solved it by driving higher up the bank, and then coasting backwards downhill. It was an operation which couldn't possibly have been judged accurately, and the stewards thought that it was a rather bad idea. However, he was let off with a reprimand.

During 1939 there was a lot of speculation about which was the fastest road car in Britain. The Press took up the question until there was only one thing to do about it, and that was to find out. A challenge was issued, with £100 and a water-colour of the winning car as the rewards. Rob Walker's Delahaye won it. But, to make sure, he had Arthur Dobson, who was very good indeed, drive it.

During the war two important things happened. One was that he joined the Fleet Air Arm. The other was that he got married. The result of the first was that he had enough flying in fighter aircraft to satisfy his aeronautical needs for a lifetime. The result of the second was that, having made a promise to his wife, he gave up driving racing cars. There was, however, an escape clause in the promise about hill climbs and speed trials.

'Going to races and not taking part in a car wasn't too easy at first,' he told me. 'But I soon found I was telling everyone else what to do, and that *is* easy—especially when you can't be proven wrong.'

Possibly motor racing was deprived of a great driver, and possibly it wasn't. We shall never really know. Nor does it matter, for Rob Walker's promise to his wife was one of the best things that have ever happened in the sport. Indirectly, it provided cars and encouragement for many drivers of promise at times when they most needed them.

There had been talk of Rob Walker going into the whisky firm, but it never came to anything. One day after the war, when he was looking for something to do, he met up with two wing commanders. They were planning to take over a house on the Chelsea Embankment and turn it into a club. Among the rewards of membership were to be boating, flying, and a car hire scheme. They invited him to join them in the enterprise. He agreed.

The club came to a rather unhappy end in 1950, when one of the aircraft crashed—killing the co-pilot and injuring one of the wing commanders. But by then Rob Walker had bought Pippbrook Garage on the London Road, Dorking, and was very heavily involved in motor racing.

There are several reasons for his continuing interest in the sport. On a purely commercial basis it provides a useful advertisement for his garage. The staff there take a great interest in the racing side. 'On the Monday after Jo Siffert came third in the 1967 Race of Champions at Brands Hatch,' he related with a mixture of pride and sorrow, 'hardly any work at all was done there. They were all too busy discussing the event.'

But the real reason is much more personal. 'It's my life,' he told me. 'All my friends are in it. I spend so little time at home that I've not much opportunity to make friends there. These motor-racing people, I see them in a different country every fortnight. There's a terrific comradeship between us. We all say "hullo" and shake hands, as if we haven't seen one another for ages. It's a fabulous thing. I think the danger element draws us together, and there's absolutely no class distinction.'

One very good year—the one in which his car won five out of the seven Tasman races—he ended with a loss of £2,000. Mostly the figure is much higher—anything up to about £12,000 depending on how things have gone. But, he admits, he goes racing in comfort. He drives a Ferrari and always stays at the best hotels.

The car itself is a Cooper-Maserati. 'It's best to race a new car for at least two years,' he said. 'It takes the first year to get the bugs out.' As a matter of fact, it is owned by Jack Durlacher (a stockbroker friend), and Rob Walker runs it. This he does on a strictly professional basis, employing three mechanics. There is no spare car.

A Walker car is always easy to spot, with its very distinctive colour scheme of dark blue and white. The main reasons for this are that he likes dark blue, and the white markings make it recognisable from a distance. And if anybody waves a book of rules in front of him he will point out that these are the colours of the St. Andrew's cross and therefore, by inference, the colours of Scotland—which is where his family came from.

At a meeting in Germany an official became depressingly articulate about the F.I.A. rules in this respect, and tried to insist that the car be painted in British racing green. Fortunately Rob Walker has a massive store of knowledge at his command. He pointed out that the colour for Germany had been white, and yet German cars habitually turned out in silver (the idea, accredited to Hitler, was that white created a glare which upset the driver's vision).

The official held his peace.

Jo Bonnier, who was also at the meeting, was less fortunate. He had a car painted in Italian red, and they made him re-paint it, on the spot, in the Swedish colours of pale blue and three yellow stripes. It looked a shocking mess in the race.

Richard Attwood does the testing for Rob Walker's car, as Jo Siffert (his currently contracted driver) is away racing somewhere every week. Indeed, the Walker-Siffert relationship seems to be a somewhat detached one. They only meet at races, where the conversation is carried out, not always without difficulty, in French. Siffert speaks no English.

It should go on record that after Stirling Moss won the Argentine Grand Prix in a Walker-entered Cooper back in 1958 the sales of British cars in South America were said to have doubled. The motor industry blinked a vaguely interested eye at the coincidence, and did nothing about it. What should have been a grateful government showed itself, as seems to be the unhappy case with motor racing, indifferent. But Rob Walker does have one honour, and that he values highly. He is a member of the Club Internationale des Ancien Pilotes de Grands Prix. Membership is limited to ex-World Champions, drivers who have won the Le Mans 24-Hour Race, and a very few other people who have made substantial contributions to motor racing. In France membership of this august body is regarded with scarcely less reverence than that accorded to members of the *Legion d'Honneur*. Among its vice-presidents are numbered no fewer than nine princes.

When he is able to use them Rob Walker has two homes. One is in Chelsea, and the other near Frome in Somerset. At the Somerset end he enjoys another distinction and one which may seem strange for a man in his position. He is chairman of the local Income Tax Commissioners. This is a kind of panel of Ombudsmen set up to hear the pleas of those who consider they are being handled with unreasonable severity by the Inland Revenue authorities. It is, he stresses, entirely neutral. But first and foremost, now and for ever, Rob Walker is a man of motor racing.

Bob Anderson: In Spite of Adversity

NOTE: *I wrote the next section of this chapter during early July 1967. About a month later, on Monday, August 14th, Bob was testing his blue Brabham-Climax at Silverstone in preparation for the Canadian Grand Prix. Travelling along the straight, his car ran over a pool of water on the track. It aquaplaned, spun off, and struck a post. Four hours later Bob Anderson died in hospital. After a lot of thought I decided to print this piece without making any changes to it. It is my tribute to a man whom I liked and admired very much indeed. R.G.*

On a crew-cropped lawn in Bedfordshire a small boy aged three is playing. Over to the left there is a group of outbuildings. Through a half-opened door one can just make out part of a Formula 1 racing car. The lawn is ringed with trees. The house, away to the right, is a pleasant, L-shaped building, which used to belong to a farmer.

It is a delightful, relaxing setting—about as far removed from the din and smell and tension of motor racing as anyone could imagine.

I approach the little boy warily and ask: 'Daddy?'

He nods solemnly and escorts me to the house. Mrs. Anderson opens the door. She suggests that her son Bruce might care to return to his game in the garden, and calls: 'Robert!' She is French, very attractive, and with a rather thoughtful way of talking—as if she is considering every statement carefully before turning it loose.

Bob Anderson comes down. He is wearing plum-coloured corduroy slacks and a dark blue shirt. He looks very fit and confident. Mrs. Anderson goes off to make coffee.

There are a number of common factors about the way in which Formula 1 teams go motor racing. The top brass and the drivers usually stay at the best hotels. They nearly always take with them spare cars and spare engines. They employ teams of mechanics, and convey this assortment of invested wealth to the circuits in large transporters.

All of them, that is to say, except Bob Anderson. By force of circumstances Anderson does his racing on a minute budget with only the barest necessities in the way of equipment. Instead of a giant transporter we see a small blue Volkswagen truck. There are no paid hands in the way of mechanics, no spare cars and no replacement engines. Socially, these outings amount to very little. He nearly always stays at inexpensive hotels away from the rest of the circus, works prodigiously hard and sleeps badly.

'I thought I'd have a go on my own for a couple of years in the hope that some works team might make me an offer,' he told me. 'Unfortunately, it hasn't worked out as I'd hoped. No team did make me an offer.'

One wonders why. Several less talented drivers have been snapped up. Anderson himself is at a loss for any explanation. 'I really don't understand,' he said. 'I wish somebody would tell me.'

Hoping to find out the truth for myself, I spoke to two people on the following day. One, the racing manager for one of the big teams, politely told me: 'No comment!' He went on to explain that his contract forbade him to discuss drivers. The other, who works for a firm involved in the sponsorship of motor racing, said: 'It is a little hard to know why. As a driver, Bob has improved enormously during the past two years. He pranged one or two cars earlier on, but that's all past. Possibly he's always been at the wrong place at the right time.'

This seems to correspond with the views of a journalist with whom Anderson once discussed the problem. The former suggested that, just possibly, those sojourns in small hotels didn't pay off. He ought to be spending more time lushing it up with the better-heeled members of his profession.

All of which is a great deal more easily said than carried out. Bob Anderson has never had any capital behind him. He is entirely dependent on racing to support his wife and himself and their two children. Furthermore, he has to do it with a car which cannot honestly be described as competitive. It has done very well in one or two races in South Africa, where the works teams were not taking part. In a big event, however, his chances of being placed are, to put it mildly, somewhat small.

There are times, indeed, when he has difficulty in getting a place on the starting grid. In the 1967 Monaco G.P., for example, he took his small ensemble all the way to the Principality, practised diligently for three days, and then learned that, in spite of finishing comfortably within the qualifying time, the regulations had debarred him from competing in the race.

'I was very bitter about it until the race was over,' he recalled, 'but then I decided that I just wasn't meant to take part. That was the way things were. It wasn't intended.'

Some of the race organisers, he agrees, are very considerate. Others are not. There was the case of a French Grand Prix at Clermont Ferrand, when he received a telegram on the Thursday before the event, telling him that he could take part. He piled the car on to the Volkswagen, and drove through most of the night. He managed to fit in one practice session. In the race itself he finished eighth.

I asked him whether he didn't find it rather disheartening, going to so many races and so seldom having a reasonable chance of finishing high up. 'Not really,' he said. 'I consider that I've achieved something if I finish eighth or fifth, or something. In my own way I may even have done better than the winner.'[1]

But, he confessed, he would certainly like to be more competitive. Unfortunately, to do so would cost him every bit of £10,000, and that is a great deal more than he could afford.

Bob Anderson was born in Hendon in 1931. His father was a doctor, his mother a pathologist who worked at the Charing Cross Hospital. When he was five years old his father died. Later his mother married again, and the family moved to Bedfordshire.

He went to a prep school at Seaford and then on to Gordonstoun. After two weeks at the latter he contracted osteomyelitis.[2] He was then fourteen. He spent nine months encased in plaster, lying on his back in a hospital at Aberdeen, and for some time afterwards he had to stagger around in a kind of strait jacket.

Soon afterwards, his academic education came to an end. It would, indeed, be interesting to have the views of the medical profession on how this illness affected his subsequent career. Did this prolonged stay in hospital, this inability to compete with his contemporaries, give him some sense of challenge which has driven him on ever since? Has he been continually

---

1. Anderson's engine is the only one in G.P. events which still depends on a carburettor as opposed to a fuel-injection system.

2. 'An infection of the bone, principally affecting the marrow. Antibiotics and surgery prevent bone destruction in the acute form; the disease may become chronic, though now only rarely.'—*The Reader's Digest Great Encyclopaedic Dictionary*

trying to catch up, to win back those lost years? The psychologists could have a field day working that one out.

Physically, the question is no less interesting. If there is one particular item of human anatomy which seems to have had a raw deal it must surely be Bob Anderson's back. Having recovered from the ordeal by disease, it was later to undergo fearful punishment from his chosen profession. On no fewer than four occasions it was very badly damaged. How does an assembly of bone and marrow and cartilage recover from such batterings? Apart from a deep scar on his right temple, he shows no outward signs of his many and fairly various injuries. He looks tough and well tuned, and the only contribution that he can make to the subject is that after that long spell on his back in Aberdeen he has been able to endure subsequent confinements to a hospital bed with a good deal of stoicism.

When, at last, he recovered from his illness he decided to go in for farming. He worked as a pupil on a farm near Winchester, later went to an agricultural college, and later still joined a firm to learn about the mechanics of farm machinery. At some stage he bought a motor cycle.

It was a Tiger '100'. It hadn't been in his possession for long when he learned that for the relatively modest sum of £25 he could buy a tune-up kit. He bought it, mainly because he thought it would be fun to do and he rather liked the idea of blazing along country lanes on a more than commonly potent machine.

He had watched motor-cycle racing and decided that 'it looked easy'. Consequently, when some of the local lads pulled his leg and more or less dared him to have a go in a race, he showed no reluctance. In 1953 he took part in an event at Castle Combe, and thoroughly enjoyed it.

'It became rather difficult,' he told me. 'To race, one had to go off on a Friday and get back on the Monday. One day my employer told me that if I took the following Friday off I could call in on the Monday and collect my money. I did just that.'

And so, with three races behind him, Bob Anderson the budding farmer gave place to Bob Anderson the professional rider.

In his chosen profession he can very reasonably be regarded as a self-made man. He once borrowed £501 2s. 6d. from his stepfather to buy a Manx Norton. But, he is quick to point out, he repaid the debt to the last penny.

On the whole, and considering he never rode for a works team, he did very well. He was placed on one occasion in the Manx Grand Prix, and on two occasions in the T.T. races. He won a number of other events of international status, and had little cause to complain. There were some people who went so far as to say that his promise put him up in the Surtees-Hailwood-McIntyre class.

At the end of 1960, however, this phase came to an end. In a race out in South Africa he damaged his back. The doctors were unanimous that, whatever else he might decide to do with his life, there must be no more motor-cycle racing.

'In a way I wasn't sorry,' he told me. 'I'd seen so many people killed on bikes.'

He sold his machines, took all his money out of the bank, and bought a Formula Junior Lotus.

Many of the motor-cycling top-liners have tried their skill at motor racing. John Surtees and Bob Anderson are among the very few who can fairly be said to have made it. 'The trouble is,' Anderson said, 'that they are not prepared to start at the bottom. They think that they can just get into a car and drive off. You can't do that. Motor racing's an entirely different medium. I'm sure Surtees realised this.'

Unfortunately, experience sometimes has to be bought at a somewhat steep price. During one of his earlier car races at Aintree, a wheel came off for reasons which have never been explained. It put him out of action for several months. All told in that year of his motor racing apprenticeship he crashed three times, damaged his back on each of them, and once nearly punctured a lung when he broke a rib. It was enough to put anyone off.

But Bob Anderson was commendably undismayed. On each occasion, after the doctors had repaired him, he patiently scooped together the remains of his car and rebuilt it. When the year came to an end his enthusiasm was undiminished.

During 1962 he drove in Formula Junior races for Team Lotus, but his heart was already set on F1.

Regarded in terms of results, his association with Lotus went very creditably. Beneath the surface, however, things weren't so good. He thought that Chapman was pushing him along too quickly. He felt tired from what he was sure was overwork.

At the end of the season he came to a big decision. Somehow he raised enough money to buy a second-hand Lola with a

1·5 litre V8 engine. After the first year he managed to rise to a Brabham chassis, which he has used ever since. When the F1 regulations were changed he invested in an ancient 2·74 litre F.P.F. 4-cylinder unit. 'With a bit of luck,' he said, 'I can get about 240 h.p. out of it, which is a good deal less than the others have.'

One day Bob Anderson promises to write a book in which he will set down the exciting and sometimes bizarre facts of his life. The chapter dealing with his marriage will certainly be worth reading. Mrs. Anderson comes from Le Havre. During a visit to Bedford she attended a dance at the Young Conservatives' Club. Bob Anderson was also present. When, later on, they decided to get married, her parents opposed the match. Things reached such a state that the only solution seemed to be a trip to Gretna Green. But by the time the young couple reached the Scottish border they seem to have got a lot of momentum behind them. At all events, Gretna Green flashed by, and so did several other towns. They finally came to a standstill on Mull, where a local clergyman carried out the rites.

Nowadays, Mrs. Anderson and their daughter Brigitte are the other directors of D.W. Racing Enterprises Ltd., which is the name they give to their motor-racing set-up. Mrs. Anderson does most of the secretarial work, and makes the travel arrangements. With two children to look after, she can seldom get to the circuits. For four years Anderson employed a full-time mechanic, but now he does nearly all the work himself. His friends—especially a farmer and the head of a plant hire firm—help him out when possible. One of them usually manages to accompany him to meetings.

Bob Anderson admits that 'I am very quick-tempered. At races I am irritable, and it gets worse and worse. But it's only momentary. I don't keep it up. Of course I'm nervous before a race. Nobody who isn't a maniac could fail to be—though, on second thoughts, I'm not sure that nervous is the right word. I think it's really excitement.'

I asked him whether he really enjoyed racing. He said: 'Fabulously.'

Which is just as well. All the money, from starting fees and the occasional bonus from his suppliers, goes back into the family company. He draws no salary at all—drinks only the odd beer, and mostly lives a life of almost spartan simplicity.

'There's no time for anything else, anyway,' he told me. 'You work like hell, trying to do the jobs of driver, team manager, mechanic, public relations man, and goodness knows what all. How can there possibly be time for anything else?'

He even adapted the outhouse which is now his workshop, and that included putting a new roof on.

There have, of course, been several occasions when he has had to rebuild his car. One of them occurred at Bulawayo in 1966 after a shunt in practice before the Rhodesian Grand Prix. He was up working all night before the race, had about an hour's sleep in the morning, and then delighted himself and a lot of other people by winning.

There are one or two writers who give Bob Anderson a great deal less than he deserves. They refer disparagingly to his position at the back of the field. If they studied the evidence more clearly they would see what a remarkably large number of times he has finished—and, indeed, has been placed much higher than his uncompetitive machinery ought to allow. Bob Anderson is a fighter. He and Rob Walker are the last of the lone wolves in motor racing. They deserve all the encouragement that anyone can give them.

PART III

End of a Year

21

What Happened in the West

WATKINS GLEN is situated in upstate New York at the end of a long finger of water called Lake Seneca. It's a pleasant place to visit in the autumn. The trees come out in a blaze of reds and russets and bronzes and browns. Anyone with an adequately thick bankroll, who is contemplating an October trip to America, would do well to put it on his list of Places to Visit. No doubt this has figured tolerably high up in the minds of those who organise the United States Grand Prix.

Conceivably those who drive Formula 1 cars pause occasionally to admire the view. I can remember Graham Hill once talking with considerable eloquence about the scenic splendours of Watkins Glen. On the other hand, one is compelled to doubt whether, in a driver's list of priorities, this receives quite such a high rating as the prize money. The Americans are very generous indeed. The total pickings amount to 142,000 dollars—which is more than all the rewards from the other G.P. events put together. But this is not all. He who does the fastest lap in practice feathers his nest to the tune of a further 1,000 dollars, and the fastest lap in the race itself earns somebody yet another 2,000 dollars. Either sum ought comfortably to cover the travel expenses and leave quite a bit to spare.

The race itself is a friendly meeting, and the jovial antics of starter Tex Hopkins add to the atmosphere. As Mr. Hopkins presents the customary view of the chequered flag to the winning driver, it is his habit to jump high in the air. Once, when an inquisitive helicopter was hovering overhead, it looked as if Mr. Hopkins would bang his head on the machine's undercarriage. Fortunately for the Hopkins head, the whirly-bird, and the

U.S. Grand Prix, there was more room than there seemed—and, therefore, no impact.

To experience the delights of the Watkins Glen autumnal tints, and doubtless with eyes on that heap of prize money, eighteen cars and drivers turned up for the 1967 United States Grand Prix. When all was done, only seven of them survived to totter across the finishing line. And totter is just about the right word. The rear suspension of Jim Clark's victorious Lotus was in a parlous condition. On the 105th lap (out of 108) the right-hand side at the rear had collapsed, canting the attendant rear wheel to a quite remarkable angle. Graham Hill (who finished second) had been without a clutch for most of the race, and Denis Hulme (third) came home gasping without so much as a drop of petrol in his tank.

So far as the non-finishers were concerned, their collective list of maladies furnishes a tolerably comprehensive list of all that can go wrong with a racing car. Bruce McLaren's V12 B.R.M. engine, for example, was none the better for an encounter with a patch of oil, which sent the car spinning away on to the grass. The oil and water pipes which pass underneath were ripped away; and, since an engine is seldom at its best without oil or water, that was that.

The battery on John Surtees's Honda went flat (sure, a lot of other uncomfortable things were also taking place within the Honda anatomy, but that was the thing which actually, and finally, stopped it). All three B.R.M.s seemed to be suffering from some nasty automotive variety of the staggers, and none of them was around when the chequered flag fluttered. A bolt came out of Gurney's rear suspension, and that dashed his hopes down on to the track. Chris Amon, who had been disporting his Ferrari and himself with considerable skill and not without success (he was mostly up in second place), came to an unhappy halt on lap 95, when his oil pressure vanished.

Indeed, the outcome of the 1967 United States Grand Prix was not so much a question of the survival of the fittest, as the survival of *anything*. For the sake of the record, however, let us commit to paper the fact that Graham Hill (when he was driving for B.R.M.) had won this race three times in succession, and Jim Clark, too, has now won it three times. Since the race was first organised in 1959, either Clark or Hill has won it on all but three occasions. Furthermore, to keep this paragraph in the realm of *significant facts*, the only 1967 F1 races in which Graham

Hill enjoyed anything approaching success were the Monaco and United States Grands Prix. And these were both events which he had been in the habit of winning.

And then came Mexico. To the credit of the 1967 World Championship series this was not one of those occasions when the outcome is certain long before it's all over, and everybody is inclined to lose interest. Not a bit of it. To be sure, there was no doubt about which team would win the constructors' award: the Repco-Brabhams tied that one up tolerably early on. Of the eleven events, there was only one (the Belgian) in which neither of the cars finished. In all the others, either Hulme or Brabham was in the first three, and in three of them (French, German and Canadian) they took first and second places.

Nevertheless, it was left to the Mexican Grand Prix to decide the outcome of the World Championship. Hulme was in a very strong position to win it, but there was one driver, and one driver only, who could beat him. And that was his employer, Jack Brabham.

To snatch the championship from Hulme, Brabham had to win the Mexican event, and Hulme had to finish no higher than fifth. If this had happened the outcome in terms of points would have been a draw. But a victory at Mexico would have given Brabham three wins (in France, Canada and Mexico) against Hulme's two (at Monaco and Germany), and that would have put Brabham on top.

However, he didn't win—he came second. And Hulme did finish better than fifth. He came third. On his own admission afterwards: 'I wasn't going to rush it. All I had to do was to stick right behind Jack and not let him get away from me—then I'd have it. That's what I did. It goes against the grain, though. It makes for an awfully long and dull race.'

Possibly it does, and not only from the driver's point of view. Still, you can't really blame him.

As a matter of fact, the two Repco-Brabhams had been the favourites for the Mexican Grand Prix. The circuit is over 7,000 feet above sea level and at that altitude the oxygen's getting a bit thin. Just as athletes seem to be threatened with respiratory troubles up there, so is a car's breathing affected. It is very difficult to get the mixture strength right, and something like 25 per cent of the power seems to be missing. This gives an advantage to a low-revving eight-cylinder engine like the Repco over a high-revving V12 or H16.

The race itself was not very exciting. It was won by Jim Clark. Once again Amon was robbed of second place by wretched luck with his car, and Hill's suspension let him down and did him out of a possible victory for what seemed to be the umpteenth time that year.

Denis Hulme went home to Surbiton. He was thirty-one years old, World Champion and, one imagines, a very happy man. He had learnt to drive at the wheel of one of his father's six-ton trucks back in his native New Zealand. He had come to Britain in 1960, sponsored by the New Zealand International Grand Prix Association. The Monaco Grand Prix of 1967 was his first victory in a *grande épreuve*. Now he was right at the top.

Ironically, Jim Clark had won four of the eleven events in the 1967 World Championship series (in Holland, Britain, America and Mexico). This works out at precisely the same number as Hulme's and Brabham's victories put together. Nevertheless, according to the point-scoring system, Clark only finished third in the table. It may seem odd, but there it is.

As a matter of fact, Clark's wins in 1967 brought his total stock of victories scored in Grands Prix up to twenty-five—one more than the number achieved by Fangio. It took Fangio eight years to amass his couple of dozen before he retired at the end of 1957. It took seven years for Clark to collect his twenty-five, though one might reasonably call it six. In 1961, his first year in G.P. racing, he only won the South African event.

You can spend hours playing around with statistics about Grand Prix racing, and I dare say you can use them to prove anything you like. Let us, however, content ourselves with recalling that 1967 was not the only year in which the World Champion was not, coincidentally, the driver to win the most races. When, in 1958, Mike Hawthorn (one G.P. victory that year) captured the top honours, both Moss and Brooks had actually won more of these races (three each). In 1964 John Surtees won the championship with two victories on his list of successes, whereas in that same year Jim Clark won three Grands Prix.

And, finally, Jack Brabham had won fourteen Grands Prix, and been World Champion thrice, whilst Jim Clark, with his twenty-five, had only held the title twice. I'm sure all this proves something, though I'm not at all certain what it is. Nor, at the conclusion of the 1967 season, did such figuring seem to be at all important. Back in Britain there had been happenings galore, which, in their own way, were quite as dramatic as anything which happened on the tracks. Indeed, there were times when the whole future of Formula 1 racing seemed to be in jeopardy.

22

Conclusions Are Not Necessarily Comfortable

One day, just before the Italian Grand Prix of 1967, I was walking down a street in the West End of London. Two young men were coming in the opposite direction. One of them was portly, pink, and bearded. As they passed me, I overheard him say to his companion: 'Of course, *I've* been on the scene a long time.'

At that particular moment I felt that *I'd* been on the scene for far too long a time. Indeed, my admission to the human race seemed to date back to the days when fossils were living, wriggling things without the slightest knowledge that, come a few hundred-thousand years, their petrified shapes would provide kicks for people who dug them up.

The reason for this somewhat sombre reverie was the current Formula 1 motor-racing scene. A year which had begun by being very neat and tidy, with the constructors full of hopes and the drivers loyally pigeon-holed into their respective teams, was (or seemed to be) steadily disintegrating into a state of confusion.

As September inched its way through the calendar, we passed into what I can only describe as 'The Zone of No Comment'— or, at any rate, not very much of it. The Formula 1 circus was making all the noises of a volcano which doesn't want, actually, to erupt—but, none the less, doesn't want to lose status. The sounds were ominous enough, and yet it was almost impossible to pull one warm fact out of the steaming crater.

Several drivers were known to be dissatisfied with their present employers, largely because they hadn't won any Grand Prix races and hadn't finished in very many. This, as a number of them not unreasonably pointed out, was not their fault so much as the shortcomings of their machinery.

There were, of course, rumours galore. One, which seemed plausible enough, was that Honda might retire from motor racing altogether. The car, even with the mechanical and driving skill of John Surtees behind it, had been remarkably uncompetitive until it won the Italian G.P. This was largely because there'd been trouble back at the factory in Japan. The firm's production-car programme had been getting behind hand. Men had to be pulled away from the racing-car project and shunted into the manufacturing departments. The Formula 1 chances had perished not from lack of ability but from neglect by the works.[1]

But the event which really triggered off this period of uncertainty had been reported in the newspapers towards the end of August. Much to most people's surprise, and to the dismay of several interested parties, BP announced that it intended to pull out of motor racing at the end of the year. The decision was described as 'an economy measure'.

The Arab-Israeli war, the closure of the Suez Canal and soaring crude-oil prices had put a particularly heavy burden on BP's economy. Obviously there had to be cuts somewhere. The first to be announced no doubt caused a minor riot among children of the company's employees. Hitherto they had been treated by a benevolent management to an annual binge at Christmas. Now, to save money, there was to be an end to these parties. Quite how much money was saved by a few hundred unordered trifles, jellies, crackers, and what-have-you was never announced.

On the motor-racing front the saving was published at £500,000 a year, though there were some fringe experts who darkly put the figure at less. Certainly, one doubts whether the withdrawal from motor racing and the cancelled Christmas beanos can have made any appreciable dent in the mountain of financial worries (£100 million, according to one estimate) occasioned by the crude-oil situation. But perhaps this wasn't the point. I have to confess that I am not in the confidence of the top men at BP—and, even if I were, it's unlikely that I'd be able to publish anything they told me in such circumstances. Nevertheless, one cannot escape the conclusion that the real purpose was to make it clear that BP was doing *something*.

1. As it turned out, Honda did not retire after all.

Nobody, of course, knows which set of interests on the BP board actually wielded the knife. A popular theory points to the Government faction, and this seems reasonable enough. Until not so very long ago, the British Government, by holding 51 per cent of the shares, actually controlled BP. In 1967, however, BP took over the chemical and plastics interests of the Distillers' Company. Stockholders in the latter were given a fresh issue of shares in the petroleum company. H.M.G. was not involved in this deal. Consequently, their share in BP was reduced to less than 50 per cent (probably about 48 per cent). Even so, it would have needed a unanimous vote by the other interests to block the proposal. Furthermore, on the lines of its thinking at the time, the Government may well have regarded motor racing as a useless frivolity, which could well be dispensed with.[1]

The one pleasing aspect of the whole business was the line taken by several of the newspapers and magazines which reported it. They praised BP's participation in the past, and they paid very timely tributes to the work done by the oil companies' motor-racing representatives. *Motor* had several kind words to say about Denis Druitt, who had looked after BP's motor-racing interests for the past fourteen years, and so had David Benson in the *Daily Express*.

Wrote Mr. Benson: 'The fact is, the men from the trade put far more into motor racing than would be expected of them in more humdrum jobs. They travel constantly, seldom see their families, often work a twenty-four hour day.

'Denis Druitt of BP is a man so familiar on the world's race tracks that it would be almost impossible to start a meeting without him.

'And one wonders if Jim Clark and Graham Hill would ever get into a racing car without Esso's Geoffrey Murdoch to look after them. He makes sure they are at the circuit in plenty of time, that they are not unduly worried by "hangers-on" before a race and they are suitably fed and relaxed by the time they get on to the grid.

'Britain has won supremacy over Europe's cars and drivers in the last fifteen years mainly because of the enthusiastic support of the trade.'

1. To my almost certain knowledge, Mrs. Barbara Castle, current Minister of Transport, has never seen a motor race and has declined all invitations to do so.

CONCLUSION

And so, to borrow a phrase minted by one of its competitors, that was BP that was! Cooper-Maserati, Honda, Rob Walker, and others suddenly knew that one of their prime economic supports was about to be pulled away from beneath them. Admittedly, BP had left it open to their operating companies throughout the world to carry on with motor sport, though strictly on a national basis. This was possibly good news for the organisers of local rallies and hillclimbs. From the point of view of people concerned with racing and rallying internationally it was useless.

Shortly after the BP announcement I spoke to Roy Salvadori on the telephone. He said: 'This is terribly serious. Without support from the oil barons we can't go motor racing.'

There were others who, at the time, took a more optimistic view. They prophesied that there were other oil companies waiting on the sidelines, which would happily take BP's place. Among those mentioned were Elf, Gulf and Castrol.

Dutifully, I investigated. Elf, which is a state-owned French petroleum company, certainly was interested in participation, but only in so far as it concerned a French revival in Formula 1 racing. For some time it had been known that the French Government was prepared to subsidise such an endeavour. The two favourites for the receipt of funds were Renault-Alpine, which had an excellent record in the Le Mans 24-Hour race behind them, and were known to be working on a 3 litre F1 engine, and Matra. Matra had produced a car which, powered variously by B.R.M. and Ford-Cosworth engines, had acquitted itself increasingly well in Formula 2 events.

The logical solution appeared to be an alliance between Renault-Alpine and Matra, with the former providing the engine and the latter the car. Political interests, however and so far as anyone could tell, were against this. State support went to Matra on the strict understanding that this should be, so far as possible, an all-French venture. The new car was likely to be ready in time for the 1968 season. Jean Beltoise and Servoz Gavin were hotly tipped as the drivers. Michelin were producing racing tyres for the project, and Elf (what more naturally) would supply fuel, lubricants, and cash.

All of which cancelled out Elf as a fairy godmother (to maintain the whimsy inspired by the name) to any of the more distressed protagonists on the far side of the English Channel.

Gulf for quite a time had been the subject of rumours, most

of which—to judge from a conversation which I had with one of their public-relations executives—were entirely false. He told me: 'This year we did supply fuels and lubricants for the Mirage as an experimental deal, and we may pursue the same course next year. But, as far as I can see, any participation in Formula 1 is out of the question.'

And that left Castrol. Castrol has a strong motor-sport tradition which stems from its founder, Lord Wakefield, who supported numerous air and land record bids during the years between the wars. The company was known to be a big spender in the fields of motor-cycle racing and rallies (both the B.M.C. and Ford rally teams used its products). Furthermore, it was this firm which came to Dan Gurney's aid, after he had spent half a year in the wilderness with backing from Goodyear tyres, but none (apart from handouts of oil, petrol, and bonus money from Shell) from a petroleum company. Was the alliance with Gurney the sign of a quickening interest in Formula 1 by Castrol? Could it be, as some people suggested, that the firm might divert some of its money from the motor-cycling scene and use it to shore up the flagging fortunes of previously BP-supported teams and drivers?

The atmosphere of that particular period was so fraught with drama that the Castrol spokesman I talked to was understandably wary of candour. Time and again he bit off slices of sentences and swallowed them before they could reach me. Nevertheless, he was prepared to feed me the following: 'We feel at present that rallying is of more benefit to us. The average motorist associates himself more with Paddy Hopkirk, say, than with Jim Clark. The former's car is the same shape as those which you see on the roads. There's no point in winning motor-sport events unless you tell the public about it. When Paddy Hopkirk wins the Monte we can cash in on it.'

And: 'At the moment we're formulating plans . . . I can't disclose them . . . I wouldn't dare.' He did conclude by saying that 'Policy is something you have to change with the market', but he left me with no expectation that the market was about to dictate a big spending spree in the world of Formula 1.

When BP disengaged itself from international motor sport the motoring correspondent of the *Daily Telegraph* wrote: 'There has been a growing feeling among the oil companies in recent years that teams and drivers were jeopardising future support by demanding unrealistic fees.' This, though it's unlikely, might have provided the inspiration for the next bombshell which burst on the already feverish motor-racing scene.

I had been away at the time. When I got back somebody said: 'Did you see that bit about Firestone?' I pointed out that I hadn't seen any newspapers for at least a week and was told: 'They're pulling out of motor racing.'

This seemed to be the ultimate catastrophe. Whatever the oil companies might decide, the tyre companies appeared certain. Indeed, the competition between them to sign on constructors and drivers seemed to be very nearly as intense as that which raged through the races themselves. And now—this!

I picked up the telephone and got through to Firestone's public-relations people. The following conversation ensued:

Me: What's all this about you pulling out of motor racing?

The Firestone Man: Firestone pulling out of motor racing? Rubbish!

Me: That's what it said in the papers.

The Firestone Man: You don't believe everything you read in them, do you? What we've done is decided to put a stop to this bidding game. We'll keep on with our existing contracts and servicing, but we're hitting out against the ever soaring retaining fee. We only have contracts with teams—we don't believe in drivers' contracts. We're doing drastic pruning. We're not going to be forced to the wall.

The dramas were still not over. As the mess of rumours and counter-rumours seemed to be clearing away, and the semblance of a picture appearing, Esso blew everything into confusion once more. On Friday, October 20th, just as the Grand Prix circus was arriving in Mexico City for the last race in the 1967 series, they announced that they, too, were quitting the ranks of oil-company sponsors.

According to the *Sun*'s report, the news was given by Mr. Frank Bowen, director and general manager of the company. He was quoted as saying: 'We deeply regret having to take this step but, despite the fact that we have been the most successful petroleum company in terms of Grand Prix honours in recent years, an operation of this sort is immensely difficult to support in terms of growing competitive and economic pressures.'

As soon as I'd read the press accounts, I telephoned Esso. 'Yes,' a public-relations man said, 'it is perfectly true. Yes, it's a question of increasing economic and competitive pressures. Suez? It's a contributing factor, but that's all.'

And so, suddenly, on that grey October day when it was trying hard to drizzle, and a row over bonuses for railway guards was playing havoc with the trains, and the dockers were still on strike, and everything seemed to be more than usually in the same old mess, Team Lotus and Jack Brabham found themselves without the prospect of a sponsoring oil company for 1968. Esso's contribution to the two teams was estimated at £30,000 each—plus perks in the way of research, free fuel and oil, and so on. It had doubtless been very nice while it lasted: but now – bang, nothing!

After talking to the Esso spokesman I phoned Phil Kerr, Brabham's manager. 'What's going to happen?' I asked.

'You tell me,' he said. 'I wish I knew. You can't go motor racing without any support. It's too expensive.'

I wished him luck, which was the least I could do, and tried to get hold of somebody at Lotus. Everybody who might have known anything was either away at the Motor Show, or else in Mexico. Not that it mattered much. As I learned afterwards, the situation there was just as uncertain as it was at Brabham's.

At the beginning of the season there had been three major oil companies sponsoring Formula 1 motor racing: Shell, BP and Esso. Now only Shell was left. Admittedly Elf was about to come on to the scene, but only to look after the Matras. There was, indeed, a certain amount of scepticism as to how Elf would manage to provide fuel for their entrants at Mexico and other events outside Europe. However, we'll let that pass. The important thing at the time was: what would Shell do?

Back to the telephone. 'At the moment Shell's policy remains unchanged,' I was told. 'You mean to go on supporting motor racing?' I asked. 'I mean just what I said,' the P.R. man said.

I gave him the benefit of the doubt. It seemed to me very likely that they would stay on in the sport, and what an intriguing situation it posed! Unless something very unexpected occurred they'd be able to take their pick from nearly all the greatest F1 cars and drivers in the world. The prospect suggested a feast of possibilities such as no oil company had ever looked upon before. Clearly, whatever bargaining they cared to do would be done from a position of enormous strength.

Firestone's action may have been an attempt to put a stop to the bidding game. Esso's withdrawal clinched it. The days of the easy money, the fat retainer, and top drivers receiving

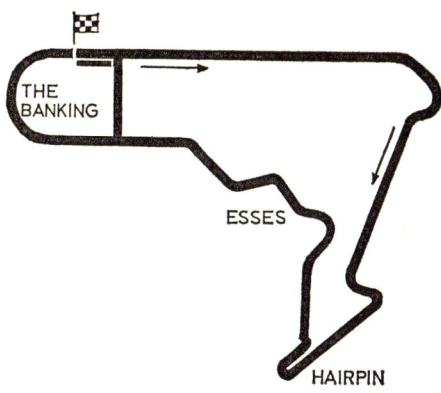

Mexico

enormously high fees were over. Formula 1 had suddenly become a Cinderella of the sports world.

Earlier on in this book, you may recall, I gave the opinion that, if necessary, the very enthusiasm of those taking part in motor racing would keep it going. Now we would see. With the tree stripped bare of so much cash, a prodigious amount of enthusiasm would be needed.

But before we shed too many tears let's look at it from another angle. What kind of return have the oil companies been getting for their money? Obviously, there have to be some rewards from such large investments. After all, if one is going to support charities, there are many better ones.

Opportunities for research, a lively image, pull with the younger generation, persuasive advertising based on the successes of their protégés, these are some of the answers. On the other hand, and with the possible exception of golf (though here sponsorship is confined to prize money), no other sport has received hand-outs on the scale of motor racing. In the entertainment industry the only thing comparable is a theatre which has received a whopping great subsidy from the Arts Council.

Naturally, the larger the attendance at Formula 1 meetings, the less need there is for any form of financial aid. Is there any way in which even bigger turn-outs could be achieved? The next step in my enquiry took me to the office of a psychologist friend of mine, David Gordon, who has carried out studies in a number of European countries, trying to discover what it is about the sport which attracts people.

He told me: 'People go to a Formula 1 race because it's exciting. There's the roar of the engines and the speed. Speed is power—human beings have always been fascinated by it. But there's very little question of spectators trying to identify themselves completely with the drivers.

'On the other hand, there must be some degree of identification; for the driver and his performance express the spectator's own wish for courage, control and power. In a sense, the spectator experiences a fantasy. He sees somebody which he can dream of being, but could never hope to be in reality. This part-identification is essential if the spectator's going to experience any excitement.

'Without it, he'd probably regard motor racing in much the same way as a visitor to an art gallery looks at a famous painting. There'd be satisfaction and joy—yes. But he wouldn't be carried away by a consuming interest and excitement.

'It is precisely this fantasy type of identification, this feeling that "I'd love to be like this driver, but it's quite beyond my reach and capabilities", which mitigates against the practical success of oil companies' sponsorship of motor racing. People can't go away from an event feeling that they'd be able, in their own lives, to apply the lessons they've learnt, or to use the same cars, tyres, or even the petrol used in the race.'

According to Mr. Gordon, the spectators take one of two views of the drivers. 'Some think that they are daredevils,' he said. 'Men who don't place much value on their lives – who are prepared to die.

'The other view is that daredevils are stupid people, and racing drivers aren't among them. This school considers that a racing driver is a man who's completely in control of his machine. He's a man of iron will, a master.'

Ninety per cent of the fun, of course, lies in taking sides. 'If there isn't a suitable driver for you to back,' Mr. Gordon said, 'you have to invent a reason for backing someone else. You need to. You need to suffer with him and enjoy success with him. The fun is saying "I want So-and-so to win". You have to find someone to take sides with.'

True to the Castrol viewpoint (though Mr. Gordon has never been employed by them), he believes that ordinary motorists find it much easier to identify themselves with rally cars and drivers. Furthermore, they're able to do it more completely.

When you discuss the motivation of going to a motor-racing meeting, you inevitably come across one or two people who see the whole thing as a mass yearning for a blood-bath. 'What people want to see is crashes,' they say. In America they have tried to pander to this supposition by inventing a contest which consists entirely of crashing cars. The vehicle which survives this clanging ordeal of colliding metal is the winner.

As a matter of fact, anyone who attends these orgies of automotive *gotterdammerung* in the hope of seeing blood being spilt is likely to be disappointed. Human casualty figures are said to be a good deal lower than those for more orthodox forms of motor sport (if 'sport', in this instance, is the right word).

Mr. Gordon's view is that motor-racing spectators do *not* want to see people hurt. 'Indeed,' he said, 'when there are accidents they want to know that nothing serious has happened. Anyway, if you're thinking of the gladiators of ancient Rome, motor racing would be very unsatisfactory to the kind of audiences who watched them.'

You may care to compare your own reactions with those laid down in what we may, perhaps, describe as the Gordon Proposition.

If Mr. Gordon is right in his suggestion that the things people go for at Formula 1 events are the roar of the engines, the speed and the power, it is tempting to wonder whether, in all honesty, the present interpretation of the formula contains the best ingredients of spectator appeal. Admittedly, the cars (when they go) are the ultimate in power and, no less, the drivers in skill and courage. On the other hand, one has only to look at films and pictures of the old racers to see that the present cigar tubes on wheels make much less impact on the imagination.

Look at any of the photographs of cars in this book, and then compare them with such projectiles as the Auto-Unions that Ferdinand Porsche designed, the whopping red Alfas, and the thunderous pre-war Mercedes. The same applies to many of the post-war cars (the original B.R.M., the Maseratis, and the early Ferraris), until one is compelled to conclude that, whereas tucking the engine away at the stern may have been the correct thing technically, it robbed the sport of much of its visual pleasure.

To some extent, one might launch a similar argument about the drivers. F1 racing drivers are the stars in what might be regarded as a spectacular and somewhat dangerous branch of show business. Like other stars, they should attract popular followings. A few of them, notably Graham Hill (who has been dubbed 'one of the last great characters of the sport'), do. Most do not. Thereby they lend support to the not infrequent suggestions that colourful personalities went out of motor racing with the death or retirement of such men as Peter Collins, Stirling Moss, Mike Hawthorn, Taffy von Trips, and others who, like their cars, were slightly larger than life. There are drivers today who, far from encouraging personal publicity, actually go to some lengths to avoid it. No other entertainment industry could endure such an attitude for very long.

Life would be a good deal more comfortable if famines were attended by diminishing appetites, but, as any Oxfam worker will tell you, that isn't so. Nor does it necessarily follow that when there's a marked absence of eager sponsors the demand for trade munificence will necessarily decline. In fact, at the end of 1967 quite the opposite was happening.

When the 3 litre formula was introduced in 1965 there were many who seriously doubted whether there would be enough cars to make up a starting grid. Two years later it seemed as if there would probably be too many. No fewer than twelve teams had announced their intention of going into F1 racing in 1968. Things had reached such a condition that, in the opinion of one informed observer, 'it looks as if we may even see works teams having to compete for a start in the Monaco Grand Prix'.

Most of the newcomers were obviously going to be sorely pressed for funds, but that was only one of their worries. The other was lack of drivers. Whilst there are many good ones, there is only about half a dozen who can be counted upon to win a Grand Prix event.

The death of Bandini and the injury of Mike Parkes had cut back the Ferrari ranks until only Chris Amon was left on the F1 side. Richie Ginther's retirement and the apparent inability to coax Foyt across the Atlantic had left Dan Gurney in a scarcely less enviable position. At one time, indeed, everybody except Lotus and Honda and Brabham seemed to be shopping for drivers, with Jackie Ickx the only newcomer of proven talent to join the Formula 1 fold.

And then, as if to make things even more complicated, along came Ken Tyrrell.

Tyrrell is, from all points of view, a remarkable person. He is an extraordinarily nice chap. He has built himself what must be a very prosperous business out of the felling and selling of trees.

This provides him with enough money to indulge his ruling passion in life—motor racing.

For most of the time he has confined his entries to Formulae 2 and 3, and in this respect he has probably contributed as much to the sport as any other individual. If you ask him about it he'll deny any pretensions as a father figure to up-and-coming young drivers, but the fact is that there are several Tyrrell discoveries gracing the current scene. Indirectly, both Bruce McLaren and John Surtees benefited from Tyrrell's help during their early days in British motor racing. More recently, Jackie Stewart was given his first single-seater driving opportunity by Tyrrell in Formula 3, and that, as everyone knows, led to a contract with B.R.M. after his first (brilliantly successful) season.

Tyrrell recalls the day at Goodwood when he gave Stewart a trial in a new F3 Cooper.

'Jackie had never been in a single-seater before,' he says. 'I lectured him. I said: "Take it steady. We've got all day. Don't go too quickly." He went off and by the third lap he was equalling Bruce McLaren's time. Bruce was also there that day, testing another Cooper. I called Jackie in and gave him another lecture. Then he went off again and went even faster.'

It seems that McLaren had been watching all this from Madgwick, which is one of Goodwood's trickier corners. He came over to the pits. 'This is ridiculous,' he told Tyrrell with a grin. 'I've never seen anything like it.'

'You think a car won't go any faster until somebody else makes it go faster,' Tyrrell continues the story. 'That's how it was that day with Bruce. He got into his car and knocked some seconds off his lap time. Then Jackie knocked off some more seconds. I called him back to the pits for the third time. "This is not a motor race!" I told him.'

Also present at Madgwick was John Cooper. Now he came running over. He took Tyrrell by the arm and said in a conspiratorial whisper: 'Sign that bloke on, quick.' Tyrrell, as it happened, needed no bidding. Jackie Stewart's future was assured.

Two of Ken Tyrrell's other discoveries are Jackie Ickx, the young wonder driver from Belgium, and the Matra. Matra swam into the Tyrrell orbit entirely by chance. He happened to be in Paris attending a reception at the end of the 1965 season. Standing next to him was a gentleman who turned out to be the managing director of Matra Sport. At the time Tyrrell hardly knew that it existed. The two men fell into conversation and the upshot was that a week later an F2 Matra arrived at Gatwick airport. It was hurried off to Goodwood, where Stewart was waiting to test it.

Stewart's verdict at the end of several laps was: 'This is the finest we've had. It puts more power on the road than any other car I've driven.' Tyrrell bought two. He installed a B.R.M. engine in one and a Ford-Cosworth in the other. Stewart and Ickx raced them throughout the 1966 Formula 2 season. In 1967, this time with Ford-Cosworth engines in both of them, they raced again, and Ickx won the European Trophy for F2 drivers.

Formula 1 is the summit of a racing driver's ambition, for there is nothing higher, nothing beyond it. It is also, one has to assume, the world in which every entrant would like to compete. Ken Tyrrell was no exception. When, during the late summer of 1967, he was offered a pair of Ford-Cosworth F1 engines, he accepted the proposition with glee. Matra were prepared to build him F1 cars to put them in. All that he needed was a couple of drivers and some sponsorship.

Ever since his Formula 3 days Jackie Stewart had been driving Formula 2 cars for Tyrrell when he was not otherwise engaged for B.R.M. Apart from saloon-car racing, and the F1 stint he put in for Cooper-Maserati after Pedro Rodriguez had injured himself at Enna, Ickx was also a Tyrrell man. And when Tyrrell was considering whether to upgrade himself into Formula 1 both of these highly talented drivers were pretty hot properties.

B.R.M. were obviously not at all anxious to lose Stewart. Enzo Ferrari was known to be bidding for him—just as he was also giving the come hither sign to Ickx. When the master of Maranello beckons it is not customary for the chosen one to refuse. Nevertheless, Stewart turned history upside down. He did what can hardly ever have been done before. He declined the maestro's offers, and opted to sign on with Ken Tyrrell. Whatever his motives may have been, and they are not the business of this book, his decision did little to ease an already difficult situation. Too many cars were chasing too few crack drivers; and here was one of the world's best performers joining a private team of which the owner was a newcomer to Formula 1. Furthermore, as if to confound the Ferrari legend of infallability, Jackie Ickx was also hesitating. He was very guarded about what he said at the time, but one had the feeling that his sympathies were on the side of Tyrrell.

On the face of it, it may sound simple enough—as if the same old firm was still in business, only this time they'd be operating Formula 1 cars instead of Formula 2. Unfortunately it doesn't quite work out like this, and there must be several people who very much rued the day that Ken Tyrrell got his hands on a 3 litre Ford-Cosworth engine, or the day when fortune placed him next to the Matra chief executive at that Paris reception.

And so the United States and Mexican Grands Prix were run, and Denis Hulme received the accolade of World Champion, just as a good many people hoped he would, and the year crept into November, which is one of the very few months (indeed, now I come to think of it, about the only one) when comparatively little happens in motor racing. Admittedly the policy-formers are up to their necks in policy-forming, the crackle of contracts is heard in the land, and the engineers are wondering what the hell went wrong with their machines and how they can be made more powerful, more reliable, more everything, for the coming year. For drivers, however, it is a month of relative peace, when they can actually enjoy the comfort of their homes for days on end.

23

What Happened in the End

THE year 1967 came to an end in a flurry of snow. On New Year's Day, the first event in the 1968 World Championship series took place in South Africa. It was won by Jim Clark, with his Lotus team mate Graham Hill taking second place.

Throughout the first half of winter, the eruption, which had brought such drama to the inner circles of Formula 1, continued. There were all manner of comings and goings, of rumours and counter-rumours, of teams in search of contracts, and of contracts hunting for drivers. Now, at last, some semblance of a picture was emerging.

Jackie Ickx didn't sign with Ken Tyrrell, for the very simple reason that, although the latter had found a petrol company (Elf) to back him, he hadn't enough cars. Matra could only supply him with a couple, and it is a simple truth about Formula 1 racing that, if you propose to race two cars, you need at least three.

This released Ickx from what might have been regarded as a moral obligation to Tyrrell; and left him free to sign with Ferrari—a state of affairs which must have pleased the Maestro of Maranello very much indeed.

Another newcomer to the Ferrari team was a young Italian driver named Andrea de Adamich, who, in 1967, had put up a very brave show behind the steering wheels of Alfa Romeos. And so, with Chris Amon, Jackie Ickx and Andrea de Adamich, there were, once again, to be three Ferraris on the starting grids.

Denis Hulme, now reigning World Champion, had also been on the move. At some point towards the end of 1967, his employer, Jack Brabham, enticed Jochen Rindt away from

Cooper's. Brabham isn't given to making announcements, but it might be a reasonable supposition to think that he proposed to retire as a driver—leaving Hulme and Rindt to drive his cars during the coming year. He had, when all is said and done, reached the great age of 42. However, this is only guesswork. The important thing is that, while Brabham was negotiating with Rindt, Denis Hulme had been busy in North America, driving for Bruce McLaren. Between the two of them, these two intrepid New Zealanders had more or less wiped the board in the Can-Am series of sports car races.

Indeed, Hulme had been so impressed by the way in which McLaren went racing, that he made it perfectly clear that, if the latter wished it, he would be more than content to join his Formula 1 team.

McLaren did wish it. He was proposing to race two cars in 1968, and they promised to be infinitely better than any he had used in Formula 1 before. Both were to be completely new designs, built around Ford-Cosworth engines, looking longer, lower and far more athletic than his previous machines. Just by way of a change, they were to be painted orange.[1]

There's an old saying to the effect that, if you shift a pebble at one point on the coastline, all the other pebbles change places and the effect becomes apparent (assuming you make a study of these things) hundreds of miles away. It is much the same thing with drivers. Stewart had left B.R.M. to join Tyrrell, and so B.R.M. had to find a replacement. The eye of Tony Rudd alighted on Pedro Rodriguez, who had made a very praiseworthy effort in the somewhat less than competitive Cooper-Maserati cars of 1967. Rodriguez, always looking for what he calls 'the good car—the good machinery', rated his chances more highly with B.R.M. than with Cooper's, and signed the proffered contract.

With Rindt moving across to the Brabham camp and Rodriguez snug in the arms of B.R.M., Cooper now had two vacancies. They invited Scarfiotti and Brian Redman to fill them. The two drivers accepted.

As I may have suggested, Cooper's were not entirely happy about their engine situation. During the long winter of 1967, they shed Maserati and bought B.R.M. V12s. 'But,' Jonathan

---

1. McLaren seems to be restless about colour. An FIA booklet, in a somewhat vain attempt to pin his colour scheme down, eventually gave up in despair and printed 'Keeps changing'.

Sieff told me at a meeting early in 1968, 'we may eventually get Alfa Romeos.'

Honda, contrary to a certain amount of expectation, did not withdraw from motor racing. In fact, the Japanese team made plans to race two cars in 1968, and signed on Chris Irwin to drive the second. They did, however, give up motor-cycle racing. It had served its purpose. They had helped themselves to a very large proportion of the market, and they couldn't reasonably expect to gain any more advantage from taking part in the sport. One must assume that the marketing emphasis was now swinging round to the cars. A cluster of Grand Prix victories might very well produce the same boost to the sales of their little minis and sports cars as their racing on two wheels had achieved for their motor-cycles.

If the drivers were on the move, so were some of the managers and designers. Much to everybody's surprise, Roy Salvadori decided to quit the Cooper camp. Derek White, the Cooper designer, also left—to join forces with John Surtees and Lola. McLaren's designer, Robin Herd, having designed the McLaren cars for 1968, departed for Ford-Cosworth and thereby aroused a lot of interesting speculations about the future of Lotus and Ford.

As if to make McLaren's team an all-New Zealand project, Phil Kerr also left Brabham and followed Denis Hulme into the McLaren camp, where he became joint managing director.

Down in Italy, Franco Lini gave up his job as Ferrari's racing manager and returned to journalism. However, right at the beginning of the 1968 season, he made a fairly substantial contribution to the array of Grand Prix hardware.

One of the odd things about the World Championship of Drivers used to be that, in spite of all the fame that winning it aroused, there was no actual trophy. Franco Lini's paper, *Autosprint*, put matters to right by providing one. Thus, at the Race of Champions at Brands Hatch in March, 1968, there was Lini with this sumptuous object, hewn from gold, and presenting it to Denis Hulme.

This race, incidentally, was the subject of one of those disputes which are not unknown in motor-racing circles. On this occasion, it had to do with advertising.

Earlier, the Royal Automobile Club had withdrawn its age-old embargo on advertisements appearing on the bodies of racing cars. The F.I.A. observed that each national automobile club could make up its own mind in this respect, but suggested that the R.A.C.'s ruling was not a bad one to follow. It stipulated that an announcement should be no more than fifty-five square inches in area, and that people mustn't cheat. In other words, you could not (say) devote one space to the word 'Coca' and another to 'Cola'. Player's, the cigarette company, were the first to cash in on this opportunity. In return for a reported sum of £100,000, they persuaded Lotus to rename its cars 'Gold Leaf Lotus', and to repaint them in the colours which appear on the Player's Gold Leaf cigarette packs.

Then the trouble started. The management of Brands Hatch, where the first F1 race of the new season was scheduled to take place, says that something like 50 per cent of its income comes from the sale of television rights. Unfortunately, the two TV companies involved wanted no part in any advertising which might appear on cars. The B.B.C. pointed to a rule which shuns publicity in any shape or form on its programmes. Independent television, on the other hand, explained that, since its income comes from commercials, it certainly wasn't prepared to provide anyone with free advertising in the form of notices on cars.

For a brief while, it looked as if the management of Brands Hatch would be unable to sell the TV rights and the race might have to be abandoned. Common sense, however, did its customary trick of prevailing. It was agreed that products used on the cars (tyres, sparking plugs, and so on) could be advertised in this way. So far as Player's were concerned, they settled for the fact that 'Gold Leaf' was part of the car's name and that, therefore, it was permissible to write these words on the body. Nor could there be any objection to the 'Gold Leaf' colour scheme.

However, the TV companies drew the line at the sailor, which is the Player's trade mark. That was totally out of order and so, for the purposes of motor racing in the U.K., a TV requirement was that a small circle of black should be pasted over this long-suffering seaman's face. It may sound childish and it probably is.

Finally—Rob Walker. He had a new car ready for 1968, powered by a Ford-Cosworth engine and with all the elements of being competitive. And then, in practice for the Race of Champions, Joe Siffert spun off the track. He was unhurt, but the car was very badly damaged. It was taken back on the transporter to Walker's racing shop at Dorking.

On the Saturday night before the race, the shop caught fire. The blaze devoured just about everything, including the F1 car and a beautiful old Delage sports car, which Walker had been in the process of restoring.[1]

But motor racing takes no heed of disappointment or even tragedy. It is tough and relentless. It goes on, no matter what has happened. As this book comes to its conclusion, the Grand Prix circus is getting ready for the first European Grand Prix of 1968, which will be at Madrid. The story is beginning all over again.

Looking back on my journeys with the Grand Prix circus in 1967, I find that I remember all manner of small things. Some of them are rather poignant, such as just before the Monaco Grand Prix, when I happened to notice how extremely well turned out Bandini looked. And there was the time when, in a hotel at Nurburg, I borrowed some of Pedro Rodriguez's tabasco sauce—a commodity he never travels without, for he finds European food underflavoured for his Mexican palate. Something else he never travels without is an extraordinary assortment of head-cold remedies. Possibly it's because he was reared in the aseptic, 7,000 feet above sea level, air of Mexico City, but young Mr. Rodriguez is a constant victim of these ailments.

I remember a small suitcase in the cockpit of Bruce McLaren's car at Monza, which made it look rather as if he were about to drive it away for a weekend by the sea; and I remember the time when, down in the A.A.R. headquarters at Rye, I actually shook hands with Juan Manuel Fangio (I was so impressed that afterwards I considered putting a commemorative plaque on my palm).

But, do you know, I can't remember a single statistic about a race. They are all written down in my notebooks, but none of them has remained in my head. That, perhaps, reflects the purpose of this book. It is, on the whole, anti-statistics and very much for people. They are the real commodities of motor racing, the creators of the excitement, the pathos, the occasional comedy and the perpetual determination, which make up the drama of the struggle for the World Championship of Drivers. People are what, in the last analysis, it's all about.

1. Walker's fortunes soon took a turn for the better. With Siffert driving a brand new Lotus, he won the 1968 British Grand Prix.

Epilogue

How does one give a book such as this a tidy ending? The politics of motor racing form and reform situations, rather like those pictures one sometimes sees of cells multiplying. Even as one writes this sentence, something, somewhere, is occurring, or has just occurred, or is being contrived to occur. We shall have to leave them to get on with it.

Unhappily, there is another aspect to motor racing, and one which is the only way of evaluating the real cost of the sport. Catastrophe. It seems to come in phases. For a while, there are no very serious accidents, and the worst disaster is a broken leg and a bent car. It is bad enough, possibly, but not final.

When Bandini was killed in the Monaco Grand Prix of 1967, it seemed to stun people. No ace of his magnitude had been killed in action for several years.

Nevertheless, one now looks back on 1967 almost with gratitude, as if it were a merciful season. Apart from the deaths of Bandini and Anderson, it did nothing to herald the horrors which were to come.

On April 7th, 1968, Jim Clark was competing in a Formula 2 race at Hockenheim in Germany. The track had been drenched by rain. Taking a relatively fast bend, something (it may have been a tyre—we shall never know precisely what it was) went wrong with the car. He shot off the circuit, into a wood, and crashed into a tree.

Jim Clark, the greatest driver of his age—and, conceivably, of any other—was dead.

The entire motor-racing world was more shaken than it cared to admit. The myth that genius is proof against disaster had been shattered. If this could happen to Clark, the man who always walked away from his smashes, the driver who was faster *and* safer than anyone else; if this could happen to him ... then every man jack who went anywhere near a racing car was in jeopardy.

They buried Jim Clark in the tiny churchyard at Duns in Berwickshire. Everyone mourned him after his own fashion. Perhaps the most moving tribute came from his own mechanics. They chartered a DC3 out of their own money to fly up to the funeral.

But the horrible toll was not yet done. Chris Irwin was seriously injured while practising for a race at Nurburgring. Mike Spence was killed while practising for the Indianapolis '500'. Ludovico Scarfiotti died after crashing a Porsche on a hill climb in Europe.

People presently turn their backs on the dead, and go off to watch the next race. But the dead are always with us: whenever their names are mentioned, we are reminded that motor racing is the most ruthless sport of them all. Clark, Spence, Scarfiotti— none of them was killed in a Formula 1 event, but that is probably a mere coincidence. There is no logic about the slaughter of a race track. It is mindless, usually inexplicable, and always unexpected. With death continually waiting in the wings, one can only admire the—what is it? Courage? The ability to exclude such thoughts? The enthusiasm which is so great that it transcends fear? Whatever it is, we can only admire it and consider that, with such a shadow upon them, these men earn every cent they are paid, for theirs is surely one of the most hazardous occupations of all.

Index

Adenauer, Dr. Konrad, 32
Aintree circuit, 117, 170
Aix les Bains bridge disaster, 13
Alfa Romeo organisation and cars, 6, 7, 8, 142, 143, 189
All American Racers Inc. (A.A.R.), 108–15, 121, *see also* Gurney, Dan
Amon, Chris, 23, 25, 37, 57, 69, 71–2, 73, 74, 90, 105, 106, 107, 116, 121, 122, 139, 150, 151, 152, 153, 157–8, 176, 178, 190
anatomy of a Grand Prix, 116–23
Anderson, Bob, 40, 57, 148, 159, 166–72
Anderson, Brigitte, 171
Anderson, Mrs., 166, 171
Argentine Grand Prix, 12–13, 165; 1953 disaster, 13
Ascari, Alberto, 6, 9–10, 14, 16
Ascari, Antonio, 9, 82
Atkins, Cyril, 55
Attwood, Richard, 20, 22, 26, 129, 148, 165
Automobilclub von Deutschland, 136
Automobile Club d'Italia, 3, 5
Automobile Club de l'Ouest, 100, 101, 102
Auto-Union, 7, 189

Baghetti, 150
Bandini, Lorenzo, 16, 21, 37, 54, 55, 56, 105, 150, 152, 190
Bandini, Mrs., 157
Baracca, Francesco, 142–3
Behra, Jean, 13, 66

Belgian Grand Prix, 4, 6, 81–90
Beltoise, Jean, 183
Benoist, Robert, 11
Benson, David, 182
Berlin Avus circuit, 132
Berthon, Peter, 44
Bira, Prince of Siam, 162
Birkin, Sir Henry, 14–15
Black, Sir John, 44
Blackburn, David, 124
Bonnier, Jo, 161, 165
Bordino, 13
Bowen, Frank, 185
Brabham, Betty, 22, 60, 61, 63
Brabham, Jack (top driver-constructor), 14, 16, 18, 20, 23, 24, 25, 34, 35, 36, 37, 38, 40, 54, 56, 57, 58–64, 66–7, 68, 70, 72, 73, 74, 84–5, 88, 90, 92, 93 fn, 104, 107, 122, 123, 129, 136, 138, 139, 147, 156, 161, 177, 178, 186; organisation and cars, 34, 35, 36, 58–64, 66–74, 104–5, 123, 136, 139, 147, 177, 186, 190
Brands Hatch circuit, 104, 117, 120, 152, 164
Breedlove, Craig, 31
British domination, 18, 125, 182
British Grand Prix, 4, 6, 8, 116–23
British Petroleum (B.P.), 29, 148, 181–3, 184, 186
British Racing Drivers' Club, 117, 119
B.R.M. company and cars, 28, 30–1, 34, 35, 36, 37–8, 40, 43–9, 50–7, 79, 121, 122, 138, 176, 192
Brivio, Count Antonio (G.P. pioneer), 5, 6, 17

Brooklands circuit, 32, 116–17, 162
Brooks, Tony, 16, 178
Brown, J. W., 117
Bucknum, Ronnie, 93, 94
Bulawayo circuit, 172

Camden, Marquess, 117
Canadian Grand Prix, 4, 147
Car, 150
Castle, Barbara, 182 fn
Castrol, 114, 183, 184, 188
casualties and disasters, 9–15
Challis, Alan, 56
champions, 16–17, 178
Chapman, Colin, 23, 25, 27–8, 35, 75, 76–80, 83, 84, 85, 86, 87, 89, 105, 123, 143, 170
Chesham, Lord, 117
Chinetti, Luigi, 110
Clark, Jim (youngest champion), 14, 16, 17, 19, 20, 22, 23, 24, 25, 26, 37, 39, 43 fn, 53, 62, 68, 69, 73, 74, 75, 76, 78, 81, 83, 85, 86, 87, 88, 89, 90, 104, 105, 107, 116, 122, 139, 152, 155, 156, 176, 178, 182, 184
Clermont-Ferrand, 103, 168
Club Internationale des Ancien Pilotes de Grands Prix, 133, 165
Collins, Peter, 10, 17, 190
Commission Sportif Internationale, 3–4, 5, 34–5, 46
Competitive Driving, 46
Connell, Ian, 162
Constructors' Championship (Formula 1), 16, 36, 47, 58, 79, 98, 125, 147, 177
Cooper, Charles, 125
Cooper, John, 39, 124, 125, 133, 136, 191
Cooper-Maserati organisation and cars, 36, 120–1, 122, 123, 124–30, 132–9, 148, 164, 183
Coppa Ciano, 5
Coquille, Emile, 102
Corriere dello Sport, 142
cost and rewards of motor racing, 23–5, 27–33, 35
Costin, Mike, 80
Costruzioni Meccaniche Nazionali, 142
Cosworth Engineering, 79–80, 87
Courage, Piers, 25, 37, 53
Coventry Climax, 34, 79

Daily Express, 32, 182
Daily Express International Trophy, 8, 45
Daily Mail, 32
Daily Telegraph, 184
Daimler, Gottlieb, 100
Delamont, Dean, 116, 117–18, 120
Dion, Count de, 100
Dobson, Arthur, 163
Dragoni, 36, 95
drivers compared with ordinary motorists, 19–21
Druitt, Denis, 182
Duckworth, Keith, 79, 83, 86–8
Dunlop monopoly, 31
Dunne, Bill, 108, 109, 114, 115, 151
Durand, Charles, 102
Durlacher, Jack, 164
Dutch Grand Prix, 4, 65–74
D.W. Racing Enterprises Ltd., 171

Elf petroleum, 183, 186
Enzo Ferrari Memoirs, 141 fn
Esso, 29, 182, 185–6
European Trophy for Formula 2 drivers, 192

Fagioli, 11
Fangio, Juan Manuel (record-holder), 6, 9, 10, 11–12, 16, 17, 18, 58, 113, 126, 132, 143, 178
Farina, Dr. Nino (first world champion), 6, 8, 9, 12, 13
Faroux, Charles, 102
Fédération Internationale Automobile (F.I.A.), 3, 6, 15, 117, 164
Fédération Internationale Motor-cycliste (F.I.M.), 3, 5
Ferrari cars and company, 8, 36, 37, 79, 110, 121, 140–6, 149, 150–8, 176
Ferrari, Dino, 141, 145
Ferrari, Enzo, 5, 7, 8, 9, 95, 106, 110, 140–6, 149, 150, 151, 152, 153, 154, 192
Ferrari, Mrs., 154
Firestone tyres, 31, 185, 186
Florio, Count, 100
Foghieri, Mauro, 144, 153, 155, 157
Ford Co., 37, 79, 80, 149; *see also* Lotus-Ford
Foyt, A. J., 69, 104, 107, 190
French Grand Prix, 4, 6, 100–2, 103–7, 168
French interest, 7, 34, 79, 100, 183

INDEX

Gardner, Frank, 129
Gavin, Servoz, 183
Gaze, Tony, 13
German Grand Prix, 4, 131–9
German predominance, 7, 17–18
Gibson, Niel Eason, 119
Ginther, Richie, 37, 68, 69, 93, 94, 95, 107, 109, 114, 151, 190
Gonzalez, 9, 12
Goodyear tyres, 29, 31, 184
Gordon, David, 187–9
Gordon, 'Flash', 88
Gott, John, 117
Gould, Horace, 15
Graded Driver, 23
Grand Prix Hospital Unit, 119–20
Grands Prix, 4, 6
Grant, Gregor, xiv
Gulf oil company, 183–4
Gurney, Arleo, 114
Gurney, Dan, 17, 20, 29, 37, 39, 58, 61–2, 68, 69, 72, 85, 88, 89, 90, 104, 105, 106, 107, 108–15, 121, 122, 138, 151, 156, 176, 184, 190; racing organisation (A.A.R.), xiv, 37, 68, 106, 107, 108–15, 151, 184, 190

Haffenden, Rouem, 115
Harris, Frank, 20
Hawthorn, Mike, 10–11, 14, 16, 18, 25, 178, 190
Hill, Bette, 22, 83, 85, 89
Hill, Graham, xi, xv, 16, 19, 20, 22, 23, 24, 25, 26, 37, 39, 43, 47, 57, 62, 69, 71, 72, 73, 76, 78, 81, 83, 86, 89, 104, 105, 121–2, 129, 136, 147, 156, 161, 175, 176–7, 178, 182, 189
Hill, Phil, 16
Hitler, Adolf, 7, 165
Honda cars and organisation, 36–7, 74, 79, 91–9, 105, 121, 123, 148, 156, 176, 181, 183, 190
Honda, Mr., 91, 92, 93, 94
Hopkins, Tex, 175
Hopkirk, Paddy, 184
Hugenholtz, John, 66
Huhnlein, Körpsführer, 7
Hulme, Denis, 37, 38–9, 40, 55, 56, 57, 61, 67, 68–70, 73, 74, 90, 104, 107, 116, 122, 138, 139, 147, 156, 176, 177, 178, 193
Hussein of Jordan, King, 62

Ickx, Jackie, 148, 151, 190, 191, 192

Indianapolis '500', 6, 37, 75
Ireland, Innes, 24
Irwin, Chris, 23, 37, 147
Italian Grand Prix, 4, 6, 8, 148–58
Italian predominance, 6, 7–8, 17, 18

Jack Brabham's Motor Racing Book, 60
Jenatzy, Camille, 11
Jim Clark at the Wheel, 22

Kerr, Phil, 58, 62, 186
Kessler, Bruce, 110
Kyalami, 38

Lascelles, Hon. Gerald, 117
Le Mans, 1955 disaster, 13; 24-Hour race, 70, 83, 102–3, 104, 105, 149, 162, 165, 182; French Grand Prix, 100–2, 103–7
L'Équipe, 144
Lini, Franco, 36, 144, 150–1, 153
Lister & Sons Ltd., George, 29
Lotus-Ford cars and organisation, 37, 75–81, 82–9, 105, 121, 122, 123, 136, 138, 139, 156, 170, 176, 186, 190
Love, John, 39–40, 57
Lowman, Mike, 115
Lucas, Oliver, 44
Lucas Ltd., Joseph, 44

McLaren, Bruce, xiii–xiv, 19, 20, 21, 23, 24, 35, 37, 40, 48, 57, 61, 69, 72, 106–7, 114, 121, 138, 151, 176, 191
McLaren, Mrs., 23
Mader, Heini, 134
Maggs, Tony, 24, 39
Maglioli, 12
marriage and the racing driver, 22–3
Matra Sport, organisation and cars, 183, 186, 191–2, 193
Mays, Raymond, 7, 8, 25, 28, 44, 45–6, 71
Men at the Wheel, 127
Mercedes Benz, xiii, 7, 29, 189
Metternich-Wineberg, Prince, 117
Mexican Grand Prix, 4, 177–8
Mexico City, 38, 185
Michelin, 183
Mieres, 12
Mille Miglia, 1957 disaster, 13
Miller, Peter, 127
Mobil, 113
Monaco, Prince and Princess of, 55

INDEX

Monaco Grand Prix, 4, 6, 8–9, 50–7, 104, 167, 177
Monte Carlo, 50–7
Montlhery, 103
Monza circuit, 1961 disaster, 13; 148–58
Mosport circuit, 147, 148
Moss, Stirling, 9–10, 12, 13, 14, 16, 25, 125, 143, 161, 165, 178, 190
Motor, 182
Murdoch, Geoffrey, 182
Murphy, Jimmy, 101
Musso, 17
Mussolini, Benito, 6
My Life and My Loves, 20

Nakamura, Yoshio, 74, 91–2, 93, 94, 95, 97, 98, 105
nerves, subject of, 20–2, 64
Neubauer, Alfred, 17–18, 45
New Zealand Grand Prix Association, 61, 178
Nurburgring circuit, 10, 32, 83, 131–9
Nuvolari, 11, 143

oil company support, 29–31, 33, 113–14, 148, 181–8
Oonk, J. H., 66
Owen, Sir Alfred, 28, 36, 44, 46, 47
Owen Racing Organisation, 46, 48

Parker, Harold, 117
Parkes, Mike, 20, 22, 24, 26, 37, 89, 105, 145, 150, 190
Parnell, Reg, 37
Parnell, Tim, 37, 38, 53, 86
Pepino, 141
Perkins, Denis, 55
Piotti, 14
points system, 3–4, 5–6
Porsche, Ferdinand, 7, 189
Portago, Marquis de, 13

Race of Champions, 152, 164
Ramirez, Joaquin, 115
Rees, Alan, 129
regulations, F1 cars, 15, 34–6; fuel, 15–16
Renault, Louis, 101
Renault-Alpine Co., 183
research aid, 30
Rheims, 103, 104
Rhodesian Grand Prix, 172
Rindt, Jochen, 37, 39, 69, 122, 128, 129, 133, 136, 137, 138, 139, 147
Roberts, Peter, 46

Robinson, Tony, 126
Rodriguez, Pedro, 37, 39, 40, 57, 74, 90, 104, 107, 122, 128, 129, 132, 133, 137, 138, 139, 148, 192
Rolt, Tony, 161
Rosemeyer, 7
Rouen, 103, 104
Royal Automobile Club (R.A.C.), 3, 23, 116–17
Rubery Owen Group, 28, 44
Rudd, Pam, 55
Rudd, Tony, 35, 46–7, 48, 52, 53, 54, 55, 73, 93, 127
rules for World Championship events, 3–4

St. Cloud Grand Prix, 7
Salvadori, Roy, 126–30, 133, 136, 138–9, 183
Scarfiotti, Ludivico, 24, 36, 37, 105–6, 145, 149, 150–1, 156
Schell, Harry, 15
Schonberg, Johnny, 59, 60
Shelby, Carroll, 108, 110, 127
Shell companies, xiv–xv, 29, 30, 113, 184, 186
Sieff, Jonathan, 124, 132–3, 134, 137
Siffert, Jo, 37, 164, 165
Silverstone circuit, 8, 32, 45, 116–23
Sommer, Raymond, 11, 45
South African Grand Prix, 4, 38–40
Southcott, Willie, 56
Spa circuit, 79–80, 81–90, 103
spectator psychology, 187–9
Spence, Linda, 55
Spence, Mike, 37, 39, 52, 53, 54, 56, 57, 122, 138
Stacey, Alan, 13–14
Standard Motor Co., 44
Stanley, Louis, 120
Stewart, Helen, 23, 55
Stewart, Jackie, 19, 20, 23, 24, 26, 37–8, 39, 43, 52, 53, 54, 55, 56, 69, 73–4, 83, 89, 90, 104, 107, 121, 122 fn, 138, 147, 151, 191, 192
Straight, Whitney, 38
Strasbourg, 101
Sun, 185
Surtees, John, 16, 17, 20, 22, 25, 36–7, 40, 54, 57, 95–7, 98, 99, 105, 106, 122, 128, 156, 157, 170, 176, 178, 181, 191
Surtees, Pat, 22, 96
Swiss Grand Prix, 6
Szisz, François, 101

INDEX

Taggart, Dr. Peter, 20-1
Targa Florio (oldest race), 100, 142
Taruffi, 6
Tasman races, 52, 164
Tauranac, Ron, 62, 67
Threlfall, Christopher, 13
Trintignent, 12
Trips, Taffy von, 13, 190
tyre company participation, 31-2, 33, 184-5
Tyrrell, Ken, 39, 148, 190-3

U.G.P. petroleum company, 183
Umberto I (King of Italy), 148
United States Grand Prix, 4, 6, 176-7

Vandervell, Tony, 25
Villoresi, 14

Wakefield, Lord, 184
Walker, Johnny, 160
Walker, Rob, 27, 28, 37, 148, 159-65, 172, 183
Wall, Tim, 115
Watkins Glen circuit, 104, 175-8
Weslake, Harry, 112, 113
Weslake Engineering, 112-13
White, Derek, 126, 133
Who's Who, 25, 26
Williams, Jonathan, 21-2, 37
Williams, W., 50
Wimille, 7
wives of racing drivers, 22-3
Woods, F. Aubrey, 112
World Championship, xiv

Youl, Gavin, 70

Zandvoort circuit, 65-74, 104